GREEK MATHEMATICAL
PHILOSOPHY

GREEK MATHEMATICAL PHILOSOPHY

EDWARD A. MAZIARZ
Professor of Philosophy, Loyola University, Chicago

THOMAS GREENWOOD
Former Professor of Philosophy, Montreal University, Quebec

BARNES
&NOBLE
BOOKS
NEW YORK

This edition published by Barnes & Noble, Inc.,
by arrangement with Continuum Publishing Corp.

1995 Barnes & Noble Books

ISBN 1-56619-954-9

Printed and bound in the United States of America

M 9 8 7 6 5 4 3 2 1

TO NINA GREENWOOD

Preface

This book offers a broad cultural survey of the mutual interaction and development of mathematics with philosophy in
Greek thought. One can readily find studies emphasizing the
purely philosophical aspect and importance of Greek thought.
Similarly, there are many books dealing with the history and
the significance of Greek mathematics. There is a need, then,
for a project which chooses to situate itself between the two
branches of learning in order to outline the course of their
development.

The first Greek thinkers were strongly influenced by the
mythopoeic thought of their neighbors. They themselves were
not without their own mystery religions, sacred objects, and
actions, and they engaged in a wide variety of magical and
ritual motions. But the cultural interchange of the Greeks with
their neighbors was a fruitful one: the Greeks gradually transmuted much of what they learned, and slowly but persistently
added the fruits of their own experience to the inheritance
they received. To supplant myth, they offered reason. For
magic and ritual, they offered abstraction and methodology.

Accordingly, it is now quite generally agreed that Greek
philosophy, mathematics, and science are at least partially
derived from religion in its forms of myth, magic, and ritual.
In fact, it has even been said that such thinkers as Plato and
Aristotle attempted to have their own philosophical systems

serve as the "myth" for their contemporaries.[1] On the other hand, the Greeks made a contribution of their own of such significance that we can still point to their culture as a point of origin for much of Western philosophy and science.

The story of this transmutation from myth to reason is told in various places, though many aspects of it are still unknown. Generally, it involves the disclosure of how the giant of mythical religion gradually yielded a place of stature and power to philosophy as human wisdom. In greater detail, the story shows further how magic and ritual activity (and philosophy itself, to some extent) were at least partially replaced by such mundane theories and practices as are to be found in mathematics and the sciences, and in medicine and the arts.

This book relates a small portion of this complex tale. It picks up the threads of mathematical philosophy in Greece with Thales and the Pythagoreans (Part I). At this time, myth, philosophy, and mathematics were not clearly distinguished. The next major development occurs during the time of Plato (Part II), where one already finds a difference between professional mathematicians and philosophers. Finally, with Aristotle (Part III), mathematics is named a science in its own right, though merely as occupying a place along with other sciences.

There is no doubt that philosophy and mathematics have always exhibited a strong liaison. One need only recall George Berkeley's attacks on the infinitesimal calculus or the more recent debates on the foundations of mathematics. It is of some interest, then, to consider the depth and the extent of this interaction in Greek mathematical philosophy—at a time when both philosophy and mathematics were in their infancy.

The great share of the responsibility for this work rests with Thomas Greenwood—a former professor and a dear friend, now deceased. His own professional life and writings symbolized the closeness of mathematics to philosophy exhibited in this

[1] Evert W. Beth, *The Foundations of Mathematics: A Study in the Philosophy of Science* (Amsterdam, 1959), pp. 34-36.

study. Unless otherwise indicated, all translations were made by Dr. Greenwood. For their friendship as well as for their help with the manuscript, my thanks are due to Richard C. Gitzinger, to Mrs. William E. Smith who typed the final manuscript, and to Cheryl M. Frank for reading the final page proofs and preparing the index.

EDWARD A. MAZIARZ

Contents

GREEK MATHEMATICAL
PHILOSOPHY

Part I

HISTORICAL BACKGROUND

The growth of civilization is a complex, evolutionary process. Miracles and revolutions in the development of knowledge generally indicate contrasts between landmarks of history. Indeed, a careful analysis of novel occurrences often shows them to be mere links in the continuous but unfinished chain of emergent forms. If extraordinary events can be explained in terms of series of facts, then they are not blindly determined by a capricious fate: the power to choose, associate, imagine, and act is an essential constituent of human progress. The operation of our will on the spiritual and material presentations of the universe is a vital part of our knowledge.

The fascinating development of Greek thought, which culminates in the doctrines of Plato and Aristotle, is often considered a miracle. But modern scholarship makes it appear more rational, more interesting, and more valuable when viewed in relation to three fundamental factors: the interactions of mind and nature, the positive traditions of Eastern civilizations which the Greeks assimilated, and the peculiar gifts of the Hellenic mind asserting itself in its own environment.

1

CHAPTER 1

The Dawn of Greek Thought

The Greeks had lived a long time before their early philosophers made their first pronouncements. As nomads, warriors, settlers, agriculturists, and colonists, they at first shared a yearning for myth and magic with primitive man. From a dim past bordering the Stone Age to the Dorian invasions and early settlements beyond the peninsula, they gradually blended with their customs and crafts abstract intuitions emerging from the reaction of mind to nature. This empirical tradition is a permanent constituent of Greek mathematical thought, though it was later overshadowed by those rational characters which became its most distinctive features.

The heritage shared by the Greeks with primitive man developed in many original directions. In those days, Greece was a country of frequent migrations—a factor which scarcely favored the pursuit of knowledge. The first settlers in the mainland soon had to yield to the pressure of various tribes pouring into the peninsula, and were forced to farther shores. A chain of Greek colonies was thus established progressively from the northern fringe of Asia Minor to the southern tip of Italy. This geographical distribution of the Greeks encour-

3

aged a close intercourse between the colonies and the mother country, and enhanced the adventurous character of the Greeks by bringing them into contact with the more developed Eastern civilizations.

Indeed, long before the emergence of a specific Greek culture, the Assyrians had made observations about the stars, the Babylonians had prepared chronological tables, the Egyptians had practiced land measurement extensively, and the Phoenicians had invented commercial arithmetic. Moreover, the myths and rituals of these Eastern races implied many remarkable psychological and cosmological observations.[1]

But though our knowledge of these ancient cultures has increased considerably in recent years, we do not find in them a deliberate or conscious effort to develop for their own sake the mathematical facts and scientific observations which supported their practical needs and religious views. For example, the Babylonians do not seem to have been interested in the rational explanation of eclipses, their discoveries being used only for astrological purposes. The Egyptians do not appear to have thought of a theory of numbers; they simply dealt with numerical problems of a practical character. The mathematical relations known to the Eastern scholars were apparently obtained by empirical considerations, and there is no proof that they were investigated much further. As the ancients scarcely differentiated their general knowledge from their practical arts, they probably never thought of systematizing the theoretical aspects of the materials they had patiently accumulated in the course of centuries.

This store of knowledge gradually found its way into the Greek world, especially when the Ionians established regular contacts with Babylon and Egypt, after Thrasybulus of Miletus concluded an alliance with the King of the Lydians in the seventh century B.C. Thus, Greek thought began to develop

[1] The influence of these earlier civilizations on Greek thought is described in the following: F. M. Cornford, *From Religion to Philosophy* (New York, 1957); Mircea Eliade, *The Sacred and the Profane* (New York, 1961); H. and H. A. Frankfort, *Before Philosophy* (Chicago, 1949).

first in Asia Minor. When the Greeks had secured a permanent foothold in Egypt with their trading station at Naucratis, many distinguished visitors from the peninsula were induced to study in foreign lands. Such was the case of Thales, who learned geometry from the Egyptian priests and was probably familiar with Babylonian knowledge, since he predicted the famous eclipse which influenced the end of the war between Lydians and Medes. Similarly, according to Isocrates, Pythagoras brought mathematics to Croton from the banks of the Nile. He probably borrowed from the East the idea of numerology, as well as the notion of an immortal soul, which he may have combined with some local Orphic doctrines. More positively, Herodotus was the first to consider Egypt as the cradle of Greek religion and culture.

Democritus is reported to have travelled widely after his first contact in Abdera with the Persian scholar Ostanes, whom the emperor Xerxes introduced to his father. About that time, Plato is said to have journeyed to Egypt; he probably learned more about ancient thought when the Academy was joined by Eudoxus of Cnidos, who had consorted with Eastern scholars. This debt to the Egyptians was acknowledged by Plato when he has Socrates repeat that Toth was the inventor of arithmetic, geometry, and astronomy.[2] These contacts with earlier cultures culminated at the time of Aristotle, when his imperial pupil Alexander was carried as far as Turkestan and India by his military campaigns. If the conquering hosts of the Macedonian scattered abroad the lofty ideals and achievements of Hellenic culture, they also brought back with them the best there was in the civilizations they had contacted.

The Greeks were thus led to improve their primitive traditions and the complex lore of the older civilizations, and were bold enough to consider the world afresh at a particularly significant time in history. The sixth century B.C. was an era of great intellectual energy and activity. Fundamental problems facing the attempt to discover the relations between reason

2 *Phaedrus* 274C.

and nature were solved differently by various religious systems: Taoism, Confucianism, Buddhism, Jainism, and Judaism, as well as the mystical rituals of the Greeks themselves. The particular importance of the Greek contributions resulted from their new orientation. Freeing themselves from the fiats of mythical religion, the Ionians fashioned anew and coordinated whatever they borrowed from others, and were soon able to soar into the abstract realm of the universalization of experience.[3]

Thus, it was the cities of Miletus, Ephesus, Samos, Colophon, and Clazomenae which gave the world its first independent thinkers. From the oldest of them came Thales of Miletus (*ca.* 624-546 B.C.), who founded the Ionian school. The rational outlook of the Ionians and their positive cosmogonies encouraged Glaucos (*ca.* 600 B.C.) and Theodorus (*ca.* 532 B.C.) to study chemistry and Hecataeus (*ca.* 550-475 B.C.) to study geography. The practical arts also flourished in Asia Minor at a time when Thales himself was one of the ablest engineers of his day.

The speculations of Thales on the origin of the world provided the startling pronouncement that water is the basic constituent of the world. It is true that water has a privileged part in the ancient cosmogonies of the Hebrews, Egyptians, and Babylonians, and in Greek mythology, but these traditions are religious. Thales attempted a rational explanation of the universe on the strength of some fundamental observations and experiments in terms of *nature,* the ultimate foundation of things. For this reason his views are given prominence in the history of thought, although he left no detailed explanation of the way things are produced. This proposal was developed further by Anaximander (*ca.* 611-545 B.C.), who proposed the *indefinite* as the ultimate element of nature, and by Anaxi-

---

[3] For accounts of the Greek transformation of science, see O. Neugebauer, *The Exact Sciences in Antiquity* (New York, 1962); Lynn Thorndike, *A History of Magic and Experimental Science* (New York, 1923), I; B. L. Van der Waerden, *Science Awakening* (Groningen, Netherlands, 1954).

menes (*ca.* 588-524 B.C.), who explained that *air* is the principle of things, while Heraclitus of Ephesus (*ca.* 540-480 B.C.) altered the Ionian monism by proposing *fire* as the constituent and principle of the world.

It is difficult to establish a definite connection between the natural philosophy of Thales and the various mathematical discoveries with which he is credited. In this field, Thales probably derived much inspiration from the Egyptians. We are told by Proclus[4] that Thales introduced geometry into Greece after his visit to Egypt. Whereas the geometrical knowledge of the Egyptians consisted of empirically obtained simple propositions about areas and volumes, Thales visualized a geometry of simple lines, an essentially abstract subject which has remained the basic part of geometry. This does not mean that Thales actually organized a body of mathematical knowledge, but simply that he stressed the abstractive and deductive process in mathematics.

According to Proclus, "he discovered many propositions himself, and he communicated to his successors the principles of many others, his method being in some cases more abstract, in other more empirical."[5] Thales had probably analyzed some empirical data of geometry into their ideal elements and established some rational connection among them; some results could thus be derived from others by logical arguments alone. This was probably the case with these few intuitive propositions about plane figures which are attributed to Thales: (1) the bisection of a circle by its diameter; (2) the equality of the angles at the base of any isosceles triangle; (3) the properties of the opposite angles of two intersecting lines; (4) the congruence of triangles having two angles and a side respectively equal; (5) the proportionality of the sides of similar triangles; and (6) the property of the angle inscribed in a semicircle.

It was practically impossible for Thales to give any proof of

[4] *In Primum Euclidis Elementorum Librum Commentarii*, ed. by Gottfried Friedlein (Leipzig, 1873), p. 65.
[5] *Ibid.*

these theorems in the sense in which we understand demonstration, as he did not possess the technical elements of such a complex logical process. In fact, Thales is said to have demonstrated only the first proposition and to have merely stated the second; while Proclus says that he discovered the third proposition without proving it scientifically, and must have known the fourth because "the method by which Thales showed how to find the distances of ships from the shore necessarily involves the use of this theorem."[6] The proportionality of the sides of similar triangles is implied in the determination of the height of a pyramid, which is attributed to Thales by Diogenes Laertius, Pliny, and Plutarch. This was accomplished by measuring the shadow of a stick fixed in the sand and comparing it with the shadow of the pyramid. Pliny simplifies the procedure by informing us that Thales took the measurements when the body and its shadow were equal in length. Plutarch states generally that by placing a stick at the extremities of the shadow of a pyramid, Thales "formed two triangles by the contact of the sunrays, and showed that the height of the pyramid was to the length of the staff in the same ratio as their respective shadows."[7]

The property of the angle inscribed in a semicircle cannot be attributed to Thales without qualification, because it involves the equality of the angles of a triangle to two right angles. It is difficult to assert that Thales knew this theorem, in spite of the striking arguments adduced by some commentators. Allman suggests that "Thales had been led by the concrete geometry of the Egyptians to contemplate floors covered with tiles in the form of equilateral triangles or regular hexagons, and had observed that six equilateral triangles could be placed around a common vertex; from which he saw that six such angles made up four right angles, and that consequently the sum of the three angles of an equilateral triangle is equal to two right angles."[8]

6 *Ibid.*, p. 352.
7 *Convivium* 2, p. 147.
8 G. T. Allman, *Greek Geometry from Thales to Euclid* (London, 1889), p. 12.

At this early stage of Greek geometry, the demonstrations of Thales must have appealed to some extent to the senses. The truth of his theorems could be recognized by such practical constructions[9] as the tentative drawing of diagrams and lines in them in order to detect possible connections from mere inspection. Analogies and similarities would then suggest generalizations of particular cases as well as simple relations between their elements. But as reasoning is more important than experiment in these processes, it may be truly said that Thales began the rational tradition which characterizes Greek philosophy and science.

[9] Paul Tannery, *La Géométrie Grecque* (Paris, 1887), p. 89.

CHAPTER 2

The Pythagorean Number Theory

The political events in Asia Minor during the sixth century
B.C. caused a migration of Greeks towards Italy, Sicily, Thrace,
and within Greece proper. But it was the intellectual reaction
against the Ionian thinkers that gave birth to the new schools
of thought in Croton, Elea, Abdera, and Athens. The first
school of its kind was founded by Pythagoras of Samos (*fl.* 570
B.C.), whose intellectual interests were enriched by his knowledge of Oriental wisdom. Similarities and analogies with
Eastern ideas appear in the doctrines and practices of the
Brotherhood he organized in Croton.

Evaluation of Pythagoreanism is made difficult by the absence of fragments of the earlier disciples. The Master himself
followed the Eastern usage of transmitting his views by word
of mouth; his spoken judgment was held as authoritative.
Moreover, the rules of the Brotherhood prevented its members
from divulging the teachings of the Master or even their own
opinions, so Pythagoras is credited with discoveries which may
have been those of his disciples. The Pythagorean doctrines
are known chiefly through their later representatives, such as
Philolaus of Croton (fifth century B.C.), who is considered the

first to have written on these matters, and Archytas of Tarentum (fifth century B.C.); from the Platonist Eudoxus of Cnidus (fourth century B.C.), whose lost works are known through extracts preserved by later writers; and from references in the works of Aristotle. Plato, who owes much to Pythagorean influences, gives only a trivial reference in the *Republic* (600*B*) to the founder of the school.

The esoteric members of the Brotherhood were called "mathematicians" because the term merely indicated the various subjects they had to learn with the Master. The modern specific meaning of "mathematics" and "mathematicians" is due mainly to Aristotle. This is shown by the wider significance of the word in the following fragment of Archytas:

> As the mathematicians seem to have arrived at correct conclusions, it is not surprising that they have a true conception of the nature of each individual thing. For having reached such correct conclusions about the nature of the universe, they were bound to see in its true light the nature of particular things as well. Thus they left us a clear knowledge about the speed of the stars, their risings and settings; about geometry, arithmetic and sphaeric; and last but not least, about music; for these studies (mathematics) seem to be sisters.[1]

Notwithstanding subsequent classifications of the sciences, arithmetic and geometry should not be separated from the rest of the Pythagorean teachings. The Master could not consider them independent of the other branches of knowledge, since they were a portion of wisdom, like music or the "bad arts" he had practiced. Moreover, Pythagoras could not study them simply as pleasant or useful subjects. A natural philosopher and religious reformer, he must have considered them the best introduction to higher wisdom: they helped the liberation of the soul from the dominion of the senses, as well as the under-

[1] Hermann Diels, *Die Fragmente der Vorsokratiker: Griechisch und Deutsch*, 5th ed. (Berlin, 1934), 47 B 1, III, pp. 431-432; (hereafter referred to as Diels, *Vors.;* trans. by Thomas Greenwood).

standing of nature and the world beyond. But the technical interest of Pythagoras in mathematics was probably conditioned by his intuitive realization that number is the essence of things. In the absence of any relevant records, we can only surmise the origin of this remarkable conception, which seems to have inspired Plato in shaping his own philosophy.

The partial solutions of Ionian thinkers concerning the nature of the primordial substance must have urged the Pythagoreans to find a more fundamental cause of things, discover a principle underlying the four elements, and give a deeper explanation of the Milesian systems. Furthermore, since nature is only a part of human experience, a more universal essence was needed to explain nature, reason, and religion as well. If the empirical aspects of knowledge could somehow be satisfied with the operations of the natural elements, its rational and mystical aspects required a different principle of explanation. Because of its rationality and permanence, mathematics could provide such a principle readily. The universal value of mathematics suggested by the naturalistic account of knowledge was confirmed by the religious requirements of action. If the emotive Orphic rituals were to satisfy the positive mind of the Pythagoreans, some rational basis was needed for their religious implications. A comparative analysis of Eastern traditions would have shown that mathematical, especially numerical, relations were essential in mystical speculations and in the interpretation of the world.

Numbers were also indispensable in many practical fields, such as commerce and everyday social intercourse. At the time of Pythagoras, numbers were not the object of a separate science. They were considered to be almost as material as the ultimate principles of things—earth, air, fire, water—of the Milesians. In fact, they were merely used for practical purposes without being considered as purely rational entities. This distinction is illustrated by Plato when he says that "logistic and arithmetic are wholly concerned with numbers,"[2] and by the

2 *Republic* 525*A*.

following passage of the scholium to the *Charmides,* wherein the object of the former is explained:

> Logistic is the science dealing with numbered objects, not numbers; it does not consider number in its essence, but it presupposes 1 as the unit, and the numbered object as number; that is, it regards 3 as a triad, 10 as a decad, and applies the theorems of arithmetic to particular cases. Thus, logistic investigates what Archimedes called the cattle-problem and also "melite" and "phialite" numbers, the latter relating to bowls, the former to flocks. In other aspects, too, it investigates the numbers of material bodies, treating them as absolute. Its subject-matter is everything that is numbered.[3]

Pythagoras would have remembered the Babylonian view that each constellation had two chief characteristics—the number of stars composing it and the geometrical figure they form. Patient observation shows how to distinguish the various constellations in that way. Thus Plato wrote in *Timaeus* that "the vision of the day and night and of months and circling years has created the art of number. It has given us not only the notion of time, but also the means of studying the nature of the universe, from which has emerged philosophy in all its ranges."[4]

Further, Pythagoras would have observed that the art of music, so steadily practiced in the Brotherhood, was ruled by rhythm and number. This may have led him to discover the fundamental harmonic relations of a vibrating string stretched over a resounding board. By means of a movable bridge, he would divide the string into different lengths and produce various high and low notes. Though unable to determine the vibrations on which the separate sounds depended, he could measure the length of the vibrating string which was the material cause of the sound and determine the ratios corresponding to the various tones. Through number, music was thus connected with astronomy.

[3] Scholium to Plato *Charmides* 165E.
[4] *Timaeus* 47B.

With every constellation and every musical note characterized by a number, the study of the heavens and of sound would
suggest by analogy the establishment of a number theory extending to ethics and religion. From trade to liturgy through
astronomy and acoustics, man's interests would be linked
together by the power of number. Merged into the things perceived by the senses as well as into the higher values of life
and destiny, numbers must have appeared to Pythagoras as
more universal than any other human conception. Stripped of
the accidents identifying them with specific objects, or even
with the astrological chart of any person, numbers could be
taken as the real constituents—the very nature of the world.
Thus Pythagoras was led to declare that number is the essence
of things.

According to Aristotle, the Pythagoreans do not place the
objects of mathematics between the ideas and material things
as Plato does, they say "that things themselves are numbers"[5]
and that "number is the matter of things as well as the form
of their modifications and permanent states."[6] As the principles
of mathematics, numbers are "the principles of all existing
things."[7] Therefore, numbers cannot be attributes of something else; they are the substance of all existing things[8] and
also "the causes of the reality of other things."[9] This follows
from their participation in the One, which is a substance and
not a predicate of something else.

But are numbers transcendent or immanent? Whereas Plato
maintained their transcendence, the Pythagoreans held that all
things possess number and are numbers. Hence numbers are
not separable from things: as all existing things are made up
of numbers, the whole heaven is number, and even abstractions
and immaterial things are numbers. The immanence of number could not be expressed in stronger terms.

5 *Met.* 987b 27.
6 *Met.* 987a 15.
7 *Met.* 985b 25.
8 *Met.* 987a 18.
9 *Met.* 987b 24.

Yet, in another passage discussing assimilation and resemblance, Aristotle attributes to the Pythagoreans the opinion that numbers are affections or relations rather than substances.

They seemed to see in numbers many resemblances to the things that exist and come into being, more than in fire, in earth and in water. Such and such a modification of numbers was justice, another was soul and reason, another was opportunity, and similarly almost all other things were expressible numerically. Again, they saw that the attributes and the ratios of the musical scale were expressible in numbers. Since all things seemed in their whole nature to be modelled on numbers, and numbers seemed to be the first things in the whole of nature, they supposed the elements of numbers to be the elements of all things, and the whole heavens to be a musical scale and a number. They collected and fitted into their scheme all the properties of numbers and scales they could show to agree with the attributes, the parts, and the whole arrangement of the heavens.[10]

Aristotle also asserts that the Pythagoreans say things exist by imitation of numbers, while Plato says they exist by participation. But he does not elaborate on this point, because "what the participation or the imitation of the forms could be they left an open question."[11] This is perhaps a reference to the views of Philolaus, for whom numbers are the *paradigms* or the substantial patterns of things—a conception apparently current among the younger Pythagoreans, which could have inspired Plato. Though the two views might have coexisted among the early Pythagoreans, Aristotle must have considered the complete identification of numbers and things to be their fundamental doctrine, as he devoted to it most of his criticism.

On the other hand, when Aristotle says the Pythagoreans "supposed real things to be numbers"[12] and "did not regard number as separable from the objects of sense,"[13] he surely

---

10 *Met.* 985b 27.
11 *Met.* 987b 13.
12 *Met.* 1090a 20.
13 *Phys.* 203a 6.

means they must have studied numbers as external objects, not as mere auxiliaries to ordinary computation. This view is emphasized by his reference to Eurytus, a disciple of Philolaus, who expressed the nature of objects by means of pebbles or counters. "Eurytus decided what was the number of an object (for example of a man or a horse) by imitating the figures of living things with pebbles, as some people bring numbers into the forms of the triangle and square."[14] Theophrastus reports the same story, which probably goes back to Archytas.[15]

A more detailed account of the method of Eurytus is given by Alexander:

> Let us assume for example that 250 is the number which defines man, and 360 that which defines plant. Having laid this down, he took 250 counters, some green and some black, others red and of many other colors; then smearing the wall with plaster and sketching on it a man and a plant, he proceeded to fix some of the counters in the outline of the face, some in that of the hands, and some in that of other parts. Thus he completed the outline of the man he was imagining by a number of counters equal in number to the units which he said defined the man.[16]

This doctrine of numbers and things prompted the Pythagoreans to collect and fit into their scheme all the properties of numbers they could discover to agree with particular experiences.

Another reason for the Pythagorean doctrine that number is immanent may be found in the general character of philosophical speculations at the time. The Ionians did not inquire about the "likeness" of things, but about the "nature" of things, their ultimate essence. The objects of sense perception were not explained through their participation with water or air, but through their ultimate identification with those elements. For example, Anaximenes considered the phenomena of the external world as the various modes of one single ulti-

14 *Met.* 1092b 10.
15 Theophrastus *In Met.* p. 6a 19.
16 Alexander *In Met.* 827-829.

mate reality, air. The Ionian monism excluded a multiplication of causes.

If things imitate numbers, the unanswered question of their ultimate cause might involve a possible multiplicity of causes. Imitation explains neither essence nor existence. Mere assertion of an analogy between numbers and the objects of experience offers no account of their nature. The Pythagoreans could scarcely fail to perceive the weakness of the argument for simple imitation. The world of experience, therefore, could not *be like* numbers; it had to *be* numbers. Instead of being mere paradigms or archetypes of things, numbers had to be the things themselves, or at least the stuff out of which things are made. By word of mouth, this intuition was transmitted from one generation to another, until Philolaus announced openly that "all things which can be known have number; for it is impossible for a thing to be conceived or known without number."[17]

With this fundamental principle, the Pythagoreans developed their views on the nature of particular things by a more intimate study of numbers. If number is the essence of things, why turn to experience for an explanation? In tracing the cause of things, the *a posteriori* method was of little help to men already convinced that they possessed the most important clue to the solution of the mysteries of the world. If number is the basis of all knowledge and if its various transformations cause the nature of everything, it should suffice to organize and analyze a variety of numbers in order to understand rationally how the world is built. Hence Pythagoras "attached supreme importance to the study of arithmetic, which he advanced and removed from the region of commercial utility."[18] This testimony is corroborated by Aristotle in his statement that "the Pythagoreans devoted themselves to the study of mathematics and were the first to advance this knowledge."[19]

What could be the stages of such a study? Establishment of

[17] This fragment is preserved by Stobaeus; cf. Diels, *Vors.,* 44 B 4, III, p. 408.
[18] Aristoxenus as quoted by Stobaeus; cf. Diels, *Vors.,* 58 B 4, III, p. 451.
[19] *Met.* 985b 23.

an adequate number theory requires first the definition of number. Following the view of Thales[20] that number is a collection of units, the Pythagoreans "made number out of one."[21] But they could scarcely regard one as a number, since a measure is not the thing measured and since one is "the beginning of number."[22] Euclid implies this view in defining a unit as that by which an existing thing is called one, while a number is the multitude made up of units.[23] Among later Pythagoreans, Thymaridas (fourth century B.C.) defines a unit as a "limiting quantity"; Chrysippus (third century B.C.) calls it "multitude one."[24] Among neo-Pythagoreans, Moderatus (*ca.* 60 A.D.) considers number as "a progression of multitude beginning from a unit, and a regression ending in it,"[25] while Nicomachus (*ca.* 100 A.D.) defines it as "a flow of quantity made up of units."[26] The assimilation of units with points will be discussed later.

The simplest operations performed with units are duplication and its reverse, bipartition or mediation. This immediately supplies a broad principle of classification of numbers into those which are divisible into halves and those which are not. As Philolaus says, "number is of two special kinds, odd and even, with a third even-odd arising from a mixture of the two; and there are many forms of each kind."[27]

Nicomachus, who represents well enough the Pythagorean tradition, gives this ancient definition: "An even number is that which can be divided both into two equal parts and into two unequal parts (except the fundamental dyad which can be divided only into two equal parts); but however it is divided, its two parts must be of the same kind without share in the other kind. An odd number is that which, however divided, must in any case fall into two unequal parts belong-

20 Cf. Iamblichus *Introductio Arithmetica*, p. 10.
21 *Met.* 985ᵃ 20.
22 *Met.* 1088ᵃ 7.
23 *Elements* vii. Defs. 1, 2.
24 Iamblichus *Introductio Arithmetica*, pp. 11-12.
25 Stobaeus *Eclogae* i. Proem. 8.
26 *Introductio Arithmetica* i. 7.1.
27 Diels, *Vors.*, 44 B 5, III, p. 408.

ing always to the two different kinds respectively."[28] This statement contains a reference to the original conception of the dyad as being not a number but the beginning of the even, just as one is not a number but the starting-point of number—a conception which must be very old, as Plato already speaks of two as even.[29] Nicomachus gives also this other definition without mentioning the dyad: "An even number is that which admits of being divided by one and the same operation into the greatest and the least parts, greatest in size but least in number (i.e., into two halves), while an odd number is that which cannot be so divided, but is only divisible into two unequal parts."[30]

As regards the term *odd-even*, Aristotle says that "the elements of number are the even and the odd" and that "the one proceeds from both of these for it is both even and odd."[31] Heath explains this strange view by submitting that the unit, being the principle of even and odd numbers, cannot itself be odd and must therefore be called even-odd.[32] According to a better explanation suggested by Archytas and attributed to Aristotle by Theon of Smyrna, the unit added to an even number makes an odd number, but when added to an odd number it produces an even number, and therefore must partake of both species.[33] On the other hand, Iamblichus uses this term for even numbers like 6 and 10, which yield an odd number after a first bipartition.[34] This conception points to Plato's distinction among "even times even," "odd times odd," "odd times even," and "even times odd,"[35] taken up later by Euclid.[36] These are examples of the possible classification of the various odd and even numbers referred to by Philolaus.

[28] *Introductio Arithmetica* i. 7.4.
[29] *Parmenides* 143D.
[30] *Introductio Arithmetica* i. 7.3.
[31] *Met.* 986a 17.
[32] Thomas L. Heath, *A History of Greek Mathematics* (Oxford, 1921), I, p. 71.
[33] *Expositio Rerum Mathematicarum,* p. 22.
[34] *Introductio Arithmetica,* p. 22.
[35] *Parmenides* 143E.
[36] *Elements* vii. Defs. 8-10.

The reciprocal operations of duplication and bipartition lead naturally to the study of numbers with regard to their divisibility in general. The Pythagoreans were not slow in discovering that certain numbers can be divided by no other number than the unit. A fragment of Speusippus based upon the writings of Philolaus[37] distinguishes "prime" and "incomposite" numbers and "secondary" or "composite" numbers. Thymaridas calls a prime number "rectilinear," and Theon of Smyrna, "euthymetric" or "linear." Theon says further that even numbers are not measured by the unit alone, except 2, which is therefore odd-like without being prime. Hence, the neo-Pythagoreans definitely exclude 2 from the prime numbers; for their predecessors, the dyad, or 2, was not a number at all, but the principle of the even, just as the one was the principle of number. Yet in defining numbers "prime to one another" as those "measured by a unit alone as common measure,"[38] Euclid accepts 2 as a prime number. So did Aristotle before him, when he speaks of the dyad as "the only prime number among the even numbers,"[39] which shows that this change was due to the immediate successors of Pythagoras. There are no reports of the early use of prime numbers for cosmical or ethical considerations.

Another early principle of combination of numbers was that of addition. By combining the unit with itself several times in succession, the series of the natural integers is obtained. Still to be considered are the results obtained from combining addition with duplication and multiplication. Such a combination yielded the *perfect* and *friendly* numbers, which result from the relations between a given number and its component parts with respect to multiplication and addition. By taking together the factors of a given number, including one but excluding that number, it may happen that their sum is equal to the given number, which is then called a "perfect" number. The

37 Kathleen Freeman, *The Pre-Socratic Philosophers* (Cambridge, Mass., 1959), p. 224.
38 *Elements* vii. Def. 12.
39 *Topica* 157ᵃ 35.

law of the formation of these numbers is described by Theon of Smyrna in this way: "If we take successive double numbers starting from the unit, add them until a prime and incomposite number is found, and then multiply the sum by the last of the added terms, the resulting number will be perfect."[40] The proof of this relation is given by Euclid,[41] who established a general connection between prime and perfect numbers.

If the sum of any number of terms of the series: $1, 2, 2^2, \ldots$ 2^{n-1} be prime, and said sum be multiplied by the last term, the product will be a perfect number—that is, equal to the sum of all its factors; in modern notation: $S_n \cdot 2^{n-1}$ is a perfect number.

When a number is smaller than the sum of its aliquot parts, it is called an *over-perfect* number; a *deficient* number is greater than that sum. The first four perfect numbers are 6, 28, 496, and 8128; for $6 = (1 + 2 + 3)$ and $28 = (1 + 2 + 4 + 7 + 14)$. The numbers 12 and 20 are over-perfect because the sum of the aliquot parts $(1 + 2 + 3 + 4 + 6)$ of 12 is greater than 12, and the sum of the aliquot parts $(1 + 2 + 4 + 5 + 10)$ of 20 is greater than 20. The numbers 8 and 14 are deficient; for 8 is greater than the sum of its aliquot parts $(1 + 2 + 4)$ and 14 is greater than the sum $(1 + 2 + 7)$ of its aliquot parts. No reference to perfect, over-perfect, and deficient numbers is found in the fragments of Philolaus or anywhere before Euclid. We are told by Iamblichus[42] that Speusippus had written about perfect numbers in "a neat little book entitled *On the Pythagorean Numbers*" based on the writings of Philolaus; the book has been lost.

Yet perfect numbers were probably known to Pythagoras if we accept a statement by Iamblichus[43] attributing to him the

40 *Expositio Rerum Mathematicarum*, p. 45.
41 *Elements* ix. 36. The algebraic proof is given by Thomas L. Heath in *The Thirteen Books of Euclid's Elements* (Cambridge, 1908), II, p. 424 (repub. in New York, 1956).
42 *Theologumena Arithmeticae*, p. 82.
43 *Introductio Arithmetica*, p. 35.

discovery of *friendly* numbers. These are pairs of numbers such that each is the sum of all the aliquot parts of the other, as 284 and 220: the aliquot parts of 284 $(1 + 2 + 4 + 71 + 142)$ together equal 220, and the sum of the aliquot parts of 220 $(1 + 2 + 4 + 5 + 10 + 11 + 20 + 22 + 44 + 55 + 110)$ equals 284. If Pythagoras investigated numbers reciprocally equal to the sums of their aliquot parts, he must also have considered the simpler class of numbers which are equal to the sum of their own aliquot parts. There is a story that Pythagoras defined a friend as "One who is the other I, such as 220 and 284." Discovery of such couples of numbers, which appear to have been known to the Hindus before the sixth century B.C., was a problem of considerable difficulty for the Greeks; because verification of such numbers usually requires the handling of very high digits. General interest in the friendly numbers seems to result from the belief that a good omen was attached to them.

The Pythagoreans considered development of the purely arithmetical properties of numbers as not only mathematically important, but also as preparation for wider application of numbers to the sensible world through their connection with figures or forms. To be sure, figures are the most natural link between purely numerical relations and presentations of the external world. From the pebbles of Eurytus to the simultaneous consideration of the numbers of stars of a particular constellation and the geometrical figure they trace out in space, many observations suggest an intimate connection between numbers and figures. If everything is number, then the figure of everything must be a number. These and similar considerations may have suggested to Pythagoras an essential relation between numbers and geometry.

On the other hand, the practical mensuration of the Egyptians and the mathematical generalizations of Thales, with which Pythagoras was presumably acquainted, could have led him to investigate the significance of his theories. For the Egyptians had not given any reason for their utilitarian geometry, nor were the material principles of things proposed by the Ionians sufficiently rational to account for the abstract properties of numbers and geometrical figures. As the technique of deduction proper was not yet established, Pythagoras probably had to work out whatever rational explanation he could in order to connect the general propositions of geometry with their practical applications. Such an explanation could be suggested by number. If number is rational and material at the same time, then extension, which is also a manifestation of matter, must be number. That is why the Pythagoreans connected the unit in arithmetic and the point in geometry, by defining the unit as a "point without position," and the point as "a unit having position." The development of a number theory should therefore embrace geometry, which should in turn account for astronomy and the general study of nature.

CHAPTER 3

Representations of Numbers

The assimilation of number and figure in a rational method of investigating nature called for a practical way of combining arithmetic and geometry. The initial step was a systematic representation of numbers, which the early Greeks accomplished in two ways. The easiest was the method of disposing dots or alphas (units) along straight lines which formed geometrical patterns; the more technical was the construction of straight lines proportional in length to their corresponding numbers. The Pythagoreans are credited with the discovery and use of both methods.

The first method is illustrated by the theory of the *figured numbers,* which assumes that any number can be represented by a rectilinear segment. Except for primes, all numbers could be expressed by straight lines drawn in two or three dimensions. Because prime numbers can be represented in one dimension only, Thymaridas called them supremely rectilinear. According to Speusippus, the study of the figured numbers dates to Pythagoras himself. Eurytus' description of living things with pebbles proves that the early Pythagoreans used dots to construct figured numbers. There is also Aristotle's statement that the Pythagoreans considered boundaries and continuity to be to the various figures, just "as flesh and bones are to man and bronze and stone to the statue; they reduce all things to number and say the line is expressed by two."[1]

By placing the right number of dots in the proper positions, one point or dot was used to represent one; 2 dots placed apart represented 2 and also the straight segment joining the 2 points; 3 dots represented 3 and corresponded to the triangle, the first plane rectilinear figure; and 4 dots, one being outside the plane containing the other 3, represented 4 as well as a pyramid, the first rectilinear solid. Through similar operations, other polygonal and solid numbers were obtained. This assimilation of numbers and figures led the Pythagoreans to investigate their mutual properties and left a lasting mark on our mathematical language, as we still speak of the "square" or the "cube" of a number.

The varieties of polygonal and solid numbers are discussed by Nicomachus and Theon of Smyrna. These numbers represent the shapes of the various polygons and solids. Polygonal numbers are obtained by adding to one the successive terms of a series with a definite difference; the product of three terms is a solid number, the cube being a special case. The simple construction of the *triangular numbers*, formed by the sum of any successive terms of the series of natural numbers, scarcely requires an elaborate explanation. A triangular number with side n is generally represented in modern notation by the formula

$$1 + 2 + 3 \ldots + n = \tfrac{1}{2}n(n + 1)$$

But the Pythagoreans *showed* each number by a separate diagram; Figure 3-1 corresponds to the first four triangular numbers, 1, 3, 6, and 10, respectively.

The *square numbers* have a peculiar construction calling for special comment. If we consider the series of the successive odd numbers, and if we add the first to the second, their sum to the

[1] *Met.* 1036b 10.

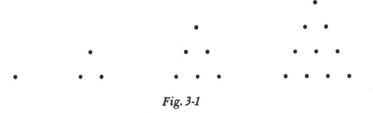

Fig. 3-1

third, and so on, we obtain a new series of numbers forming successive squares (Figure 3-2). Moreover, if we have a number of dots forming and filling up a square, for example, 9 dots, the next higher square, or 16, can be formed by adding rows of dots around two sides of the original square (Figure 3-3), and so on. In modern notation, the expression of a square number is

$$1 + 3 + 5 \ldots (2n - 1) = n^2$$

The addition of the next odd number makes the next higher square $(n + 1)^2$, and so on.

1	= 1	
1 + 3	= 4	
1 + 3 + 5	= 9	
1 + 3 + 5 + 7	= 16	
1 + 3 + 5 + 7 + 9	= 25	

Fig. 3-2   *Fig. 3-3*

The Pythagoreans would thus define an odd number as the difference of two square surfaces having for their sides two successive integers. This geometrical representation of odd numbers probably suggested their being called *gnomons* by analogy with the primitive astronomical instrument measuring time, consisting of an upright stick casting a shadow on a surface. Owing to its shape, the gnomon was used to describe what remained of a square when a smaller square was removed from it. Euclid extended the geometrical meaning of gnomon by applying it to figures similarly related to parallelograms.[2] Heron of Alexandria and Theon of Smyrna used the term in a more general sense, defining it as that which, added to a number or figure, makes a whole similar to what it is added to. In this sense, the gnomon can be applied to polygonal and solid numbers.

The generation of triangular and square numbers led naturally to the kind of numbers produced by adding the successive terms of the series of even numbers beginning with 2. Taking two dots and placing an even number of dots around them, gnomon-wise and successively, we obtain the *oblong numbers* with sides or factors differing by a unit. The diagrams in Figure 3-4 give the first four oblong numbers beginning with 2. The successive numbers of this kind are 2; $2 \cdot 3 = 6$; $3 \cdot 4 = 12$; $4 \cdot 5 = 20$; $5 \cdot 6 = 30 \ldots$ and generally $n(n + 1)$.

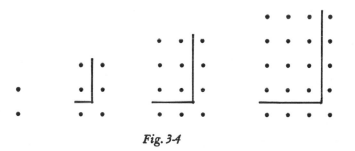

Fig. 3-4

Any oblong number is twice a triangular number (Figure 3-5) and any square is made up of two triangular numbers (Figure 3-6), the sides of the triangles differing by a unit. The oblong numbers are dissimilar, the ratio $n:(n + 1)$ being different for every value of n. By adding the successive odd numbers to one, we obtain always the form of the square; by adding the successive even numbers to 2, we get a series of oblong numbers all dissimilar in form.

2 *Elements* ii.

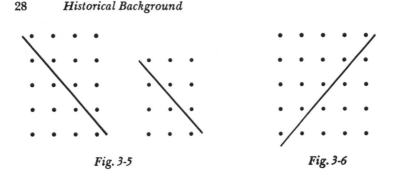

Fig. 3-5   Fig. 3-6

These relations may explain some Pythagorean views reported by Aristotle. One is the identification of "odd" with "limited"[3] and the inclusion of "square and oblong" in the Pythagorean scheme of the 10 pairs of opposites where odd, limited, and square are opposed to even, unlimited, and oblong, respectively.[4] Another is the identification of the unlimited with the even, which provides things with the element of indeterminacy. Thus, when gnomons are placed around the unit and then around any other number, the resulting figure in the latter case is always different or undetermined, while in the former it is always the same.[5] The figure referred to as being the same is, of course, the square formed by adding the odd numbers as gnomons around the unit.

The words "without the unit" are quite proper, provided their elliptic meaning is adequately understood. Aristotle surely refers to gnomons placed around the numbers beginning with the unit, and then around the numbers beginning without it, in other words, around any number other than the unit. In Figure 3-7 we start respectively with 3 dots placed in a row, then with 4, then with 5 dots; by placing gnomons around these linear groups of dots, we still obtain oblong numbers. Such an interpretation requires "without the unit" to mean "separately" from the one, or other than the unit.[6] This ren-

3 *Met.* 986a 18.
4 *Met.* 986a 23.
5 *Phys.* 203a 10.
6 W. D. Ross, *Aristotle's Physics* (Oxford, 1930), p. 544.

dering is confirmed by Iamblichus in a passage dealing with the unity of shape preserved in figured numbers beginning with one, and the diversity of shapes obtained with series beginning with numbers other than the one.[7] Further, both Plato and Aristotle give the word "oblong" the wider meaning of any non-square number with 2 unequal factors. This interpretation is fixed by the term *prolate* in the writings of Nicomachus and Theon of Smyrna, possibly using much earlier sources.

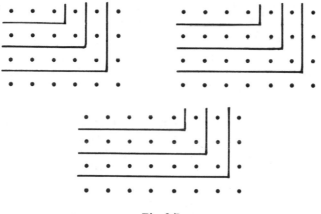

Fig. 3-7

We have no details about the Pythagorean investigations concerning solid numbers, although later commentators discussed them in detail. Nicomachus speaks of the "pyramid" as the first solid number; he argues that the base of the pyramid may be a triangular number, a square, or any polygonal number. But he only mentions the first triangular pyramids 1, 4, 10, 20, 35, 56, and 84, and he explains the formation of pyramids on square bases. He also classifies other solid numbers, speaking of cubes and of "scalene" solid numbers such as beams, columns, and tiles, as well as other combinations.

---

[7] *In Nicomachii Arithmetica* 73 (15) *sq.*

The early Pythagoreans probably thought of the solid numbers in connection with the construction of regular solids, which they may have identified with the material elements of the universe.

The manipulation of figured numbers alone could not provide a comprehensive interpretation of the world, especially as the Pythagoreans had no means of generalizing the relations among the various figured numbers. For a closer assimilation of number and figure, they could propose to represent numbers with straight segments proportional in length to their corresponding numbers. When two such segments formed a plane right angle, their product was the rectangle having them as adjacent sides; when three such segments formed a solid right angle, their product was the parallelepiped having them as adjacent sides. This method, used extensively by Euclid, is implied in Plato[8] and in the Pythagorean use of the proportionals and of the application of areas. These theories represent the culmination of the earliest combination of arithmetic and geometry as urged by the Pythagorean doctrines.

The discovery of proportionals attributed to Pythagoras[9] is a natural extension of his number theory. If a point is a unit in position, then a line is made up of points, just as a necklace is made up of beads. Disregarding later disputes about the continuous and the discrete, homogeneous and identical points may be taken as the ultimate units of spatial measurement. Consequently, the ratio of 2 given segments is merely the ratio of the numbers of points in each. Moreover, because any magnitude involves a ratio between the number of units it contains and the unit itself, the comparison of 2 magnitudes implies 2 ratios, or 4 terms. When any 2 pairs of terms have equal ratios, these 4 terms are said to form a *proportion*.

Development of the theory of numerical proportion leads

8 Cf. *Theaetetus* 147D-148B.
9 Proclus *Commentary on Euclid*, p. 65. There are two readings of the Greek text, one for proportionals and the other for irrationals. The latter is dismissed, as it was difficult to believe that Pythagoras developed a "theory of irrationals." But either reading may be true, as Pythagoras did discover both the proportionals and the irrationals.

to the consideration of *means* which the Pythagoreans studied, probably for their musical experiments. They knew of 3 means: the arithmetic, the geometric, and the harmonic, which Archytas explained for the first time.[10] In the arithmetic mean, the first of the 3 terms exceeds the second by the same amount as the second exceeds the third. In the geometric mean, the first term is to the second as the second is to the third. In the harmonic mean, the 3 terms are such that, by whatever part of itself the first exceeds the second, the second exceeds the third by the same part of the third. Their corresponding algebraic expressions are as follows:

Arithmetic $\dfrac{a-m}{m-b} = \dfrac{a}{a}$ or $2m = a + b$

and m is the arithmetic mean between a and b.

Geometric $\dfrac{a-m}{m-b} = \dfrac{a}{m}$ or $m^2 = ab$

and m is the geometric mean between a and b.

Harmonic $\dfrac{a-m}{m-b} = \dfrac{a}{b}$ or $\dfrac{2}{m} = \dfrac{1}{a} + \dfrac{1}{b}$

and m is the harmonic mean between a and b.

The name "harmonic mean" was adopted by Archytas in accordance with the views of Philolaus concerning geometrical harmony, instead of the older name "subcontrary," which may imply a previous arithmetical definition before its discovery in the intervals of the octave.[11] This name was applied to the cube because it has 12 edges, 8 angles, and 6 faces, while 8 is the harmonic mean between 12 and 6, as the following expression shows:

$$\frac{a-m}{m-b} = \frac{a}{b}, \quad \text{hence} \quad \frac{12-8}{8-6} = \frac{12}{6}.$$

[10] Quoted by Porphyry in his *Commentary on Ptolemy's Harmonics:* Diels, *Vors.*, 47 B 2, III, pp. 435-436.

[11] In his *Commentary on Plato's Timaeus* (Oxford, 1928), A. E. Taylor shows how the Pythagoreans would have observed the 3 means in their musical studies.

The relation of this proportion to musical harmony can be explained thus: "If 6 is made to correspond to the first note of the scale, so as to have exclusively integers in the relations between the tones of the scale, then 8 corresponds to the fourth instead of 4/3 and 12 corresponds to the octave instead of 2."[12]

The generalization of this proportion, called the "musical mean," is considered by Iamblichus after Nicomachus as the "most perfect proportion." It consists of 4 terms so combined that the two middle terms are the arithmetic and harmonic means between the extremes:

$$a : \frac{a+b}{2} = \frac{2\,ab}{a+b} : b$$

While the Babylonians are credited with its discovery, Pythagoras introduced it into Greek science and Plato used it in *Timaeus*. This numerical connection between geometrical and musical harmony was another link in the cosmic significance of the number theory.

The doctrine of means developed by later Pythagoreans consists of 10 types described by Nicomachus[13] and Pappus,[14] 7 of them elaborations of the 3 fundamental means already mentioned. No information is available about the developments of the early Pythagorean theory of proportion, except that it was based on considerations involving integers only. When the irrationals were discovered, the Pythagoreans did not build a more adequate theory of proportion. This was left to Eudoxus, who was probably influenced by Plato's views. But the Pythagoreans used their own restricted method of proportionals, especially in their theory of application of areas.

This method is thus outlined by Proclus:

These ancient things, says Eudemus, are discoveries of the Pythagorean Muse: I mean the application of areas, their exceeding and

12 Gaston Milhaud, *Les Philosophes Géomètres de la Grèce*, 2nd ed. (Paris, 1934), p. 93.
13 Cf. *Arithmetica Introductio*, p. 141 *sq.*
14 *Collectio*, p. 102.

their falling short. These men inspired later geometers to give their names to the so-called "conic" lines, calling one of these the parabola (application), another the hyperbola (exceeding), and another the ellipse (falling short). Those godlike men of old saw the things signified by these names in the construction of areas upon a given straight segment in a plane. For when you take a segment and lay the given area exactly alongside the whole of it, they say you apply that area. When you make the length of the area greater than the segment, it is said to "exceed"; and when you make it less, so that after drawing the area a portion of the segment extends beyond it, it is said to fall short. In the Sixth Book, Euclid speaks in this way both of exceeding and falling short.[15]

The general form of the problem involving application of areas is as follows: "Given 2 figures, to construct a third equal to the one and similar to the other." The ratio of one area to the other, or the ratio of the contents of the 2 figures, can be expressed as a ratio between straight segments, and such ratios can be manipulated in various ways. The application of areas is an important part of Greek mathematics; it is the foundation of the Euclidian theory of irrationals and of the Apollonian treatment of the conics. In performing the geometrical operations involved, the Greeks did the equivalent of the algebraical processes of addition, subtraction, multiplication, division, squaring, extracting roots, and solving mixed quadratic equations with real roots.

The method of application of areas has been systematized by Euclid, who used the Eudoxian theory of proportion in the *Elements* to prove such Pythagorean problems as the following:

I, 45—To construct in a given rectilinear angle a parallelogram equal to a given rectilinear figure.[16]

II, 5—If a straight line is cut into equal and unequal segments, the rectangle contained by the unequal segments of the

---

[15] *Commentary on Euclid* i, p. 419.

[16] Proclus observes that ancient geometers were led to investigate the squaring of the circle as a consequence of this problem.

whole and the square on the line between the points of
section equal the square on the half.[17]

II, 11—To cut a given straight line so that the rectangle contained
by the whole and one of the segments equals the square
on the remaining segments.[18]

VI, 28—To apply on a given straight line a parallelogram equal to
a given rectilinear figure and deficient by a parallelogram-
mic figure similar to the given one; the given rectilinear
figure must not be greater than the parallelogram described
on half the segment and similar to the defect.[19]

VI, 29—To apply on a given straight line a parallelogram equal
to a given rectilinear figure and exceeding by a parallelo-
grammic figure similar to the given one.

These examples show how the Pythagoreans could use
geometry as a substitute for modern algebraic operations, and
why a large part of their geometry may properly be called
"geometrical algebra." When dealing with problems involving
similar figures, their method of applying areas required the
notion of proportionals. But when dealing with mere elementary problems of simple transformation of a given area
into another of a different form, the Pythagoreans could use
their theory of figured numbers.

Such methods may be linked with the remarkable theorem
of the square of the hypotenuse, which illustrates all of these
other methods. Tradition attributes it to Pythagoras, who may
have obtained it either by generalizing particular Babylonian
and Egyptian cases, by means of purely numerical considera-

[17] This theorem yields the Pythagorean rule for finding integral square
numbers. Thomas L. Heath obtains through it the geometrical solution
of the equation $ax - x^2 = b^2$; but there is no direct evidence that the
Pythagoreans or even Euclid used this proposition for such a solution.
Cf. *The Thirteen Books of Euclid's Elements* (Cambridge, 1908), I, p. 384
(repub. in New York, 1956).

[18] This problem gives a geometrical solution of the equation $x^2 + ax$
$= a^2$.

[19] The condition of the solution of this problem is proved in the
preceeding proposition (VI, 27), which is a good example of a *diorismos*.
This problem and the following one correspond to the solution of
quadratic equations.

tions, by the application of areas, or by a restricted use of proportion. According to the method of obtaining square numbers explained by Heath,[20] the sum of any successive terms of the odd numbers series is a square. It then suffices to pick out the odd numbers which are squares and to find an expression for all sets of such 3 numbers giving the hypotenuse relation. More specifically, the right-angled triangle with sides (3, 4, 5) illustrates the case of a square with side 5 being transformed into 2 others of sides 3 and 4 respectively, and together equivalent to the first. This fact may have led Pythagoras to state the more general theorem in terms of the theory of application of areas, the problem being to transform a given square into 2 squares together equivalent to the first; or, conversely, to transform 2 given squares into one square equivalent to the sum of their areas.

Several proofs by proportion can be given of this theorem. One of the simplest is as follows (Figure 3-8). Let ABC be a triangle right-angled at A, with AD perpendicular to BC. The similarity of the triangles DBA and DAC to the triangle ABC gives the relations $BA^2 = BD \cdot BC$ and $AC^2 = CD \cdot BC$; hence $BA^2 + AC^2 = BC^2$. In this proof, the square on BC is equal to the sum of 2 rectangles, which is precisely what Euclid proves in Book I by a different method. Although the Pythagorean theories of proportion and of numbers in general were applicable to commensurable quantities only, the restricted use of proportion in a special proof was possible;

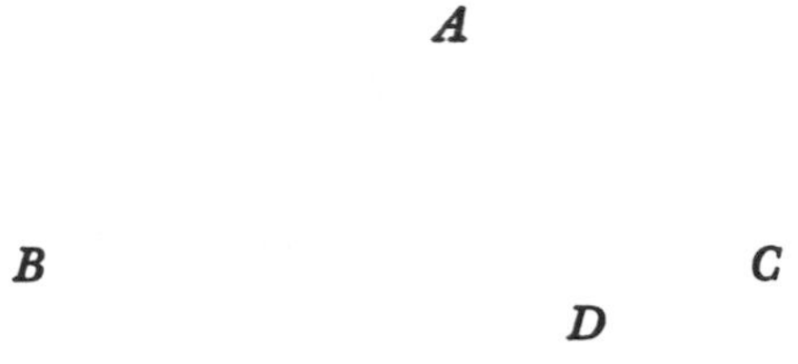

A

B   C
                    D

Fig. 3-8

[20] Thomas L. Heath, *A Manual of Greek Mathematics* (Oxford, 1931), pp. 46-48.

when the discovery of the irrationals made revision of the Pythagorean proof necessary, neither the Master nor his immediate disciples tried any substitute for it. Indeed, the invention of irrationals was so far-reaching that it demanded revision of the number theory itself, a momentous task the early Pythagoreans could not undertake with their restricted methods.

CHAPTER 4

Cosmic Significance of Mathematics

While the world was still unaware of the critical developments of Pythagorean mathematics, the numerical theory of the Brotherhood was diligently applied to the various aspects of the cosmos. The initial step in this process was conditioned by the distinction between odd and even numbers. The Pythagorean assimilation of the odd with the limit and of the even with the unlimited or indefinite was probably connected with the theory of bipartition. As an odd number is not divisible by two, it sets a limit to bipartition and is therefore limited, while an even number is unlimited, as it does not set a limit to bipartition. Thus the limit and the indefinite become the ultimate principles of the universe. The one is identified with the limit; by drawing towards itself more and more of the indefinite, it sets a limit to the latter and transforms it into a definite thing.

The Pythagoreans developed this original distinction into a table of 10 fundamental principles:[1] the limit and the unlimited (or indefinite), odd and even, one and many, right and

---

[1] *Met.* 986ᵃ 22.

left, resting and moving, straight and curved, square and oblong, light and darkness, male and female, good and bad. The Pythagoreans used the limit and the indefinite in a way which makes of these opposites an expression of form and matter, and indeed the elementary constituents of the world. They thought of matter as unlimited, and probably imagined it in much the same way as the indefinite of Anaximander or the air of Anaximenes. Such a view appears justified by the primitive belief of an endless expanse of air beyond the cosmos, from which the world draws its breath. The connection between the Pythagorean opposites and the Milesian doctrines seems to find a striking confirmation in Plato's cosmogony,[2] where mist and darkness are given as forms of air.

To the Ionian conception of a primary stuff, the Pythagoreans added the notion of the limit which plays a part similar to that of form. The generation of things out of Anaximander's "indefinite" becomes easier with a limit shaping the amorphous energy of the indefinite. Discussion of the views of Anaximenes about the rarefaction and condensation of air may have shown how these processes imply the quantitative ideas of more or less. The next step was to consider quantity and air as two separate principles producing the world when combined. This is precisely what the Pythagoreans did by assimilating air with the void, the boundless and abstract extension emanating from the even, and by identifying with the limit the principle of number, the one exemplifying the odd. Thus, under its dual aspect of odd and even, number was the principle of matter as well as of the form which limits and shapes it. Indeed, number was the essence of everything.

An interesting hypothesis about the generation of the Pythagorean monad is put forward by Enriques.[3] The boundless and formless matter of the cosmos, as conceived by Anaximander, would produce the various elements by rarefaction and condensation, as imagined by Anaximenes. Condensation

---

2 *Timaeus* 58D.

3 Frederigo Enriques, *Il Mondo Antico*, trans. Jerome Rosenthal (New York, 1929), II, p. 17.

of a gas in a vessel spreads all over its cold surface clusters of minute drops which are themselves many centers of condensation. This phenomenon might have led the Pythagoreans to consider each of these monadic centers as a small solid nucleus separated from the others by the surrounding rarefied medium. The monad would thus be formed by the mechanical variations of the shapeless matter. Enriques believes his suggestion to be consistent with the description of the Pythagorean doctrines given by Aristotle, and with the method used by Eurytus in identifying things with the number and position of material points.

The main difficulty of this explanation is that the Pythagorean monad is not the result of any material process, but the principle of all such processes. We may quote here the reported testimony of Alexander Polyhistor about the beliefs of the Brotherhood:

> For them, the principle of all things is the monad; arising from the monad, the undetermined dyad acts as matter to the monad which is cause; from the monad and the undetermined dyad arise numbers; from numbers points; from these, lines out of which arise plane figures which produce in turn solid figures; from these, material bodies whose constituents are four—fire, water, earth, air. These elements interchange and turn into another completely; out of them arises a world which is animate, intelligent, spherical and has the earth as its center, a spherical body inhabited round about.[4]

These remarks summarize the relations established by the Pythagoreans between their number theory and their physical and astronomical observations, although very little is known about their method of generating the universe. Because Plato used the 5 regular solids for this purpose,[5] some of the early commentators believed that the Pythagoreans held a similar opinion. Probably on the authority of Theophrastus, Aetius says that Pythagoras "considering the five solid figures, also called the mathematical figures, maintains that the earth arose

[4] Diogenes Laertius viii, p. 24-25.
[5] *Timaeus* 53C-55C.

from the cube, fire from the pyramid, air from the octahedron, water from the icosahedron, and the sphere of the universe from the dodecahedron."[6] This opinion agrees with this fragment of Philolaus quoted by Stobaeus: "There are five bodies pertaining to the sphere, the fire, water, earth and air in the sphere and the vessel of the sphere itself as the fifth."[7] This fragment does not mention specifically identification of the regular solids with the elements in the sphere, but it is consistent with this doctrine.

This view attributed to Philolaus does not differ greatly from the theory of Empedocles, who was the first to consider water, air, fire, and earth as the material principles of the universe. Empedocles may have taken the matter of his intuition from the philosophers of Croton, and his two principles of Love and Hate fit well in the Pythagorean table of opposites. But as number was the principle of things, the Pythagoreans had no need to stress the generating virtues of the 4 material principles as presented by the Milesians. Hence, they emphasized the geometrical or mathematical nature of the four elements, while Empedocles insisted on their material character.

Consequently we would not attribute to Plato, as does Heath,[8] the original assimilation of material elements with regular solids. This identification was probably implied in the construction ·of the regular solids attributed to Pythagoras by Proclus and other commentators. But the early Pythagoreans were unable to construct the regular solids as systematically as Euclid did in Book XIII of the *Elements,* because the Euclidian method of constructing and calculating their sides in terms of the radius of the circumscribed sphere calls for a mathematical knowledge the Pythagoreans did not possess. But they could have "put together" the regular polygons in the manner Plato puts them together in *Timaeus*—by bringing

6 *Placita* ii, 6.5; Diels, *Vors.,* 44 B 12, III, pp. 412-413.

7 Diels, *Vors., op. cit.*

8 Thomas L. Heath, *A History of Greek Mathematics* (Oxford, 1921), I, p. 158.

together several angles of equilateral triangles, squares, or pentagons at one point so as to make a solid angle, and then by completing all the solid angles in that way.

According to Proclus, the Pythagoreans put angles of certain regular figures around a point, and showed how only 3 kinds of such angles fill up the space in one plane around the point.[9] The scholiast mentions "the five so-called Platonic figures which do not belong to Plato, three of the five being due to the Pythagoreans, namely the cube, the pyramid, and the dodecahedron, while the octahedron and icosahedron are due to Theaetetus."[10] The last two solids mentioned were probably known to the Pythagoreans, as their construction is not difficult.

Some have questioned the Pythagorean origin of the dodecahedron with its pentagonal faces, as the construction of the regular pentagon entails the cutting of a segment *in extreme and mean ratio*. But this special problem is a simple case of the Pythagorean method of applying areas. Iamblichus even attributes this particular construction to Pythagoras when recounting the story of Hippasus, who perished by shipwreck for being "the first to divulge the construction of the sphere with the twelve pentagons; though he received credit for the discovery, it really belonged to Him, as they refer to Pythagoras whom they do not call by name."[11] This story recalls the one mentioned by Proclus about the Pythagorean who perished at sea for revealing the irrational. He may have been the same Hippasus, for the irrational is involved in the solids inscribed in the sphere. To be sure, the construction of the dodecahedron by means of 12 pentagons may be plausibly attributed to the earlier Pythagoreans, who were familiar with the star-pentagon. Both Lucian[12] and the scholiast to Aristophanes[13] mention the "triple interwoven triangle" called the

9 *Commentary on Euclid,* p. 304.
10 Thomas L. Heath, trans., *The Thirteen Books of Euclid's Elements,* ed. Heiberg (Cambridge, 1908), V, p. 654 (repub. in New York, 1956).
11 *De Vita Pythagorica,* p. 88.
12 *Pro Lapus in Salutando* ii. 330.
13 *The Clouds,* 609.

pentagram or pentalpha, the symbol of health used by the Brotherhood as a sign of recognition.

The physical experiments of the Pythagoreans relating to acoustics are of particular interest. Since number ruled the world, it must explain the various phenomena of nature, especially the art of music, for which Pythagoras had a great predilection. We have no definite information about the discovery of the fundamental harmonic relations of a string vibrating over a resounding board. But it is probable that Pythagoras himself found the numerical ratios determining the concordant intervals of the scale. In those days, the most common instrument was the lyre with 7 strings; the eighth string was probably added after the Pythagorean discoveries. Yet Pythagoras did not use the lyre for his experiments, but the *monochord,* an instrument he made with one string which could be stopped at different intervals by a movable bridge.[14] He could have also used some details of Eastern music he may have learned during his Egyptian travels.

Although Pythagoras could have been aware that the pitch of notes depends on the rate of vibrations communicating impulses to the air, he had no means of measuring the rate of vibration. But as the rate of 2 similar strings are inversely proportional to their length, the experiment could be reduced to a simple comparison of length along the single string of the monochord. He could discover in this way how the fifth and the octave of a note are produced on the same string by stopping at $2/3$ and $1/2$ of its length, respectively. This harmony may have suggested the name of harmonic proportion, since

$$1 : \frac{1}{2} = 1 - \frac{2}{3} : \frac{2}{3} - \frac{1}{2}$$

The interest of the Pythagoreans in number and music accounts readily for their wonder at this unexpected but intimate connection between number and sound. A simple experiment

14 An account of the Pythagorean discoveries in acoustics is given in Boethius *De Institutione Musica* i, chaps. 10-11.

with a primitive instrument had revealed the most remarkable operation of law in a field hitherto closed to systematic investigation. Intervals between sounds perceptible only to the fine ears of professional musicians, which could be neither explained to others nor referred to definite causes, were now reduced to clear and fixed numerical relations. The rule of spatial quantity was thus imposed on a most intangible and delusive phenomenon affecting the ear: sound was shown to be measurable in space, to be subject to number. Having established a basic principle of the mechanics of sound, Pythagoras may have thought that all other mechanical systems could be investigated according to similar principles. Hence, he may have sought to explain the motion of the heavenly bodies by means of some numerical regulative law.

The Pythagorean views on astronomy might be considered, indeed, as an extension of experiments with sound. Here again we may quote Aristotle, who recounts how the idea of harmony was applied to nature.

> Some have supposed that the motion of the (heavenly) bodies of that size must produce a noise, since on our earth the motion of bodies far inferior in size and speed has that effect. When the sun, the moon and all the stars so great in number and in size are moving with such a rapid motion, they say, how should they not produce an immensely great sound? Starting from this argument and from the observation that their speeds as measured by their distances are in the same ratios as musical concordances, they assert that the sound produced by the circular movement of the stars is a harmony. And since it appears unaccountable that we should not hear this music, they explain that the sound is in our ears from the very moment of birth and is thus indistinguishable from its contrary silence, since sound and silence are discriminated by mutual contrast.[15]

A reference to this view, generally known as the *harmony of the spheres*, is found in Plato's myth of Er, where the whorls representing the spheres of the heavenly bodies "together form

[15] *De Caelo* 290b 15.

one harmony,"[16] and also in the formation of the world-soul,[17] where ratios are given to the planets on the pattern of a musical harmony. Aristotle rejects this "melodious and poetical" theory, saying that any sound emitted by the heavenly spheres would be so great in proportion to their size that it would shatter any solid body. "If the heavenly bodies moved in a generally diffused mass of air or fire, as every one supposes, their motion would necessarily cause a noise of tremendous strength, which would necessarily reach and shatter us. Since this effect is evidently not produced, none of them can move with the motion either of animate nature or of constraint."[18] Hence, there cannot be any noise, for sound is created by friction alone.

The weight of tradition notwithstanding, it is not certain that Pythagoras believed in a celestial harmony. He probably developed his astronomical conceptions from the cosmic systems of the Milesians. Anaximander considered the sun, moon, and stars as 3 wheels of fire surrounding the earth and encased in air or mist, although we only see the single aperture through which the fire escapes "as through the nozzle of a pair of bellows." At this stage, Burnet suggests that "everything points to the conclusion that the Pythagoreans retained the rings of wheels of Anaximander"[19] and improved on the arbitrary distances assigned by him between the earth and these 3 rings by making them correspond to the fourth, the fifth, and the octave. In such a natural explanation of the harmony of the spheres, there is no question of a musical harmony, but only of concordant intervals expressing a numerical law of the world. Furthermore, when the cause of eclipses was known, "it was natural to infer that the earth was a sphere; and we may probably attribute that discovery to Pythagoras, himself."[20]

[16] *Republic* x, 617B.
[17] *Timaeus* 35B.
[18] *De Caelo* 291a 18.
[19] J. Burnet, *Early Greek Philosophy* (London, 1914), p. 56.
[20] *Ibid.*, p. 44.

A simpler view is put forward by Heath, who says that
Pythagoras "attributed spherical shape to the earth as to the
universe, for the simple reason that the sphere is the most
beautiful of the solid figures. For the same reason, Pythagoras
would surely hold that the sun, moon and the other heavenly
bodies are also spherical in shape."[21] Indeed, the astronomical
conceptions of the Pythagoreans have a strictly mathematical
character, as they do not involve any forces causing the respective movements of the heavenly bodies. Astronomy is
geometry combined with arithmetic and harmony. All the stars
are spheres, the most perfect solid figures, and they move in
circles.

This is also the opinion of Aristotle, in whose view the
Pythagoreans simply held the universe to be spherical, with
fire at the center, and the earth as one of the stars creating
night and day by its circular motion about the center. However, the view that the earth and the other heavenly bodies
revolve about the central fire is probably due to Philolaus and
other later Pythagoreans. Aristotle mentions this interesting
addition to the revolving bodies: "they further constructed
another earth in opposition to ours, to which they gave the
name of counter-earth."[22] This counter-earth was conceived
in order to bring up the number of the moving bodies to 10,
because the Pythagoreans liked to fit into their scheme "all
the properties of numbers and scales they could show to agree
with the attributes and parts and with the whole arrangement
of the heavens; and if there were a gap anywhere, they readily
made such additions as to make their whole theory coherent.
For example, because the number 10 is thought to be perfect
and to comprise the whole nature of numbers, they say the
bodies moving through the heavens are ten; but as the visible
bodies are only nine, they invent a tenth, the counter-earth."[23]
The number 10 is said here to be perfect because it signifies
the Decad, which has many mystical and numerical perfec-

21 Heath, *A History of Greek Mathematics,* I, p. 163.
22 *De Caelo* 293ᵃ 21.
23 *Met.* 986ᵃ 3.

tions, and not in the numerical sense of being the sum of its aliquot parts, which is not the case for 10.

Before closing this discussion, it may be useful to indicate some early applications of number to psychology, as the mathematical analogies used by Plato in the construction of the soul and of the universe obviously display Pythagorean influences. Considering knowledge as a whole, the Pythagoreans used number as a cause in all the branches of their teaching. In fact, their mathematical conceptions enabled them to combine the naturalism of the Milesians, the mysticism of the East, and some of the religious practices of Orphism into one system.

The revival of the Orphic traditions introduced into Greek philosophy the germ of a dualism between matter and mind, body and soul, God and the world. These distinctions were unknown to the earlier generations, for whom nature was animate and every living creature somehow infused with mind. The incorporation of the Orphic doctrine of transmigration into a philosophic system showed the aim of life to be liberation from the circle of rebirths in order to enjoy the divine state of bliss: the road to salvation was purification from sensuality and renunciation of worldly interests. The ritualistic character of this Orphic purification was intellectualized and given a moral value by the Pythagoreans, who supplemented their ascetic observances with silence, daily self-examination, and mental effort. Hence, science, music, gymnastics, and medicine were studied systematically by members of the Brotherhood, who recommended them for the purification of the soul and the body.

The purgative function of music, which originated in the practices of the Corybantic priests, was fully recognized in ancient psychotherapy. The introduction of a mathematical element into music, through the connection between sound and number, encouraged the use of mathematics for purification of the soul. If ordinary music was a soul purge, a similar effect could be obtained by cultivating the "highest music," the name given to philosophy in Plato's *Phaedo* (86B). Just as Pythagoras discovered the means to blend such apparently elusive things as the high and low notes of the octave, so could he determine numerically the blend of opposites in order to find a "mean" point fair to both, and to remove the "injustice" affecting the soul when one opposite encroaches upon the other.

Similarly, the health of the body must depend on the adequate blend of opposites, such as hot and cold, and wet and dry, traditionally considered as the principles of human life. According to Plato, the Pythagoreans held the body to be tuned to a certain pitch, like an instrument, the high and low notes in music identified with hot and cold, wet and dry. Consequently, health is just being in tune, and disease arises from the ill adjustment of hot and cold, wet and dry. The medical school founded by Alcmeon of Croton, which flourished at the same time as the Pythagorean Brotherhood, held similar views about health and disease and many associated topics, such as diet and climate. As friendly relations prevailed between their respective members, it is difficult to distinguish clearly what belongs to each school from the little evidence in our possession.

The proper function of the Pythagorean physician was to adjust an adequate blend of opposites in the human body, just as the curative function of music was to produce a proper blend of opposites in the human soul. The doctrine of mathematical means helped to determine their correct proportions and to combine efficaciously their various differences according to the constitution of individual patients. But such combinations depended ultimately on the restriction of the indefinite by the limit entailing number. Life and death themselves are thus ruled by number: if life is health, it is also harmony of the opposites; if death is the last phase of disease, it is also the result of the final elimination of the correct proportions of opposites in the human being.

In this primitive psychology, the principle of the harmony of the opposites is the soul, which "brings number and harmony into the body," according to Philolaus. An accurate account of the Pythagorean theory of the soul is not easy to formulate, for the statements handed down by tradition imply differences of opinion between earlier and later Pythagoreans. The following passage of Aristotle seems to represent the views of the older members of the school:

> There is yet another theory about the soul: for its supporters the soul is a kind of harmony, for harmony is a blend or composition of contraries, and the body is made of opposites. But harmony is a certain proportion or composition of the constituents blended, and the soul can be neither of these. Further the power of originating movements cannot belong to a harmony, while almost all regard this as a principal attribute of the soul. It is more appropriate to consider harmony as health or generally as one of the good states of the body, than to predicate it of the soul.[24]

The Pythagorean theory of the soul is also connected with the doctrine of rebirth or transmigration, which Pythagoras may have learned from Orphism and the East. Xenophanes made fun of him for pretending to recognize the voice of a departed friend in the howls of a beaten dog,[25] and Empedocles seems to refer to him when he mentions a man who could remember what happened 10 or 20 generations before. The doctrine of transmigration may have inspired the Platonic doctrine of Reminiscence, which plays so great a part in *Meno* and *Phaedo*. Burnet suggests that Pythagoras was probably familiar with the idea of Reminiscence, for he must have noticed that "the realities he was dealing with were not perceived by the senses."[26] But such an interpretation is excessive, since the Pythagorean mathematical conceptions were less pure and abstract than those of Plato. Since material things seen, heard, or touched by the early Pythagoreans were essentially numbers, it was unnecessary for them to recall what their souls may have known before incarnation. The direct vision of a higher mathematical reality may be considered as a proper Platonic doctrine.

24 *De Anima* 407b 30.
25 Diels, *Vors.*, 21 B 7; I, p. 130.
26 Burnet, *op. cit.*, p. 43.

CHAPTER 5

The Crisis of the Irrationals

There are strong reasons to believe that Pythagoras discovered the irrationals when considering the relation between the diagonal of a square and its side. His method of obtaining square-numbers may have prompted him to question why every number is not a square, when he had found some exception to his practical rule. But geometry offered the best examples of the existence of irrationals, as in the cases of the isosceles right-angled triangle and the numerical relation between the diagonal of a square and its side. The very names of *side-numbers* and *diagonal-numbers* seem to justify this view.

If the primitive treatment of the theorem of the right-angled triangle was arithmetical, the impossibility of finding a root for the square of the hypotenuse of an isosceles right-angled triangle would naturally yield the notion of $\sqrt{2}$, the first irrational. According to a scholium to Euclid, the Pythagoreans discovered the irrationals by observing numbers; for "though the unit is a common measure of all numbers, they were unable to find a common measure of all magnitudes."[1] This

[1] Thomas L. Heath, trans., *The Thirteen Books of Euclid's Elements*, ed. Heiberg (Cambridge, 1908), I, p. 415 (repub. in New York, 1956).

was because magnitudes are endlessly divisible, without leaving any part too small for further division.

After this discovery, the Pythagoreans probably investigated the properties of such magnitudes, but nothing definite seems to have been done before Theodorus of Cyrene and Theaetetus of Athens. The title of the lost work of Democritus, *On Irrational Lines and Solids,* suggests that surds were known before his time. The irrationality of $\sqrt{2}$ is alluded to in Plato's *Republic* as a well-known fact; in *Theaetetus* we are told that Theodorus was the first to prove the irrationality of $\sqrt{3}$, $\sqrt{5}$ ... $\sqrt{17}$, which implies that $\sqrt{2}$ has been dealt with earlier.

The traditional proof of the irrational character of certain numbers is indicated by Aristotle as an example of *reductio ad absurdum:* "All who effect an argument *per impossibile* infer syllogistically what is false, and they prove the original conclusion hypothetically when something impossible results from the assumption of its contradictory; for example, the diagonal of the square is incommensurate with its side because odd numbers are equal to evens if it is assumed to be commensurate."[2] This is evidently the proof interpolated in the tenth book of Euclid's *Elements,* where the fraction m/n in its lowest terms is supposed to equal $\sqrt{2}$; then both m and n must be even because $m^2/n^2 = 2$ and $m^2 = 2n^2$; yet this cannot be, because of the condition of the fraction. With this contradiction, no fraction m/n can have 2 as its square.[3]

Their fruitless effort to find the exact root of $\sqrt{2}$ led the Pythagoreans to prove its incommensurability, and to determine any number of successive approximations to its value by finding the integral solutions of an indeterminate equation (of the form $2x^2 - y^2 = -1$ in modern notation). The pairs of values of x and y were called *side-numbers* and *diameter-numbers* or *diagonal-numbers,* respectively; as these values increase, the ratio of y to x approximates $\sqrt{2}$ more closely. Theon of Smyrna[4] gives an interesting explanation of the formation

2 *An. Priora* 41ᵃ 23.

3 Cf. Bertrand Russell, *Introduction to Mathematical Philosophy* (New York, 1938), p. 67.

4 *Expositio Rerum Mathematicarum,* pp. 43-44.

of these numbers, whose names are justified by their particular function and purpose.

The Greeks treated the irrationals in general as a part of geometry rather than arithmetic, because of the difficulty of handling irrationals arithmetically and of the successful Pythagorean combination of geometry with number theory. For want of a notation, any irrational was represented by a rectilinear segment or a combination of lines. This is illustrated in the tenth book of Euclid's *Elements,* where simple and compound irrationals are dealt with geometrically. Yet the Pythagoreans could not develop the theory of irrationals on this basis, precisely because their geometry depended on their restricted number theory. Furthermore, as their arithmetic involved a theory of proportion applicable to commensurable magnitudes only, discovery of the irrationals must have dealt a severe blow to its whole structure. In fact, it involved the restriction of their method of proportion, pending the discovery of the generalized theory of proportion established by Eudoxus during Plato's time. The discovery of surds also shattered the geometrical methods of the Pythagoreans, as the proof of several geometrical theorems rested on their primitive theory of proportion.

When the invention of surds became known to members of the Brotherhood, a rift was opened between arithmetic and geometry; this led to the investigation of various problems involving irrational magnitudes. Pythagorean and other schools of mathematicians tried laboriously to find whether the rift could be bridged by purely mathematical methods. This might explain why such problems as the squaring of the circle, trisection of the angle, and duplication of the cube were popular after the death of Pythagoras. In spite of the interesting results obtained by some mathematicians, these circumstances may account for the setback suffered by mathematics at the end of the fifth century B.C.

It may be questioned whether the Pythagoreans knew the incommensurability of a circumference in relation to its diameter, although the circle played an important part in their cosmogonies. Tradition mentions Anaxagoras of Clazomenae (*ca.* 500-428 B.C.) as the first to deal openly with the problem of squaring the circle. But he may have heard of it from the early Pythagoreans, of whom he was a younger contemporary, and who could not have dealt openly with this question because of their oath of secrecy. To be sure, discovery of the irrationals must have been kept secret a long time, as it had far-reaching consequences for the practical and philosophical doctrines of the Brotherhood. The esoteric disciples must have heard with awe from the Master that number, which was and explained everything, could not account for some simple geometrical magnitudes related to their number theory.

This situation must have weakened the cosmic and moral applications of the number theory as a whole. The square, a most fundamental and beautiful type of number, was found to bear within itself an element of irrationality. By using a square number as a physical explanation of facts, reason was appealing, so to speak, to "unreasonable" elements. It may also have been observed that many rules of harmony apparently subject to number entailed irrationals. When the irrationality of π was established later, many must have thought that the laws of the heavens themselves could not be as true as Pythagoras said they were, for if the distances between the heavenly bodies were proportional to the lengths of the vibrating strings which produced the musical scale, the perfect circular paths of these bodies had no common number with the proportional distances between the center of the world and the various bodies moving in space. Consequently, it was impossible to maintain any longer that number was the essence of all existing things, or that all things were made of number.

This awkward crisis encouraged the Pythagorean esoterics to maintain their oath to withhold from the public the existence of irrationals. This accounts for the legend that the first Pythagorean who made it public, whether it was Hippasus or another, perished at sea for his impiety. According to Proclus,[5] the unutterable and the formless were to be concealed; those

5 Cf. Iamblichus *De Vita Pythagorica* xviii, 88.

who uncovered and touched this image of life were instantly destroyed and shall remain forever the play of the eternal waves.

Meanwhile, destruction of the primitive mathematical balance between the cosmos and man called for new conceptions to satisfy man's yearning for truth. If nature contained elements beyond reason, then man himself should be studied in order to find out his limitations and their eventual remedy. This task was performed by the Socratic schools, although the serious interest of the Pythagoreans in the practical rules of life was originally responsible for introducing ethics and social theory into the range of philosophical inquiry. This interest was intensified with Xenophanes and Heraclitus, and it reached its highest mark with Democritus and the Sophists.

The Pythagorean experiment was certainly discussed at the time. If the existing fragments of the pre-Socratic thinkers were not so scanty, we could probably trace many more references to Pythagorean doctrines before the time of Plato. The founder of the Academy must have borrowed a good deal from them, although he scarcely mentions them in his Dialogues. We have to turn to Aristotle, who disagreed with both Platonism and Pythagoreanism, for the first serious criticism of these views. In the first book of his *Metaphysics,* Aristotle says the Pythagoreans treat of principles and elements stranger than those of the Ionian philosophers, for these principles are taken from non-sensible things, since the objects of mathematics are things without movement. Yet the Pythagoreans claim to discuss and investigate nature, for they generate the heavens and explain their parts and functions by observing the natural phenomena and referring them to principles and causes. This attitude was shared by the Ionian philosophers, for whom the real is all that is perceptible and contained by the so-called heavens.

For Aristotle, the causes and principles mentioned by the Pythagoreans may lead gradually to the higher levels of reality, but they are less suited to theories about nature. Elaborating this view, he criticizes the Pythagoreans for neglecting to make clear whether the limit and the indefinite, the odd and the even are the only principles assumed. As a result, they are unable to account for the existence of motion and the facts of generation and destruction. Consequently, they offer no explanation of the particular movements of the heavenly bodies and of the difference between light and heavy objects. Although Plato assimilated the elements with the regular solids, the Pythagoreans apparently said nothing about fire, earth, air, or water. Engrossed with the problem of motion, Aristotle fails to see how number and its attributes are causes of what exists and of what happens in nature, when the only acknowledged numbers are those out of which the world is composed. Similar difficulties may have led Zeno to formulate his famous arguments.

Referring to some aspects of Pythagorean mysticism, Aristotle cannot reconcile its implications with his logical vision of the world. He fails to see why opinion and opportunity are placed in one particular region, while injustice and mixture are above or below. He also disagrees with the alleged proof that each of these is number, and that a plurality of the extended bodies composed of numbers is already in those places because the attributes of numbers are attached to various places. In this case, one cannot determine whether or not the number identified with each of these abstractions is also the number exhibited in the material universe. Although Plato says it is different, for him both the bodies and their causes are numbers.[6]

Notwithstanding the effectiveness of Aristotle's criticism, the Pythagorean doctrines and methods have suggested a basic approach to the problems of the world which has greatly influenced the development of philosophy and science. Commenting upon the Pythagorean doctrine that mathematical entities are the ultimate stuff of existence and experience, Whitehead asserts that, with this bald and crude statement, Pythagoras had hit upon

[6] *Met.* 900ᵃ 8-30.

a philosophical notion of considerable importance, a notion which has a long history, and which has moved the minds of men and has even entered into Christian theology. About a thousand years separate the Athanasian Creed from Pythagoras, and about two thousand four hundred years separate Pythagoras from Hegel. Yet for all these distances in time, the importance of definite numbers in the constitution of the Divine Nature, and the concept of the real world as exhibiting the evolution of an idea, can both be traced back to the train of thought set going by Pythagoras. . . . So today, when Einstein and his followers proclaim that physical facts such as gravitation are to be construed as exhibitions of local peculiarities of spatio-temporal properties, they are following the pure Pythagorean tradition.[7]

In short, the Pythagorean conception of science corresponds definitely to a fundamental attitude of the mind in its search for truth.

[7] A. N. Whitehead, *Science and the Modern World* (New York, 1941), p. 36.

CHAPTER 6

The Eleatic Reaction: Zeno

Philosophy and mathematics moved towards idealism when the early Pythagoreans refined the Milesian materialism by hypostatizing number. The pace was quickened when thinkers strove to avoid the anti-intellectual consequences of Heracliteanism and the technical shortcomings of Pythagoreanism. The latter inspired the negative arguments of Zeno and the constructive intuitions of Plato, while the former called forth the twin reactions of the Eleatics and the Atomists. The extreme idealism of the Eleatics asserted itself by rejecting the Ionian doctrines and, later, exploiting the Pythagorean inability to account for the irrationals. The Atomists vindicated the main implication of the Milesian cosmology, the indestructibility of matter, with a theory which took into account the Eleatic criticism.

The spiritual founder of the Eleatic school was Xenophanes (fl. 540 B.C.), who went from Asia Minor to Elea in Italy. But it was his disciple, Parmenides (fl. 476 B.C.), who openly opposed the Heraclitean doctrine of change and shaped the Eleatic philosophy. For him, not only was the divine being changeless, as Xenophanes had proclaimed, but being as such was immutable, since one thing cannot arise from another thing essentially unlike itself; to think otherwise is self-contradictory. Sense-perceptions are non-being, unreal, and untrue; thought alone is real and true. Being is the single permanent essence underlying apparent differences in bodies; by eliminating these differences, we conceive the only reality, eternal and unchangeable, limited only by itself, but nevertheless evenly extended and therefore spherical.[1]

Hence, the real problem of knowledge is to discover the true world of being beyond the appearances of common experience. It is difficult to say whether Parmenides thought of a rational method leading to such knowledge; in his philosophical poem, a goddess guides him toward truth. But in spite of its mystical or symbolical presentation, the problem of Parmenides expresses the basic quest of these philosopher scientists. The search for what is constant and permanent beyond the world of appearance asserted its importance beside the Ionian conception of the perpetual and unlimited transformations of material substances. For the Eleatics, the 4 elements themselves were mere appearances; it was beyond them that reality was to be found. But little could be done with the motionless and changeless being of Parmenides. These extreme characteristics of being subsequently had to be abandoned; the atoms of Democritus, the ideas of Plato, and the forms of Aristotle gave a better explanation of change.

In the meantime, the position taken by Parmenides influenced considerably the mathematical conceptions of the Greeks. It was not the arithmetical and geometrical generalizations of the Ionians which were affected by it, but the conceptions of the Pythagoreans. The town of Elea, where Parmenides had his School, was not very far from Croton, where the Pythagoreans held their meetings. There is little doubt that Parmenides was familiar with the leading doctrines of the Brotherhood. Although he did not discuss their mathe-

---

[1] The geometrical shape imputed to the changeless world by Parmenides indicates a compromise with intuition and involves all the difficulties of the continuum which Zeno denounced soon after.

matical ontology, he used the Pythagorean cosmology when he described the unreality of the world of appearances by way of contrast with the realm of being. The mathematical implications of these views were developed by Zeno when the Pythagorean difficulties were divulged to the world.[2]

As Zeno was neither a mathematician nor a physicist, his arguments on divisibility and motion had a wider aim than the one suggested by their technical interpretation. In fact, we are told[3] that he wrote a book upholding the views of Parmenides against the common conceptions of things. Although many absurdities may follow from the doctrine that only the "One" exists, Zeno could show that still more contradictions are entailed in the popular view that "Many" exist. This is probably why Zeno is considered the founder of Dialectic.

The method developed by Zeno was to make the same thing appear like and unlike, one and many, at rest and in motion.[4] For example, he would say that if multiplicity exists, it must be both infinitely small, its last divisions being without magnitude, and infinitely great because of the infinite number of these divisions.[5] The meaning of this dilemma is clear. If it is argued that a continual division does not necessarily end up in *nothing*, then the assumption that the final elements of a division have *some* size also involves a contradiction. For the original magnitude to be divided would be infinite in size, as it would have an infinite number of such parts. This dilemma

2 The ideas of Parmenides do not necessarily involve any conception of the infinitesimals or of the relativity of motion as understood today.

3 Plato, *Parmenides* 128C.

4 Plato, *Phaedrus* 261D. The dialectical ability of Zeno is illustrated by the following passage in the *Life* of Pericles, who was a frequent listener of the Eleatic thinker: "The two-edged tongue of mighty Zeno who, say what one would, could argue it untrue" (Plutarch *The Lives of the Noble Grecians and Romans*, p. 185).

5 Cf. Simplicius, *Commentary on Aristotle's Physics*, p. 139.5 (Diels). Another form of this argument is the following dictum attributed to Zeno: "That which being added to another does not make it greater, and being substracted from another does not make it less, is nothing"— E. Zeller, *Die Philosophie der Griechen* (London, 1931), I, p. 540.

is elaborated in Zeno's famous arguments against motion: the *Dichotomy* and the *Achilles* imply the indefinite divisibility of space and time, while the *Arrow* and the *Stadium* assume that space and time are not infinitely divisible, but are formed of indivisible elements.

These famous enigmas have been preserved by Aristotle in the following ter. is:

I. *Dichotomy.* "There is no motion, because what moves must arrive at the middle of its course before it reaches the end."[6]

II. *Achilles.* "The slower in a race will never be overtaken by the quicker; because the pursuer must first reach the starting point of the pusued, so that the slower must always be some distance ahead."[7]

III. *Arrow.* "The flying arrow is at rest";[8] because a thing is at rest when occupying its own space at a given time, as the arrow does at every instant of its alleged flight.

IV. *Stadium.* This argument[9] concerns 2 rows of bodies equal in number which pass one another on a race course as they move with equal speed in opposite directions, one row starting from the end of the course and the other from the middle. This is said to imply, as will be shown presently, that half a given time is equal to its double.

The implications of these 4 arguments seem to be wider than Aristotle thought when he proved their fallacy by means of his own views about motion and the infinite, which will be mentioned later. On the other hand, commentators do not always agree about their meaning and aim.[10] For a long time they were thought to be paradoxes against the existence of

6 *Phys.* 239b 11.
7 *Phys.* 239b 14.
8 *Phys.* 239b 29 (also 239b 5).
9 *Phys.* 239b 33.
10 Cf. Cajori, *The History of Zeno's Arguments on Motion,* which appeared in 1910 in the *American Mathematical Monthly*; Bertrand Russell, "The Problem of Infinity Historically Considered," Lecture VI in *Our Knowledge of the External World* (New York, 1929), pp. 169-198.

motion, but in recent years they have been rehabilitated and even considered as the basis of some modern mathematical conceptions.

These sophisms were reinstated and made the foundation of a mathematical renaissance by a German professor who probably never dreamed of any connection between himself and Zeno. Weierstrass, by strictly banishing all infinitesimals, has at last shown that we live in an unchanging world, and that the arrow at every moment of its flight is truly at rest. The only point where Zeno probably erred was in inferring (if he did infer) that because there is no change, the world must be in the same state at one time as at another. This consequence by no means follows.[11]

The fact that it took 24 centuries to answer satisfactorily Zeno's arguments proves their fundamental importance in the history of mathematical philosophy.

The *Dichotomy* and the *Arrow* refer to absolute motion; they assume an object to be moving and prove it cannot even begin to move. The *Achilles* and the *Stadium* deal with relative motion; by comparing the motions of 2 objects, they show they cannot continue to move even if they had started. All 4 involve the continuity of space and time. The *Dichotomy* and the *Achilles* give more prominence to space and consider the continuum to be divisible indefinitely. As Aristotle had shown, the difference between them is the ratio of each distance to the preceding one, 1:2 for the former and 1:n for the latter. The *Arrow* and the *Stadium* stress the notion of time and assume the continuum to be composed of indivisible elements. Taken in pairs, these 4 symmetrical arguments form the horns of a dilemma set against the possibility of any continuum, and of motion in particular.

Both the *Dichotomy* and the *Achilles* contend that motion

11 Bertrand Russell, *The Principles of Mathematics* (New York, 1938), p. 347.

is impossible if space is continuous and divisible indefinitely, because any assumed motion presupposes another motion, this in turn another, and so on indefinitely. Yet, this series of divisions, by hypothesis inexhaustible, must be exhausted to make motion possible. But no assigned motion can actually be obtained with this endless regress by adding up the inexhaustible quantity of its parts. Zeno's difficulty resulted from his assumption that the existence of a magnitude (or of a convergent series) depends on the possibility of perceiving separately each part of the magnitude (or each term of the series). Instead of considering the regularity of the genetic law of a progression, Zeno required all its terms to be visualized separately in a spatial intuition. As this cannot be done, either motion does not exist or there is no discontinuous plurality of elements.

The difficulties involved in these first 2 arguments cannot be explained away by suggesting, with Aristotle, that Zeno did not consider time as divisible indefinitely like space, or by showing with Leibniz and others that the 2 spatial and temporal series are exhausted simultaneously, or by calculating with Descartes and others the moment *when* Achilles will overtake the tortoise, and the sum of the infinite series of $1 + 1/2 + 1/4 \ldots$ which converges to a definite limit. The question actually involved is *how* the infinite can be exhausted. Zeno was probably aware that the *Dichotomy* and the *Achilles* would be no longer valid if limits and discontinuity were taken into account, as the nature of the continuum would then be altered. Hence there is a development of the second alternative in the *Arrow* and the *Stadium* where space and time involve indivisible elements. Zeno's first alternative could be dismissed by pointing out that infinite convergent series are not involved in our intuition of continuity, and cannot be justified in terms of sense impressions.

The argument of the *Arrow* asserts that an object cannot move in an indivisible instant, because any change of position would divide the instant; and as time is composed of indivisible instants, the moving object is always at rest.[12] Zeno's contention here is true up to this point, and it has been likened by Russell to the "very widely applicable platitude" that every possible value of a variable is a constant, and that the values of a variable cannot have the variability which belongs to it exclusively. But the Eleatic failed to see that velocity is not a physical fact or a property belonging at each instant to a moving object, but the numerical expression of the limit of certain ratios. "This static theory of the variable is due to the mathematicians; and its absence in Zeno's day led him to suppose that continuous change was impossible without a state of change, which involves infinitesimals and the contradiction of a body being where it is not."[13] In fact, the paradox of the flying arrow can be answered readily in terms of the modern conception of the derivative.

With regard to the *Stadium*, Aristotle's description of the process by means of letters makes its meaning clear, although there has been some doubt about its exact interpretation. This

$$A \quad A \quad A \quad A \quad A \quad A$$
$$B_6 \quad B_5 \quad B_4 \quad B_3 \quad B_2 \quad B_1 \longrightarrow$$
$$\longleftarrow \quad C_1 \quad C_2 \quad C_3 \quad C_4 \quad C_5 \quad C_6$$

Fig. 6-1

argument may be illustrated by Figures 6-1 and 6-2, in which the A's represent a stationary row, while the B's and C's move with equal velocity alongside the A's and in opposite directions. Starting to move from their first positions (Figure 6-1),

$$A \quad A \quad A \quad A \quad A \quad A$$
$$B_6 \quad B_5 \quad B_4 \quad B_3 \quad B_2 \quad B_1$$
$$C_1 \quad C_2 \quad C_3 \quad C_4 \quad C_5 \quad C_6$$

Fig. 6-2

there will be a moment when the B's and the C's will be exactly under the A's (Figure 6-2). In that case, B_1 would have passed

12 Kathleen Freeman, *The Pre-Socratic Philosophers* (Cambridge, Mass., 1959), p. 157.
13 Russell, *The Principles of Mathematics*, p. 351.

alongside the 3 *A*'s and the 6 *C*'s during the same time and without changing. The same would be true for C_1 with respect to the other rows.

As *A*, *B*, and *C* stand for equal intervals, the time taken by B_1 in passing all the *A*'s is the same as the time it needed in passing half of them: hence, a given time is equal to its half, and any quantity equals its double. It follows that every instant is divisible as it is equal to its half. But if one wishes to maintain its indivisibility, the only way to avoid the alternative of its being equal to its half is to reject the possibility of motion. The point of this argument is clear, but it has been asked whether Aristotle asserts that half the given time would be double the half or equal to double the whole. The latter interpretation does not seem to affect the basic issues significantly.

The technical difficulties involved in the *Stadium* and in the *Arrow* can be disposed of now by the assumption that space and time intervals contain an infinite number of subdivisions, as the notion of an infinite class is not self-contradictory according to modern analysis. But if the arguments of Zeno can now be solved by means of the recent theories of continuity, limits, and infinite sets, they were real problems for the Greeks, who had not thought of these abstractions. For them, the realms of sense and reason, of intuition and logic were not clearly separated, hence their belief that mathematics was the study of situations generally thought to subsist in nature. Under these circumstances, Zeno's dilemmas must be regarded as effective arguments against the Democritean, the Heraclitean, and especially the Pythagorean doctrine of multiplicity, where the geometrical and the physical are not distinguished clearly and where a point is a unit having position. This was shown convincingly by Tannery,[14] for whom these 4 arguments indicate that the controversy between the philoso-

14 Paul Tannery, *La Géométrie Grecque* (Paris, 1887, p. 124 *sq.* This view was accepted by Milhaud, Zeuthen, and Cajori. The objections directed against it by Thomas L. Heath, *A History of Greek Mathematics* (Oxford, 1921), I, p. 283, seem to follow from a technical misunderstanding. Yet the monadic conceptions of the Pythagorean mathematics gradually disappeared after Zeno's controversy.

phy of being and the philosophy of change had widened enough to involve as well the quarrel between Pythagoreans and Eleatics.

The Pythagoreans identified the ultimate elements of reality with the integers derived from the empirical concept of extended points or monads. Hence, the universe was made of integral numbers; geometrical figures were concrete aggregates of monads; lines consisted of a definite number of points; and the intervals of time were sets of a definite number of instants. Furthermore, to these monadic assumptions were added the commensurability of any 2 segments in order to make measurements possible. The Pythagorean discovery of the irrationals shattered these doctrines. When it was found that no integral number accounted for the relation between the side of a square and its diagonal, or between the circumference of a circle and its diameter, it became obvious that discontinuous plurality and the continuity of motion could not be made coincident. To be sure, Pythagorean mathematical philosophy was more concerned with form and structure than with flux and variability. But if the principles established to account for permanence could be extended to account for change, then motion could be described in terms of the conceptions denounced by Zeno. Hence, the original Pythagorean views about the nature of magnitudes had to be abandoned.

In the meantime, a last attempt to rationalize the concept of the infinite was undertaken by Melissos (*fl.* 440 B.C.) the Eleatic, who endeavored to prove the main thesis of Parmenides by a direct method, rather than by indirect means like Zeno's arguments. Such a procedure was closely related to the geometrical problems of the day. But it had to be used more carefully here than in science, as its purpose was to express verbally what is true, and principally to arrive at a proper notion of being as such. We are thus told that being is eternal, homogeneous, true, infinite, unchanging, immobile internally.[15] Fragment 9 in particular indicates a strong ideal-

---

[15] Diels, *Vors.*, 30 B 9, II, p. 275.

istic trend: "If being is, it must be one, and being one, it must be without a body; for if it had dimensions, it would have parts and it would not be one." The various interpretations of this text are metaphysical rather than mathematical. Melissos seems to disagree here with the corporeal sphere with which Parmenides identifies being: as a sphere is not infinite, being cannot be a sphere, and, by extension, it is not space.

Though it is difficult to discover a mathematical meaning in the views of Melissos, it is now possible to visualize the gradual development of some basic attitudes towards mathematics. The Ionians failed to logicize their naturalism, thus showing the difficulty of reconciling the diversity of experience with the unifying power of logic. The most they could achieve with abstractions was to reach knowledge by successive generalizations from sensible data. Going a step further, the Pythagoreans did perceive the intelligible, but they did not disentangle it completely from experience, as they insisted that numbers are things. Even though Philolaus improved this view by asserting that everything *has* a number, it was still through its number only that a thing could be known.

The first expression of a real difference between the sensible and the intelligible realms came from the Eleatics, who introduced idealism and rationalism in philosophical speculation. For them, what exists is the intelligible only—whether concrete and material or abstract and ideal—which is conceived by itself and can be defined by itself. To support this view, both Parmenides and Zeno emphasized the irrationality of multiplicity and of motion. With Melissos, who introduced the indefinite in the notion of the one, Eleaticism exhausted itself in the vain attempt to rationalize the empirical elements of knowledge. By exposing its weaknesses in trying to mend them, Melissos elaborated a syncretic eclecticism which dissatisfied his contemporaries and caused various reactions. Future discussions will center around the 2 Pythagorean opposites of the indefinite (continuous) and the finite (discrete). But no synthesis of these two principles has yet been found to satisfy equally mathematicians and philosophers.

CHAPTER 7

The Empirical Tradition:
Atomists and Sophists

In the pre-Socratic controversies, the Atomists made a strong stand against the ontologism of the Pythagoreans and the Eleatics. They vindicated the basic Ionian doctrine of the indestructibility of matter with a theory which took into account the main Eleatic arguments. In attempting to emancipate thought from the determinations of being as viewed by the Eleatics, the Atomists (Leucippus, *fl.* 500 B.C., and Democritus, *ca.* 520-440 B.C.) were considerably influenced by the demands of experience. This is shown by the materialistic character of their atomic theory, which combines a belief in the reality of atoms (Eleatic view), or unchanging elements, with a belief in the reality of local motion (Heraclitean view), which accounts for change. As Aristotle puts it, the only reality acknowledged by the Atomists is matter, which is characterized by its 3 accidents of form, order, and position, and which is determined by motion.

All substances are composed of extremely small and indivisible particles or *atoms* formed of the same and only matter. Atoms are separated by the void which takes a kind of material reality by allowing them to have form and shape. The perceptible differences in substances are caused by the various shapes and combinations of the atoms, for all atoms have magnitude (for example, the atoms of the soul are small and spherical). Furthermore, the atoms are in a perpetual state of motion, as their weight causes them to "fall" in the infinite void. This motion produces their different formations, and consequently the various aspects of the resulting substances are already accounted for by their material cause. As Leucippus says: "Nothing can be produced without a purpose; but everything results from a cause and by reason of necessity."[1] This is the first explicit statement of scientific determinism.

As magnitudes and shapes lead to an interest in mathematics, after the fashion of the Pythagoreans and in keeping with the discussions of the period, it is not surprising that Democritus revealed himself as an able and original mathematician. According to Clement of Alexandria,[2] Democritus boasted that no one of his time, not even the so-called Arpedonats of Egypt, had surpassed him in constructing figures from lines and in proving their properties. Democritus probably developed his interest in mathematics through his association with Anaxagoras his master, Philolaus, and other Pythagorean friends. Though none of the works of Democritus has survived, some of their titles transmitted by Diogenes Laertius[3] form 3 tetralogies concerning mathematics and astronomy. The mathematical books dealt with geometrical questions, the contact of the circle and sphere, incommensurable lines and solids, and numbers. But these titles do not indicate the developments and methods of Democritus. Fortunately, some fundamental propositions are distinctly attributed to him by tradition, and his accepted philosophical views give a likely ground for their interpretation.

We are told by Archimedes[4] that Democritus was the first to

[1] Diels, *Vors.*, 58 B 4, III, pp. 451-452.
[2] Kàthleen Freeman, *The Pre-Socratic Philosophers* (Cambridge, Mass., 1959), p. 291.
[3] Diogenes Laertius ix. 46-49, 55a 33.
[4] *The Method* 55b, 155n; also in Heiberg's edition, *"Eine neue Archimedes Handschrift,"* published in *Hermes* (1907), pp. 245-246.

state that the volumes of any pyramid and of any cone are one-third of the volumes of the corresponding prism and cylinder having respectively the same base and height. This property was proved later by Eudoxus with the method of exhaustion. Though it is not known how Democritus substantiated this important intuition, he may have heard of the Egyptian formula for the volume of the square pyramid; then he may have generalized it to include all polygonal pyramids, finally applying the result to the cone by increasing indefinitely the number of sides of the polygon at the base of a pyramid.

Another problem which preoccupied Democritus was the relation in size between 2 sections of a cone parallel to the base and very close to each other. If 2 such consecutive sections are unequal, the surface of the cone would be dented like steps; if these are equal, the cone would become a cylinder.[5] Difficulties of a similar kind were involved in the discussion of the nature of the sections of a pyramid of an increasing number of sides. Democritus may have tried to solve such paradoxes by means of thin laminae, as Cavalieri did later with his theory of indivisibles. Equally complicated was the study of the horn-angles formed by the contact of a circle or sphere with a tangent, or even by the contact of the circle and sphere, as the title of a Democritean work suggests. At any rate, such interests involve basic problems of mathematics leading to the concepts of the calculus.

The Democritean attempt to account for the continuous through the discrete in mathematics as well as in physics was rather·premature. His reasonings probably involved the very type of fallacies which made Democritus suspect to both Plato and Aristotle, and which explain in part Plato's alleged remark that he wished he could burn all his books. If we assume that Democritus tried to solve the Pythagorean difficulties concerning the incommensurables by means of his mathematical atomism, then a mathematical atom must be conceived as an indivisible. On the other hand, Democritus was too good a

5 Plutarch *The Common Notions*, 39 (1079*E*).

mathematician to be unaware of the snares of the indivisible lines. Yet according to Simplicius,[6] he held to the indefinite divisibility of all lines. This view involves discrimination between mathematical and physical atoms, which was maintained later by Epicurus,[7] though Aristotle made no such distinction. But even if Democritus could not solve the paradoxes of the infinite, his notion of a fixed infinitesimal magnitude remained a permanent fixture of mathematical intuition, until its supersession by the modern concepts of the derivative and the integral.

Meanwhile, the logical discrepancies which analysis revealed in the leading mathematical concepts in the materialistic framework of Atomism probably led Democritus to deny the truth of the common notions of the mathematicians. Such an attitude tended to emancipate thought from ontologism and favored a tendency towards logical formalism. This accounts for the opinion of Sextus Empiricus that both Democritus and Plato upheld the truth of thought-objects in contradistinction to the empiricism of Protagoras and of the Sophists in general.

Indeed, the value of mathematical knowledge was weakened by the arguments and methods of the Sophists, whose polymathic and confusing teaching was encouraged by the variety of doctrines already in favor at their time.[8] The brilliant century of Pericles, who consorted with their ablest representatives, favored freedom in matters of speculation and encouraged learning and debate. The empirical and critical outlook of the Sophists gave them little faith in the abstract conceptions of the mathematicians. Arguing against them that no such straight lines or circles as they assumed exist in nature,

---

6 *Commentarii in Aristotelis physicae libros* (Venice, 1551), p. 7.

7 In his *Letter to Herodotus,* in Whitney J. Oates, ed., *The Stoic and Epicurean Philosophers* (New York, 1940), p. 5, Epicurus admits "the existence of extreme and indivisible limits of the lengths which are the original measure of magnitudes."

8 This type of erudition was denounced by Heraclitus; Diels, *Vors.,* 22 B 40, I, p. 160, and 22 B 129, II, pp. 180-181; and by Democritus, Diels, *Vors.,* 58 B 65, III, p. 462.

Protagoras said that "a hoop touches a straight edge not at one point only,"[9] meaning that a material circle does not touch a material ruler at one point only.

These empirical strains in Greek mathematics account for the quaint names and etymologies of many fundamental geometrical concepts. Such is the case of the *horn-like* angle made at the point of contact of a circle with a tangent, or, as Protagoras would say, at the place where "a hoop touches a straight edge." Just as suggestive is the Greek word meaning "skin" or "color" which the Pythagoreans used to denote a surface. Again, the word *parallel* means "alongside one another"; in defining parallels in a plane as lines which are "neither converging nor diverging," Posidonius surely had some material examples in mind.

The story of the word *pyramid* is most interesting. As it occurs in the Rhind Papyrus, the Greeks probably obtained it from Egypt. In comparing the 4 elements with geometrical solids, the pyramidal form of a flame must have prompted them to identify the pyramid with fire. These circumstances, coupled with their ignorance of Egyptian mathematics, caused the late medieval writers to derive the word "pyramid" from the Greek word for fire and occasionally to call a pyramid a fire-shaped body. Burnet insists on another Greek etymology of pyramid. He derives it from an expression which means a "wheat cake," with the remark that the Greeks had a tendency to give humorous names to things Egyptian.[10] It is now established that the word *pir-em-us,* which is used in the Rhind Papyrus, denotes the vertical height of the pyramid. Heath believes that the name "pyramid" may have been derived from this strictly Egyptian word.[11]

Experience also suggested many of the initial problems of Greek geometry. Thales laid the foundations of the theory of

9 Aristotle *Met.* 998n 1. Cf. Diogenes Laertius ix. 55, who mentions a work where Protagoras may have presented a criticism of mathematics.
10 J. Burnet, *Early Greek Philosophy* (London, 1914), p. 21, note I.
11 Thomas L. Heath, *A Manual of Greek Mathematics* (Oxford, 1931), p. 79.

proportion by measuring the distance of ships at sea, and by calculating the height of a pyramid with the shade of his stick fixed in the sand, a method reminiscent of the Egyptian technique of the *gnomon*. In discussing the Pythagorean claims to the general theorem of the square of the hypotenuse, we explained how this early proof could have been a generalization of a number of experiments with concrete triangles.

Empirical considerations are also involved in the 3 classical problems of squaring the circle, trisecting the angle, and duplicating the cube. Simple cases of mensuration would lead gradually to the more difficult questions of finding a square equivalent in area to a given circle, and of dividing an angle into 3 equal parts. As to the duplication of the cube or Delian problem, it was a request of the oracle at Delos to double Apollo's altar which led to the quest for the side of a cube twice as large as the volume of a given cube. As these problems involved so-called irrational relations, they could be solved neither by means of integers nor with constructions involving exclusively the ruler and the compass, the only instruments allowed by rigorists in geometry. For this purpose, it was necessary to invent "mechanical" curves such as the *quadratrix* of Hippias and of Dinostrates, the *conchoid* of Nicomedes, the *cissoid* of Diocles, the *spirals* of Archimedes, and the *method of exhaustion* of Antiphon, developed and systematized later by Eudoxus. Although Plato strongly objected to the use of mechanical curves, which were due mainly to the ingenuity of the Sophists, the Greeks felt instinctively that practical analogies of experience could offer better means of solving certain problems when rational methods proved inadequate.

If the Greeks were prompted to turn to experience for the basic notions of science and treatment of special mathematical problems, we could also find empirical traces even in the abstract postulates of their systems. For example, the Euclidian *axioms* may be considered as general expressions of practical experiments with objects representing integers or with simple cases of mensuration. Yet, in spite of the interest and value of the empirical tradition in Greek mathematics, which made itself felt in subsequent developments, the main characteristic of the Greek mind is its deliberate use of mental operations in systematizing knowledge.

A reaction against strict empiricism is found in the constructive views of Anaxagoras (born *ca.* 500 B.C.), who is considered a Sophist, although he has a place of his own in the history of thought. In endeavoring to solve the Heraclitean and the Eleatic antinomies, he tried to reconcile the logical and the real by asserting that absolute becoming is impossible and that change is only relative. In this he agreed with Empedocles, that other pluralist (born *ca.* 490 B.C.), although he differs from him about the 4 primary elements and their mode of combination. For Anaxagoras, the real constituents of the world are indefinite in number and combined according to the purpose of the universal mind. As everything is given from the beginning, Anaxagoras could say, with Parmenides, "The whole can neither decrease nor increase, for it is impossible that more things exist than the whole; indeed the whole is constantly equal to itself."[12]

This view involves rejection of the Democritean atomism, because the continued division of an object cannot yield any atoms and, even less so, the 4 primary elements. In any case, it is impossible to obtain indivisible elements, because there is no actual minimum of smallness,[13] although the whole is definite and immutable. This belief was probably corroborated by the logical arguments involved in the problem of squaring the circle, to which Anaxagoras gave much thought. For the first time in the history of thought, infinitesimal considerations were expressed positively when Anaxagoras asserted the possibility of infinite regression.

From these general remarks, it appears that pre-Socratic mathematical knowledge and methodology, however developed at the time, did not rest on secure grounds. Yet both

12 Diels, *Vors.*, 58 B 5, III, p. 470.
13 *Ibid.*

Eleaticism and Atomism had a vital bearing on the development of mathematical philosophy, as they provided basic elements which Platonist thinkers developed into mathematical concepts. It is true that Proclus mentions neither the Eleatics nor the Atomists in his historical summary; and that earlier historians of mathematics take no notice of these schools, unless they merely connect them with Greek philosophy exclusively. But this may be due to the Eleatic contempt for mathematics because of the many inconsistencies discovered in its assumptions.

CHAPTER 8

The Development
of Greek Mathematics

The time of Socrates and Plato was an important period of philosophical and mathematical activity. Although speculative thought had crystallized around the teaching of Socrates, various aspects of the older doctrines had found their way into the Schools of the Megarics, the Cynics, and the Cyrenaics. In particular, the views of the Eleatics (Zeno) and the Atomists (Democritus), who were actively aware of the mathematical discussions of their time, had an important influence on the later systematization of arithmetic and geometry. But more decisive was the influence of the Pythagoreans who had left Southern Italy and settled in various Greek cities. This partly explains why the various branches of science were steadily developed by independent mathematicians mostly connected with the Pythagorean message.

The lesser Socratic schools developed the teachings of their common master, each in a specific field and in a definite direction; they also combined earlier doctrines with those of Socrates in the elaboration of their own systems.

74

The Megarians had shown how much room there was for Eleatic metaphysics in the Socratic doctrines; Aristippus had indicated its points of contact with Pythagoras, and hence the physics of Heraclitus and the Atomists; finally Antisthenes had proved the possibility of being an adherent of Socrates, and yet remaining a dialectician after the fashion of a Gorgias trained by Zeno and Empedocles. None of these facts were forgotten; and at the same time the last of the pre-Sophistic views of the world, that of the Pythagoreans, is consciously incorporated with Socratism.[1]

As a disciple of Socrates who was to excel his master, Plato was fully informed about the philosophical trends and the mathematical knowledge of his time. He had heard of the geometrical work of Anaxagoras of Clazomenae and of his younger contemporary Oenopides of Chios, both of whom he mentions in a dialogue where two youths argue about them by drawing circles and by placing their hands at an angle;[2] this incident may be a reference to the former's attempt to square the circle and the latter's discovery of the obliquity of the ecliptic. Again, though Plato ignores Democritus in his dialogues, he probably knew his mathematical views, for he is said to have wished to burn all his works. He must have been familiar also with the results of Hippocrates of Chios, who was in Athens from about 450 to 430 B.C. Hippocrates won his fame by squaring the *lune* or *meniscus* with a rudimentary use of *exhaustion,* by reducing the duplication of the cube to the finding of 2 mean proportionals, and by being "the first of those mentioned as having compiled Elements."[3] These Elements were probably used as a textbook in the Academy, as were those of Leon and of Theudius written a little later.

At that time also lived the Pythagorean Archytas, the Sophists Antiphon and Bryson, who attempted to square the circle, Leodamas of Thasos to whom Plato transmitted his method of analysis, Theodorus of Cyrene who was the teacher

[1] Karl Erdmann, *History of Philosophy* (New York, 1892), I, pp. 94-95.
[2] *The Rivals* 132*A*-*B*.
[3] Proclus *Commentary on Euclid* i, p. 66.

of Plato and of Theaetetus of Athens, and Eudoxus of Cnidos (*ca.* 408-355 B.C.), who joined the Academy after studying and traveling abroad. Among the younger contemporaries of Plato, many were encouraged by his enthusiasm to study mathematics. Proclus recounts that Philip of Medma was diverted to mathematics by Plato, and that he not only made his own investigations according to his directions, but also set himself to do such things as would fit in with the philosophy of Plato. We are also told that Menaechmus, who discovered the conic sections, his brother Dinostratus, Theudius, and other mathematicians conducted in common their investigations in the Academy. The discoveries of these mathematicians and their philosophical interpretation undoubtedly influenced Plato's thought.

The theory of irrationals and the theory of proportion play an obvious and important part in the Platonic doctrines. After the failure of Pythagoreanism to account for the irrationals, their theory was neglected to such an extent that Plato denounced the "shameful ignorance" of most Greeks regarding the incommensurability of many geometrical magnitudes with one another.[4] Yet the Pythagoreans had discovered the irrationality of $\sqrt{2}$ and Theodorus had proved the irrationality of the roots of the integers up to 17 which were not squares. Most likely his method was applied afresh to each case owing to the different numbers used in the proofs, and he stopped at $\sqrt{17}$ when he realized that the process would probably never end.

The idea of defining all these roots under one term was due to Theaetetus, who generalized the theory of the roots. Plato explained in a dialogue between Theaetetus and Socrates how this advance was made.

Theodorus was proving to us a certain thing about square roots, I mean the square roots of three square feet and five square feet, namely that these roots are not commensurable in length with the foot-length, and he proceeded in this way, taking each case in turn up to the root of seventeen square feet; at this point for

4 *Laws* 819D.

some reason he stopped. Now it occurred to us, since the number of square roots appeared to be unlimited, to try to gather them into one class by which we could henceforth describe all the roots.

S.–And did you find such a class?

T.–I think we did; but see if you agree.

S.–Speak on.

T.–We divided all numbers into two classes. The one, consisting of numbers which can be represented as the product of equal factors, we likened in shape to the square and called them square or equilateral numbers.

S.–And properly so.

T.–We likened to oblong shape the numbers between these, among which are three and five and all that can not be represented as the product of equal factors, but only as the product of a greater by a less or a less by a greater and are therefore contained by greater and less sides; and we call them oblong numbers.

S.–Excellent. And what after this?

T.–Such lines as form the sides of equilateral plane numbers we called lengths; and such as form the oblong numbers we called roots, because they are not commensurable with the others in length, but only with the plane areas they can form. And similarly in the case of solids.[5]

An additional testimony of the discoveries of Theaetetus is found in a *Commentary* on Euclid attributed to Pappus, where it is said that the theory of irrationals "was considerably developed by Theaetetus the Athenian, who gave proof in this part of mathematics as in others of an ability justly admired, and who established rigorous demonstrations of the propositions concerning the theory of irrationals."[6] The discoveries of Theaetetus were probably incorporated in the *Elements* of Leon and in those of Theudius, finding their way later into Euclid's *Elements,* where the theory of irrationals is systematically expounded.

[5] *Theaetetus* 147D-148B. In other words, the roots of oblong numbers are always irrational. They cannot be expressed in terms of linear measurement, but only in terms of areas, as they form squares when raised to the second power.

[6] Pappus of Alexandria, *La Collection mathematique* (Paris, 1933), I, p. 34.

These investigations made possible the capital discovery of Eudoxus concerning the general theory of proportion. The Pythagorean theory of proportionals and means was restricted to integers and did not apply to irrationals. This restriction made inconclusive most proofs depending on the Pythagorean doctrine of proportion. A general theory was required, covering equally integers and irrationals and applicable to arithmetic, geometry, harmonics, and all mathematical sciences. This method, as expounded in Book V of Euclid's *Elements,* is considered by the scholiast as "the discoverer of Eudoxus, the pupil of Plato." Its intrinsic importance is emphasized in the results of Dedekind and Weierstrass, who adopted the basic views of Euclid's Book V almost without modification.

The widespread interest of the Greeks in the irrationals during Plato's time is evidenced by the variety of problems investigated by the mathematicians. Besides the incommensurability of the diagonal of a square with its side, many other geometrical constructions involving irrationals were investigated by Plato's contemporaries and their successors. In particular, the squaring of the circle, the duplication of the cube, and the trisection of the angle influenced the course of Greek mathematics for at least 3 centuries, as new curves and constructions were invented for their solution. According to Plutarch, Anaxagoras wrote on the squaring of the circle while in prison. The first quadrature of curves was made by Hippocrates of Chios, who squared certain types of *lunes* (figures included between two intersecting arcs of circles) and who found the sum of a lune and a circle.[7] Perhaps Hippocrates attempted these quadratures in the hope of squaring the circle.[8] The earliest attempts to solve the problem by means of higher curves were those of Hippias and Dinostratus, a contemporary of Plato, who invented the quadratrix for the purpose.[9]

[7] Simplicius *Commentary on Aristotle's Physics* 60-68, in Diels, *Vors.*
[8] Cf. W. D. Ross, *Aristotle's Physics* (Oxford, 1930), p. 466.
[9] The *spiral* of Archimedes, the *conchoid* of Nicomedes, the *cochloid* (cylindrical helix) of Apollonius, and the *double-motion curve* of Carpus were used later for quadratures.

The first tentative solutions by means of approximation by polygons were given by Antiphon and Bryson, two contemporaries of Socrates. The method of Antiphon consisted of inscribing a regular polygon in a circle and doubling continually the number of its sides until they become so small that they coincided practically with the circumference. Since a square could be made equal to any polygon, then a square could be made equal to the circle. Bryson improved this method by using both inscribed and circumscribed polygons, and by assuming between them an intermediate polygon to which the circle would be ultimately equal. The objections raised by early commentators against Antiphon and Bryson seem to be more verbal than real. At any rate, both methods seem to involve the idea of exhausting an area by means of inscribed regular polygons with an ever-increasing number of sides. These loose attempts were transformed later into the rigorous *method of exhaustion* founded by Eudoxus, expounded by Euclid, and applied skillfully by Archimedes to many problems.

The method of exhaustion showed that mathematics does not require actual existence of the infinitely small, but only the simple assumption of reaching a magnitude *as small as we please* by a continual division of a given magnitude. This conception saved geometry from the difficulties involved in Zeno's arguments and established the principle of exhaustion as a regular method in Greek mathematics. In the preface to his first book of *The Sphere and Cylinder*, Archimedes assigns to Eudoxus the proof of the 2 theorems due to Democritus about the volume of a pyramid and of a cone, for which he used the same lemma required by himself in determining the area of a segment of a parabola. This lemma, known as the Axiom of Archimedes, states that "of unequal lines, surfaces or solids, the greater exceeds the less by a magnitude which is capable by addition to itself of exceeding any of the magnitudes compared to one another." It has its equivalent in certain principles given by Euclid.[10]

10 *Elements* v. Def. 4, and x. 1.

The problem of trisecting any angle other than a right angle, which is a natural generalization of the fact that any angle can be trisected, is connected particularly with construction of a regular polygon of 9 sides. A practical trisection was attempted at first by means of the method of inclination, and later by the use of conics.[11]

One problem of particular interest to Plato was the duplication of the cube, involving 2 mean proportionals. To be sure, the founder of the Academy is mentioned in the legends attached to its history, as recounted by Theon of Smyrna and Eutocius on the authority of Eratosthenes. It is said that certain Delians who were asked by an oracle to double the altar of Apollo vainly tried to find how a solid could be made the double of another solid. When they asked Plato about it, he told them that "the god had given this oracle, not because he wanted an altar of double the size, but because he wished in setting the task before them to reproach the Greeks for their neglect of mathematics and their contempt for geometry."[12] On the other hand, Eutocius sent the perplexed Delians to the geometers who were with Plato in the Academy. This agrees with Plutarch's account that Plato directed the Delians to Eudoxus or Helicon of Cyzicus, who could solve the problem for them.

The question of duplication of the cube had already been reduced·by Hippocrates of Chios to the finding of 2 mean proportionals in continued proportion between 2 straight lines of which the greater was double the smaller. The problem has been so treated ever since. At the time of Plato, the solutions attempted were those of Archytas, Menaechmus, and Eudoxus, the last being unfortunately lost. The method of Archytas, according to Eudemus, involved a three-dimensional construction determining a certain point as the intersection of a right cone, a cylinder, and a tore. But most important of all was the solution of Menaechmus, who invented *conic sections*

[11] Pappus *Collectio* iv. 36, iv. 43.
[12] Theon *Exposition Rerum Mathematicarum* ii. 7-12 (ed. Hiller).

for the purpose, and who used for duplication of the cube the ordinate property of a parabola. Eutocius, who gives the solutions of Archytas and Menaechmus,[13] considers both of them theoretical, as they could not lead to a practical construction. But he makes exception to a "certain small extent" in favor of Menaechmus. Other solutions were proposed by Eratosthenes, Nicomedes, Heron, Diocles, and Eutocius himself.

This short account of the development of early Greek mathematical thought indicates sufficiently the technical sources used by Plato and Aristotle in organizing their systems. But it may be useful to add a few remarks about the techniques used by the Greeks for their numerical operations. In common with most early races and with their Eastern neighbors, the Greeks followed the decimal system of numeration without attempting to improve effectively its technique. Traces of quinary reckoning are found in Homer,[14] who used the Greek term meaning "to five" for reckoning, although counting by 5's was probably auxiliary to counting by 10's.

The development of trade and other interests prompted the Greeks to evolve 2 more convenient systems of symbols. The first one was used in early times and is known as the *Attic* system, because of its prevalence in Attic inscriptions.[15] With 10 symbols, corresponding to 1, 10, 100, 1000, and up to 50,000, this system allowed the ordinary operations of reckoning. But it was soon superseded by the more concise system using an alphabet of 27 letters (α representing 1) currently employed in the available Greek texts. As there is no place value in this system, operations usually started with the highest symbols. Instead of using the Egyptian practice of doubling and halving, the Greeks employed a multiplication table attributed to Pythagoras to simplify their calculations. They were thus able to perform additions, multiplications, divisions,

---

[13] *Commentary on Archimedes Sphere and Cylinder* ii, in Heiberg, pp. 78 and 84.

[14] *Odyssey* iv. 412.

[15] Also called the *Herodiantic* system, because it is described in a fragment attributed to Herodian (eleventh century A.D.), the grammarian.

and extractions of roots, although they had no knowledge of the zero and of the place-value method of reckoning.

It may be of interest to mention that a pre-Socratic thinker would scarcely dissociate completely abstract concepts of numbers and figures from their concrete applications. Although arithmetic and geometry considered as theoretical sciences were essential parts of philosophical speculation, many of their details were obtained by induction or generalization from the actual practices of logistics and mensuration. This must have been the case with the prime and polygonal numbers and the rectangular triangle. The processes involved in the actual manipulation of concrete cases could thus be extended or transferred to abstract generalizations. Such practices and methods were inherited by Plato and Aristotle, who used them as patterns or examples of their abstract speculations.

Part II

THE MATHEMATICAL
ONTOLOGY OF PLATO

The main incidents of Plato's life (427-347 B.C.) are inferred from his own dialogues and from details given in his *Epistles*.[1] As a young man, Plato was interested in poetry and public affairs. He had looked forward to a political career,[2] but he was discouraged by the excesses of the Thirty Tyrants, which made the former democratic constitution of Athens seem like gold in comparison to theirs.[3] To the ruthless measures imposed by this oligarchy, he preferred the technical remedies of competent leaders and the moral education of the people. But he could do little, as he was born "late in the day for his country,"[4] so he devoted himself to the study of philosophy and mathematics.

Two deciding events in Plato's life influenced the development of his doctrines. One was his acquaintance with Socrates,

---

[1] The authenticity of the *Epistles* and the life of Plato are discussed in J. Burnet, *Early Greek Philosophy* (London, 1914), pp. 205-219.

[2] *Epistles* vii. 324*B*.

[3] *Epistles* vii. 324*D*.

[4] *Epistles* v. 322*A*.

who saved him from the Heracliteanism taught by Cratylus and the Sophists. The other was his connection with the Pythagoreans, who convinced him of the universal value of mathematics.

Plato became intimately connected with Socrates at the age of 20. The old master could not be responsible for Plato's scientific interests, as he was not much versed in science, although he may have been familiar with mathematics.[5] Yet the influence of Socrates on science was not destructive, although he turned the attention of the mind from the study of external phenomena to introspective and moral considerations. On the other hand, the Socratic method and teachings did make systematic science possible. To be sure, the objective knowledge denied by the Sophists is the guiding motive of the Socratic inquiries. For Socrates, truth is known to the subject only insofar as it is universal in character and therefore objective. Hence, learning is mere recollection and teaching should elicit knowledge from the learner. That is why the Socratic method sets out from particular instances and gradually reaches the universal elements enshrined in them. Plato emphasized this method by use of the dialogue, instead of the monologue which expressed the authoritative manner of the Sophists. And it is no accident that Plato usually expressed his views through the person of Socrates, as a tribute to his teaching and inspiration.

While the early philosophers inquired about the nature of things in a rather superficial way, Socrates taught Plato to direct his attention primarily to what is permanent in things and to strengthen his speculations with universal definitions. Indeed, the Socratic method of discovering and understanding the universals[6] enabled Plato to reject the philosophical doctrines of his predecessors and build his own system.

5 Xenophon *Memorabilia* iv. 7 (3).

6 Strictly speaking, Socrates could only seek *forms*, for the term *universals* was not yet invented; there was no Greek word to express a concept. The *Parmenides* rejects conceptualism after putting it forward as a possible solution of the problem of participation.

Soon after the death of his master, Plato began his travels. In Southern Italy, his discussions with the Pythagoreans[7] convinced him of the universal value of mathematics. Plato seems to have known Philolaus and to have maintained friendly relations with Archytas of Tarentum. In one of his *Epistles* Plato writes to Archytas: "We have been wonderfully pleased at receiving the treatises which have come from you, and we felt the utmost possible admiration for their author; indeed we judged the man to be worthy of his ancestors."[8] The Pythagorean assimilation of mathematics to abstract knowledge set Plato's thoughts in a definite and final direction. When he returned to Athens, he founded the Academy and gave a prominent part to mathematics in its program of studies. Tradition reports that the front doors of the Academy displayed these words: "Let no one unfamiliar with geometry come under my roof."[9] Whether true or not, this story illustrates the essential importance which Plato attached to mathematics in the training of philosophers and statesmen, and in the establishment of a universal system of knowledge.

[7] Cicero *Tusculans* i.17.
[8] *Epistles* xii. 359D.
[9] Tzetzes *Book of Histories* viii. 972.

CHAPTER 9

Scientific Interests of Plato

The impetus given to philosophical speculation and mathematical research during the rule of Pericles provided Plato with many details for his own system. Although he did not specialize in the exact sciences, he knew and used their technical results. In fact, his mathematical speculations account considerably for his method and for the final expression of his thought. In discussing the nature of true knowledge after the *maieutic* method of Socrates, he could use no better examples than those of mathematics, for such truths are approved by reason and are not a matter of opinion. As Proclus says, Plato "filled his writings with mathematical arguments and stimulated admiration for mathematics in all those who took up philosophy."[1] In fact, many propositions and definitions are given in the dialogues, in *Parmenides,* the *Statesman,* and *Timaeus* especially, which are valuable for the assessment of Plato's technical knowledge and for the history of ancient science.

Plato dealt most skillfully with questions specifically mathe-

[1] *Commentary on Euclid,* p. 66.

matical, such as construction of the regular and semi-regular solids, finding of geometric means between 2 squares and 2 cubes, the rule for finding a series of square numbers the sum of which is also a square, and minor questions relating to acoustics, optics, astronomy, and irrationals in general. The regular solids investigated by the Pythagoreans and by Theaetetus were called "Platonic" because they are described and used in *Timaeus,* where Plato constructs them by putting together the necessary number of plane faces.[2] These are made up of elementary triangles "derived from two, each having one right angle and the other angles acute. Of these triangles, one has on either side the half of a right angle the division of which is determined by equal sides; the other has unequal parts of a right angle adjoining unequal sides."[3]

Isosceles right-angled triangles form each one of the 6 faces of the cube. A square is obtained by putting together the vertices of four such triangles around a point; and the solid angle of the cube is formed by 3 right angles. Equilateral triangles form the tetrahedron, the octahedron, and the icosahedron by placing their vertices in such a way as to enclose entirely the 4, 8, and 20 solid angles of these figures respectively. The equilateral triangle is made up of 6 equal right-angled triangles, formed by drawing a perpendicular from each vertex to the opposite side. The pentagonal face of the dodecahedron requires the isosceles triangle having each of its 2 equal angles double the vertical angle.[4] The construction of such a triangle, which is reducible to 2 scalene right-angled triangles, required a more complex geometrical method which is not given by Plato, probably because he did not use it for any primary body.

According to Archimedes, quoted in Heron's *Definitions,* Plato knew at least one semi-regular solid inscribable in a sphere out of the 14 investigated by Archimedes. It was a

2 *Timaeus* 53C-57D.
3 *Timaeus* 53D.
4 Cf. Thomas L. Heath, *The Thirteen Books of Euclid's Elements* (Cambridge, 1908), p. 98 (repub. in New York, 1956).

figure with 14 faces of which there are 2 sorts, one made out of 6 squares and 8 triangles, the other made out of 8 squares and 6 triangles. Heath explains how the former is obtained by cutting off from the corners of a cube pyramids on smaller equilateral triangles as bases, the triangles being such that regular octagons are left in the 6 faces. The latter, which seems to be more difficult to obtain, is arrived at by cutting off from the corners of an octahedron pyramids with square bases such that hexagons are left in the 8 faces.

The first of the 2 geometrical problems in *Meno*[5] is given to illustrate the doctrine of reminiscence. It states that twice the square on a straight line equals the square on the diagonal of the square having the straight line for its side; it is not equal to the square of twice the original length. This is an instance of the Pythagorean theorem concerning the right-angled triangle. The second geometrical problem in *Meno* offers an example of a hypothesis, which considers the conditions for a possible solution of a problem. Here Plato asks whether a given area can be inscribed in the form of a triangle in a given circle. This is his answer:

> I do not know whether this is the case, but I think I have a useful hypothesis. If this area is such that when applied (as a rectangle) to the given straight line in the circle it is deficient by a figure (rectangle) similar to that which is applied, then one result seems to me .to follow; while another result follows if what I have described is not possible. Accordingly, the use of a hypothesis allows me to conclude whether or not it is possible to inscribe the given area in the circle.[6]

One of the interpretations of this involved passage is the suggestion of Heath[7] that Plato seeks a criterion for inscribing in a circle a triangle equal in area to a given figure of any shape. The real condition is that the given area must not

5 *Meno* 82*B*-85*B*.
6 *Meno* 86*E*-87*B*.
7 Thomas L. Heath, *A History of Greek Mathematics* (Oxford, 1921), I, pp. 298-303.

exceed that of the inscribed equilateral triangle. More precisely, such a triangle can be inscribed only if "the given area is such that when applied to the given straight line in the circle, it is deficient by a figure similar to the one which is applied." All these expressions involve the method of application of areas with which Plato was familiar.

Various passages in *Timaeus* indicate Plato's knowledge of proportionals and geometric means. One of them states that "if the universe should be a plane surface without depth, a single mean would be enough to connect its companions with it; but in fact the world was to be solid in form, and solids are always conjoined by two and not by one mean."[8] According to Heath,[9] square and cube numbers are meant by Plato when using the words "plane" and "solid." So if m^2 and n^2 are 2 squares, then $m^2 : mn = mn : n^2$; and if m^3 and n^3 are two cubes, then the means are in continued geometric proportion:

$$m^3 : m^2n = m^2n : mn^2 = mn^2 : n^3$$

Another passage describes how the Demiurge divided the world-soul into harmonic intervals: "First he took one portion from the whole, and next a portion double of this; the third half as much again as the second, and three times the first; the fourth double the second; the fifth three times the third, the sixth eight times the first; and the seventh twenty-seven times the first."[10] Two progressions are involved in this description, starting with the numbers 2 and 3 respectively, although they are arranged in a single series of 7 terms beginning with the unit, which the Pythagoreans held to contain both the even and the odd which are the elements of number. The two progressions give the even (1,2,4,8) series and the odd (1,3,9,27) series.

Interpreting this passage, Cornford remarks that "in Plato's description the numbers are spoken of as measuring corre-

8 *Timaeus* 32A-B.
9 Heath, *A History of Greek Mathematics*, I, p. 89; Euclid proves these properties of square and cube numbers in Book viii. 11-12.
10 *Timaeus* 35D.

sponding lengths of a single long strip of soul-stuff. We must imagine them as placed in one row at intervals answering to these lengths, in the order 1, 2, 3, 4, 9, 8, 27. The intervals are, of course, of very various lengths. They are presently to be filled in with additional numbers until we finally obtain a series representing musical notes at intervals of a tone or a semitone."[11] The compass of these notes is determined by the decision to stop the series at 27, the cube of 3, the first odd number, because the cube symbolizes a body in 3 dimensions. But this decision, as Cornford points out further, has nothing to do with the theory of musical harmony: "Continuous geometrical proportion was chosen as the most perfect bond to connect the four solid bodies of the world. It is obvious that these considerations are concerned with theories about the nature of number and with the functions of the soul as a bond holding the world's body together; they have nothing to do with music."[12] No one would start to construct a musical scale with the series (1, 2, 3, 4, 9, 8, 27). If Plato had intended merely to form a musical scale, he would have used the traditional Pythagorean Tetractys which contains the numbers forming the ratios of the perfect consonances. Furthermore, the composition of these series is very similar to the results of the generation of numbers proposed in *Epinomis*, which will be discussed later.

The harmonic proportions used in the shaping of the world and the soul are the only indication of Plato's knowledge of acoustics.[13] Unlike the Pythagoreans, who turned to actual experiments in their study of sound and music, Plato simply accepted the results of his predecessors and used them in his rational method of world building. His views on optics illustrate the same dogmatic outlook of his natural philosophy. According to Plato's theory of *synaugia,* vision results from the union and combination of the fire contained in the atmos-

11 F. M. Cornford, *Plato's Cosmology: The Timaeus of Plato,* translated with a running commentary (Cambridge, 1937), p. 67.
12 *Ibid.,* p. 68.
13 Cf. Plutarch *On Music,* chap. 22.

phere with the more subtle part of the fire emerging from the pupil of the eye. This conception is an addition to the theories of vision proposed by earlier thinkers.[14]

Plato's astronomical ideas likewise involve a disregard for direct experimental methods. Taking the sphere to be the most perfect form, he conceived the universe as spherical and the heavenly bodies as moving around in properly combined circular paths. It may be doubted that Plato had realized in his old age that a moving Earth would give a simpler account of the astronomical phenomena, for this Pythagorean view, which was worked out later by Aristarchus, scarcely agrees with the anthropomorphic inspiration of the Platonic natural philosophy.

[14] The Pythagoreans considered vision as resulting from the impact on the perceptible things of rays emanating from the eyes. The Stoics explained it by the pressure exerted on the eye by the surrounding air, and the Epicureans by the assumption of light images discharged from the sensible objects and penetrating the eye. A better account of vision is given by Aristotle in *De Sensu,* where he puts forward the idea of a medium between the eye and the physical objects.

CHAPTER 10

Mathematics and Education

The function of education is conversion of the soul from the awareness of Becoming to the contemplation of Being. This Pythagorean principle, which permeated the program of studies of the Academy, carried with it the distinction among the 4 sciences which later formed the medieval quadrivium: arithmetic, geometry, astronomy, and harmonics, regardless of the further distinction made by Plato between plane and solid geometry.

Arithmetic was studied for the sake of knowledge and not for any utilitarian or commercial end. The philosopher must learn the art of numbers "because he must rise up out of the sea of change and lay hold of true being."[1] Although arithmetic has nothing to do with action, Plato acknowledged that arithmetical training sharpens the mind for other kinds of knowledge. As one must understand the nature of numbers by thought alone, one should not learn arithmetic like an amateur or a merchant. Indeed, arithmetic produces an elevating effect by compelling the soul to reason about abstract

1 *Republic* vii. 252 or 524C.

number, without drawing visible or tangible objects into the argument and without being perplexed by the ambiguities of sense perception.

As visible and tangible units can be divided, they are many as well as one; they may even be unequal and vary in size. But the real units are absolutely equal, invariable, and indivisible. As such, they cannot be apprehended by the senses, but only by thought. The apparent contradictions of sense perception draw the soul towards real being. If a simple unit could be properly perceived by any sense, there would be nothing to attract the soul towards real being. "But if some opposite is seen along with it, so that it appears to be no more than the opposite, then . . . the perplexed soul would be forced to inquire by stirring thought within itself and to ask what is the one in itself. So the study of the one would lead and divert the soul towards the contemplation of real being."[2]

Similarly, geometry is important because it studies objects eternal and unchangeable and thus lifts the soul toward true being. A slight knowledge of it suffices for practical ends, as in the art of war. But its more advanced parts should help to apprehend the idea of the good. This conception of science is entirely different from the implications of the ordinary language of geometers, who think in practical terms only. "They talk loudly about squaring, applying, adding and the like; whereas knowledge only is the real object of the whole science."[3] This knowledge, which concerns the eternal and not the transient, determines the spirit of philosophy.

The objects of geometry do not become real by construction; points, lines, triangles, or squares are objects of pure thought which the mind contemplates. Geometry uses diagrams as illustrations only, for the triangle we draw is an imperfect representation of the triangle of which we think. It follows that constructions, or the processes of adding, squaring, and the like, are not of the essence of geometry, but are actually

[2] *Republic* vii. 524.
[3] *Republic* vii. 527A.

opposed to it. In this connection, Plutarch recounts the story that Plato blamed Eudoxus, Archytas, and Menaechmus for trying to reduce the duplication of the cube to other constructions by means of mechanical instruments, on the ground that "the virtue of geometry is thereby lost and destroyed by reverting to things perceived by the senses, instead of being directed towards eternal and non-corporeal images."[4]

Although these considerations refer to plane geometry, they apply equally well to solid geometry or "stereometry," as it is called for the first time in *Epinomis* (990D). According to Plato, stereometry is a science intermediate between plane geometry and astronomy, insofar as it deals with the third dimension "which is concerned with cubes and dimensions of depth" as well as length and breadth. Stereometry appears to be necessary to astronomy because the study of solids in themselves should precede the study of solids in revolution, which is the object of astronomy. Apparently, stereometry was not considered as an independent science in Plato's time, although Theaetetus had then completed the theory of the 5 regular solids. Plato complained that "no government patronizes this subject, which leads to a want of enthusiasm in its pursuit; moreover students cannot learn it without a teacher, who is difficult to find."[5] But he believed that if the state seconded the efforts of an instructor, stereometry would soon impose itself by its natural perfection.

A typical mathematical theory Plato wished to incorporate into the education of young Athenians was that of the irrationals. He denounced as a national crime the fact that young people were left ignorant of the distinction between rational and irrational quantities.[6] He thought this was largely due to the inappropriate teaching of mathematics in Greece, adding that the greatest evil was not total ignorance but misdirected learning and teaching. For him the study of the irrationals

4 *Convivium* viii. 2. 1.
5 *Republic* vii. 528C.
6 *Laws* 820B.

becomes easier when they are shown to be the natural complement of the more elementary questions of mathematics. Plato's insistence on introduction of the study of the irrationals into Greek education was prompted not only by his view that science is incomplete without them, but also by his belief that a comprehensive study of these magnitudes is indispensable to the elaboration of a universal and coherent philosophy free of the difficulties which wrecked the Pythagorean system. The material for such a study was prepared in Plato's lifetime by Theodorus of Cyrene and Theaetetus of Athens, but their discoveries were extended and systematized by Eudoxus and incorporated later in the *Elements* of Euclid, who developed a general theory of irrationals.

A nobler purpose is also attributed to the 2 principal sciences dealing with motion—astronomy and harmonics. Astronomy should not be studied merely for its use in agriculture, navigation, or strategy, or even because it turns our thoughts to the heavens. The visible and intricate motions of the celestial bodies are related to true astronomy as the diagrams analyzed by the geometer are related to his science; hence, these apparent motions must be regarded merely as a pattern pointing to a higher wisdom.

> Only knowledge of being and of the unseen can make the soul turn upwards. Whether a man gazes at the heavens or blinks on the ground seeking to learn what his senses perceive, I would deny that he can learn; for nothing of that sort is real knowledge. His soul is looking downwards not upwards, whether his way to knowledge is by land or by sea, whether he soars or lies on his back. The starry heavens we behold are wrought upon a visible ground; and though they are the fairest and most perfect of visible things, they must necessarily be deemed inferior to the true motions of absolute swiftness and absolute slowness. For these are relative to one another and carry with them what they contain, namely true numbers and figures which cannot be apprehended by sight, but only by reason and intelligence.[7]

[7] *Republic* vii. 529D.

Hence the right approach to astronomy, with the proper use of natural reason, is to study problems as in geometry and leave the heavens alone.

The proper knowledge of harmonics, the Pythagorean counterpart of astronomy, is also obtained by abstraction. Harmonics deals with motions apprehended by the ear, just as astronomy deals with motions apprehended by the eye. But it is not enough to say that a given interval is expressed by a particular number; one must consider which numbers agree together and which do not, and find reasons for both cases. Plato considers that teachers of harmony and practical music do not really deal with harmonics, because they only compare the sounds and the consonances heard. "These people tease and torture the strings and rack them on the pegs of the instrument." [8] Harmonics must be studied for the good, and not as the empiricists or even the Pythagoreans, who express the harmonic intervals by numerical ratios without emancipating themselves from the sound as heard. "They, too, are in error like the astronomers; they investigate the numbers of the harmonies heard, but they never reach the natural harmonies of number, nor do they consider why some numbers are harmonious and others are not." [9]

This dissociation of mathematics from their immediate or remote applications enables Plato to define one of the permanent ideals of the mathematician: number and figure should be studied in themselves, independently of the heavens and even of diagrams. Furthermore, the study of the mathematical sciences in relation to one another and the similarity of their general characteristics led Plato to believe that he could construct the heavens by mathematical methods alone, and determine the principles of harmonics without using the natural relation of sounds to the ear. This attitude is completely different from the practice of modern science, which is built on physical observations expressed in mathematical structures.

8 *Republic* vii. 531*B*.
9 *Republic* vii. 531*C*.

These general views about mathematics, as expressed in the seventh book of the *Republic,* do not represent Plato's final thought on the relation between mathematics and true knowledge. What this dialogue asserts about arithmetic, geometry, astronomy, and music is in line with the needs of adult education. In fact, mathematics strengthens the power of attention, develops the sense of order, and enables the mind to grasp by simple formulas the quantitative differences of physical phenomena. The development of the mental powers of man is most important and useful for the statesman, whose education the *Republic* has more particularly in view.

But this educational purpose provides a link between mathematics and the idea of the good, which is the supreme object of the philosopher's study. The allegory of the prisoners in the cave, at the beginning of the seventh book of the *Republic,* shows that abstract or universal concepts like those of mathematics correspond to the reflection of the sun in the water. Consequently, ultimate reality must be found beyond mathematics as such. Yet, as education trains the mind for the apprehension of the idea of the good, it is necessary to determine whether the various sciences provide the elements required for that further effort. A proper assessment of mathematics thus calls for a discussion of the methods of the sciences. From such a debate will emerge the necessity of a discipline more effective than mathematics, to which the name *dialectic* is given, and which will lead to the proper apprehension of numbers and forms.

CHAPTER 11

Organization of Rational Methods

The mathematical theories known in Plato's time were not rigorously systematized, in spite of their logical coherence. The Academy probably used the *Elements* of Hippocrates of Chios, but no copy of that work has reached us. The theories and problems discussed or solved by earlier Greek mathematicians were based to some extent upon intuition or experience, hence Plato's criticism of their methods. Such discussions encouraged the enormous work of compilation and correlation undertaken by the mathematicians of the Academy, and paved the way for the remarkable systematization of Euclid and of Apollonius of Perga.

In discussing mathematics, Plato used the analytical method which reaches ultimate hypotheses by successive reduction. Ancient mathematicians had already used the method of proving a theorem by reducing it successively to other theorems or problems, until a proposition already known was reached. The Pythagoreans employed analysis in proving certain properties of numbers and in their method of applying areas. Hippocrates of Chios reduced the problem of duplicating the cube to that of finding 2 mean proportionals.

Plato's contribution was to show the importance of analysis from the point of view of logical rigor, and to develop it as a universal method in mathematics. This is confirmed by Proclus.

> Certain methods have been handed down. The finest is analysis which carries the thing sought down to an acknowledged principle. It is said that Plato communicated this method to Leodamas who used it in discovering many things in geometry. The second method is division which breaks into its parts the genus proposed for consideration, and which gives a starting-point for the demonstration by eliminating the other elements in the construction of what is proposed. Plato considered this method as being of assistance to all sciences.[1]

There is also the testimony of Diogenes Laertius, who says that Plato "explained to Leodamas of Thasos the method of inquiry by analysis."[2]

The method of division mentioned by Proclus is closely related to the method of synthesis which Plato gave as the reciprocal of analysis. This is confirmed by Aristotle.

> There is a difference between arguments from and those to the first principles. For Plato was right in raising this question and asking, as he used to do, "are we on the way from or to the first principles?" There is a difference as there is in a race-course between the run from the judges to the turning-point and the way back. For while we must begin with what is known, things are objects of knowledge in two senses, some to us and some without qualifications.[3]

The method of synthesis was more widely used before and during Plato's time. By directing attention to analysis and to the reciprocal connection between analysis and synthesis, Plato did a great service to mathematics and to science in general.

1 *Commentary on Euclid* i, p. 218.
2 Diogenes Laertius iii. 24.
3 *Ethica Nicom.* 1095ᵃ 30.

The Platonic method of analytical regression is not concerned merely with the simple reduction of a proposition to one known or already proved, but also with the discovery of the ultimate hypotheses of science. Plato explained it when discussing the difference between images and hypotheses. He maintained that hypotheses are used in the sensible as well as in the suprasensible world; in the former they take the form of images, while in the latter the soul ascends above hypotheses to the idea of the good. He took as an example the hypotheses of mathematics.

> Students of geometry, arithmetic and the like take for granted the odd and the even, figures, three kinds of angles and other similar assumptions in their several sciences. As these are their hypotheses, which everybody is supposed to know, they do not deign to give any account of them, but they go on until they finally reach their conclusion in a consistent manner. Yet, although they use the visible forms and reason about them, they rather think of the ideas which they resemble; they do not concentrate on the figures they draw, but on the absolute square and the absolute diameter, and so on. The forms they draw or make, which have shadows and reflections in water, are converted by them into images; but they are really seeking to behold the things themselves, which can only be seen with the eye of the mind.[4]

Analysis and synthesis are required by the various problems in which Plato was interested, such as construction of the regular and semi-regular solids, which have an important function in *Timaeus*, the use of irrationals, and the finding of means. Moreover, the progress of mathematics in the Academy was largely due to the clearer conception of its objects and methods fostered by Plato's discussion of the mathematical hypotheses, and also of definitions, which may be considered as a kind of hypotheses.[5] The art of clarifying concepts by various processes leading up to their definition is decidedly Socratic. If we accept Xenophon's testimony that his master

4 *Republic* vi. 510D.
5 Cf. *Epistles* vii, to the friends of Dion.

was not unfamiliar with mathematics, Socrates probably gave his followers various illustrations of his dialectic and maieutic methods by applying them to ethical or practical ideas and, occasionally, to current mathematical notions.

Meno offers a remarkable example of the treatment of a concept leading to its definition. Socrates attempts to define a "figure" by arguing whether there is anything equally true of the round, the straight, and the other things called figures, and which is the same for all. He suggests at first that "figure" might be associated with color alone. But, says Meno, suppose the interlocutor does not know what color is? Well, replies Socrates, there are things in geometry which we call a surface or a solid and so on, and from these examples we may learn what we mean by figure; consequently, "figure" is that in which a solid ends, it is the extremity of a solid.[6] Here "figure" is equivalent to surface from a practical point of view, an association which connects this concept with the Pythagorean and Aristotelian definitions of surface.

Several definitions of mathematical concepts are found in the dialogues of Plato. An "even" number is defined as a number divisible into 2 equal parts. Various distinctions between different kinds of numbers were already known to the Pythagoreans. The "round" or "circle" is defined as "that in which the farthest points in all directions are at the same distance from the middle";[7] a similar definition is given of a sphere. *Parmenides* contains a number of mathematical statements, such as the definition of a straight line as "that of which the middle covers the ends,"[8] and the axiom that "if equals be added to unequals, the sums differ by the same amount as the original magnitudes do."[9] This is a more complete enunciation of a similar axiom given later by Euclid.

Plato considered that definitions are fundamental elements of knowledge: "The right opinion with a rational definition

6 *Meno* 75A-76A.
7 *Parmenides* 137E.
8 *Parmenides* 137E.
9 *Parmenides* 154B.

or explanation is the most perfect form of knowledge."[10] The *Sophist* and the *Statesman* give examples of the method leading to a definition. In the *Laws*, Plato refers to a threefold knowledge of things: "We know the essence, the definition of the essence, and the name."[11] This statement gives to the definition its place in the structure of knowledge. It is amplified by Plato in a letter addressed to the friends of Dion, which also contains a vague but significant hint about his ultimate conception of true knowledge.

There Plato says that every existing object carries 3 necessary means by which a knowledge of it is acquired. First comes the name, second the definition, third the image. Knowledge as such follows up fourth, and we must postulate as fifth the object itself, which is cognizable and real.

> Take a single example and learn from it what applies to all. There is an object called a circle, which has for its "name" the word just mentioned, and secondly, it has a "definition" composed of nouns and verbs; for "that which is everywhere equidistant from the extremities to the center will be the definition of that object having for its name "round" and "spherical" and "circle." Thirdly, there is that object being portrayed and obliterated, or being shaped with a lathe, or falling into decay; but none of these affections is suffered by the circle itself, to which all these others are related, even though it is distinct from them. Fourthly comes knowledge, intelligence and true opinion concerning these objects which must be assumed to form a single whole. As this does not exist in vocal utterance or in bodily form but in the soul only, it is plain that it differs both from the nature of the circle itself and from the three items previously mentioned. Of those four, intelligence approaches the fifth most nearly in kinship and similarity.[12]

This is a remarkable example of the Platonic doctrine of knowledge, with special reference to the intimate connection between things mathematical and the vision of truth. The

[10] *Theaetetus* 206C.
[11] *Laws* 895C.
[12] *Epistles* vii. 342B-C.

remarks applied to the circle can be extended to everything else: "The same is true alike of the straight and of the spherical form, of color, of the good and the fair, of all bodies whether manufactured or naturally produced, such as fire and water and all such substances, of all living creatures, and of all moral actions or passions in souls. For unless a man somehow or other grasps the four of these, he will never acquire a perfect knowledge of the fifth." [13]

Dealing next with the 4 items just distinguished, Plato observed that there is nothing essential in the name which is merely conventional: there is nothing to prevent our assigning the name "straight line" to what we now call "round," and vice versa; nor is there any real preciseness about the definition, which is made up of parts of speech, nouns and verbs. The particular circle drawn or turned is not free from admixture of other things, it is not the mathematical or essential circle. Heath remarked that this classification makes no place for the particular mathematical circles corresponding to those we draw, and which are intermediate between these imperfect circles and the idea of circle which is "one." [14]

Plato's main purpose was to stress the existence of something beyond science and knowledge, of something unutterable, apprehended only by a spiritual vision. He thus says of the philosopher that "the force of his desire will not abate until he has attained the knowledge of the true nature of every essence, by a sympathetic and kindred power in the soul, by that power drawing near and mingling and becoming incorporate with very being. Having begotten mind and truth, he will have knowledge and will live and grow truly." [15] But if the study of mathematics clears the ground for the ascent of the mind towards the higher truths of life, dialectic alone leads to the direct vision of the good, the highest form which is beyond description.

[13] *Epistles* vii. 342D-E.
[14] Thomas L. Heath, *A History of Greek Mathematics* (Oxford, 1921), I, p. 289.
[15] *Republic* vi. 490B.

CHAPTER 12

Mathematics and Dialectic

According to *Phaedo,* mathematics is concerned with forms, which are the objects known through it. Mathematicians facilitate our acquaintance with forms by leading our mind from the sensible figures used as aids to the knowledge of these forms themselves. The *Republic,* however, mentions a supreme idea, the form of the good, and it examines the hypotheses of mathematics in the light of that higher principle.

As to those who study the mathematical arts, which give some apprehension of true being, they only dream about being. They can never behold the waking reality so long as they leave undisturbed the hypotheses used without being able to account for them. For when a man does not know his first principle, and when his conclusion and intermediary steps are constructed out of he knows not what, how can he imagine that such an arbitrary agreement will ever become science? Dialectic alone goes back to a principle; it is the only science which eliminates hypotheses in order to establish them.[1]

1 *Republic* vii. 533*B.*

Mathematical reasoning thus entails 2 basic defects: it depends upon sensible things as sources of suggestion, although not as objects of demonstration, and it makes no attempt to reach self-evidence in its initial postulates. The hypotheses of mathematics are neither immediately self-evident nor technically demonstrated; they are synthetic *a priori*. Mathematical reasoning shows that the theorems of mathematics, from first to last, follow by logical necessity from a group of unproved premises; but it is also compelled to accept these hypotheses as true. Consequently, the whole body of mathematics is left hanging in the air; for this reason, it scarcely can be called knowledge. Furthermore, the use of concrete diagrams weakens knowledge, for in all the sciences the objects actually studied are objects we think about without actually seeing or perceiving them. Yet all the sciences direct attention to these objects, which are really forms, by appealing first to the senses. The geometer draws a figure he calls a triangle and a line he calls a diameter, but when he demonstrates a proposition about the triangle or the diameter, these objects are not this visible figure and this visible line, but the triangle and the diameter which are not seen except with the eye of the mind. He is not even dealing with this visible figure and an indefinite plurality of others like it, because he cannot construct any visible figure fitting exactly the definition of the triangle or of the diameter.

This general criticism of mathematics applies equally to the more concrete sciences and to the whole fabric of knowledge. The path is thus clear for recognition of the possibility and necessity of the higher and more rigorous method of *dialectic,* which should help to rebuild the existing sciences on a stronger basis. In *Euthydemus*[2] we were told that arithmeticians, geometers, and astronomers must hand over their discoveries to the dialectician for examination. After Plato's remarks in the *Republic,* this necessity becomes more pressing.

[2] *Euthydemus* 290C.

The hypotheses of mathematics must be somehow "destroyed" in order to cleanse them of their concrete characteristics; such is the case of the hypothesis of the 3 kinds of triangles, which implies the images of 3 different triangles, while the idea of the triangle itself is one. This "destruction" of the hypotheses widens the application of the general concepts of science. In arithmetic, for example, the fundamental postulate of the series of the natural integers makes no allowance for any irrational quantities, although these have been established as the subject of a regular mathematical theory. The prominence given to the study of quadratic surds in *Theaetetus* indicates the necessity of extending the idea of number to include quantities which are neither odd nor even. When irrationals are regarded as numbers, the old hypotheses of arithmetic are destroyed.

Mathematics becomes the starting point of dialectical reasoning when "the soul passes out of hypotheses and goes on to a principle above them, making no use of images but proceeding only through the ideas themselves."[3] The power of dialectic enables reason to attain that other knowledge by using hypotheses, not as first principles, but as "steps leading into a world which is above hypotheses; so that reason may soar beyond them to the first principle of the whole, and then descend again by successive steps and without the help of any sensible object, by leaning on that principle then on that other which depends on the first, thus beginning and ending in ideas."[4]

Hence the ideal of knowledge is that mathematics and the other sciences, after the elucidation and reconstruction of their special postulates, should become one and the same science, having for its object the first principle, which is no longer a postulate—the form of the good. When reason has ascended to the idea of the good by means of a dialectical process, it may then descend once more to any particular conclusion of

3 *Republic* vi. 510*C*.
4 *Republic* vi. 511*B*.

the special sciences without using concrete diagrams. Knowledge would thus be reduced to a sort of algebra, a mighty conception taken up later by Leibniz and illustrated eminently by the founders of mathematical logic.

Although dialectic is not fully explained by Plato, it appears to be more than the art of reasoning in the Socratic sense; it is more comprehensive than the method of learning by means of question and answer; it is wider than the process of giving a rational account of things and receiving such an account from others. It shows which forms will harmonize with one another and which forms will not. Those who possess that art "will be able to distinguish a single form pervading many single and separate things; many forms distinct from one another but comprehended from without by one; and a single form pervading in turn many such wholes and binding them together into one, while many other forms are quite separate and apart from it." [5]

Here is the foundation of Plato's logic as implied in the dialectic, although not developed independently. According to Burnet's interpretation of this passage, Plato distinguishes clearly between genus and species when he uses the terms "form" and "kind." He also describes as single forms the "highest kinds" such as being, rest, and motion; these are "manners of participation" or "forms of predication," as Aristotle calls them. Plato's principal problem is that of the compatibility or incompatibility of the "highest kinds" or forms. Burnet also thinks that Plato was the first to discover the ambiguity of the copula, although he did not express this clearly.[6] We are led to believe that the mathematical interests of Plato could scarcely allow him to discover specifically the structure of deduction; for his mathematical mind, the logical pattern of mathematics seemed too perfect to require any separate and more general organon.

If Plato saw the possibility and necessity of a universal sci-

5 *Sophist* 253D.
6 J. Burnet, *Early Greek Philosophy* (London, 1914), p. 284.

ence of reasoning, it must have been a science transcending value and fact, the essence as well as the existence of things. In attaining wisdom through dialectic, one would find the reason why and what anything is in the sole character of a self-evident and self-explanatory supreme being, the source of all reality and knowledge, the ultimate good. Accordingly, all human knowledge would be transformed into what Burnet called a "teleological algebra." The vision of such a science is perhaps implied in the remark in *Phaedo* that a particular solution of the problem of the position and shape of the earth would be acceptable if its proof could show that the earth must have that shape and position and no other.[7]

Yet, Plato did not work out the details of this comprehensive science, and he never assumed the task of doing the world's scientific thinking. He indicated the proper line to follow in the progressive rationalization of the world, but his Socratic conception of the modesty of human knowledge in proportion to the vastness of scientific problems made him aware of his limitations. In particular, he knew that, in his effort to "mathematicize" as much as possible, the means he used were not as perfect as they ought to be. This is perhaps one of the reasons why Plato did not commit to writing his final views concerning the deduction of the forms from the idea of the good.

---

7 *Phaedo* 97D.

CHAPTER 13

Irrationals and Indivisibles

The progressive rationalization of knowledge by means of mathematics demands as a prerequisite the rationalization of mathematics itself. This operation became particularly urgent for Plato, as he knew that geometry involved many notions inexpressible in the arithmetic of integers. It was necessary not only to explain the generation of the integers, but also to show how the discontinuous series of integers can generate the geometrical continuum, for this entity involves all the real numbers, especially those which may express such geometrical relations as the ratio between the sides and the diagonals of a series of squares.

The difficulties of the early Pythagoreans were due to their inability to establish such a generalized arithmetic and to avoid the kind of inconsistencies exemplified by Zeno's arguments. This failure became evident when the irrationals were discovered: the earlier parallelism between geometry and arithmetic was broken, for the Pythagorean concept of number could not account for all geometrical forms and the empirical things corresponding to such geometrical patterns. If the truth of mathematics was to save the rational value of knowledge, it

109

was necessary to revise the conception of number, to widen its definition so as to cover irrational numbers as well, and to formulate laws for their addition and multiplication in terms of the arithmetic of integers.

To be sure, the irrational quantities were not beyond reason for Plato, as he used them to illustrate his doctrine of Reminiscence. In the passage in *Meno* already quoted, Plato tried to explain that teaching is only reawakening the memory of something in the mind of the learner: a slave is introduced into a room containing objects which should rouse him, with the help of the dialectical treatment, to some universal truths concerning them. Meno watches to see whether the boy answers by way of reminiscence and out of his own mind, as the reasonable questions of Socrates fall "like water on the seed-ground." By putting to the slave a carefully prepared series of questions, Socrates leads him to recognize that double the square of any straight line is not the square on double the line, but the square on the diagonal of the original square.[1] Surely the so-called irrationals must be rational somehow if the mind, having contemplated their patterns in the world of ideas, "remembers" them when confronted with their actual geometrical illustrations. "See him now; how he remembers in the logical order, as he ought to remember." And again, "Just now, as in a dream, these opinions have been stirred up within him." Socrates assures us the slave will perform similar acts of reminiscence on demand with any and every problem.

The same view is expressed in *Phaedo:* the theory of an innate knowledge independent of our experience holds "as much about two equal lines as about the absolute Beauty, the absolute just and good and all things whatever." For if we are born with certain mathematical principles apprehended before birth, then we can say that "we have knowledge, both before and immediately upon our begetting here, not merely about the equal, the greater and the less, but also about all other things of the kind." [2] Incidentally, this doctrine appears

1 *Meno* 82B-85B.
2 *Phaedo* 75C.

to be closely related to the implications of the Pythagorean teaching concerning the memory of past lives.[3]

There is another reason for the necessity of the irrationals and consequently for their rationalization. In the *Laws*, we are given the qualifications and duties of the "nocturnal council" which looks after public safety: the public piety which must be the primary concern of its members requires some knowledge of the heavenly bodies which exemplify the wisdom of the Creator by their conformity to mathematical law. This regularity can be ascertained by observing the rhythmic periods of each planet's motion, and by expressing them in terms of the period of any other, an operation which might require something more than the arithmetic of integers.

Hence the necessity of studying integers and surds. But the latter must be considered as pure and not as embodied, and an account of their derivation must be given before discussing their application. That is how "astronomical problems force on us the extension of arithmetic by the discovery of a method of evaluating quadratic and cubic surds, and a corresponding enlargement of our conception of number which will enable us to include these surds among numbers."[4] Although geometry can always represent the motions of the heavenly bodies, its processes are less satisfactory to reason, as they are more pictorial than those of arithmetic. When the discovery of irrational lines had placed geometry in a higher position than arithmetic, there was no choice but to apply geometry to astronomical problems. Even in generalizing the Pythagorean theory of proportion, Eudoxus used geometrical rather than arithmetical concepts; but if geometry is considered only an illustration of the arithmetic of the quadratic and cubic surds, this parallelism of arithmetic with geometry preserved the primacy of arithmetic over all the sciences.

Plato may have worked out a numerical interpretation of the discoveries of Theaetetus and Eudoxus, thus reverting to

[3] Cf. A. Cameron, *The Pythagorean Background of the Theory of Recollection* (Madison, Wis., 1938).

[4] A. E. Taylor, *Philosophical Studies* (London, 1952), p. 103.

the earlier priority of arithmetic over geometry. This is implied in *Epinomis,* which goes beyond the mathematical considerations of the *Republic.* "The first and most important 'study' is of numbers in themselves; not of corporeal numbers, but of the whole genesis of the odd and even, and the extent of their influence on the nature of things."[5] There comes next geometry and stereometry, which permit "an evident likening of numbers unlike one another by nature." According to the following fragment of *Archytas,* this view was predominant at the time: "In respect of wisdom, arithmetic surpasses all the other arts and especially geometry, seeing it can treat the objects it wishes to study in a clearer way. Where geometry fails, arithmetic completes its demonstration in the same way even with regard to figures, if there is such a thing as the study of figures."[6]

An illustration of the primacy of arithmetic over geometry may be found in the Platonic notion of indivisible lines. The Pythagorean method of filling the geometrical continuum with points defined as monads having position implied that a point has a minimum volume, but this view has been refuted by Zeno's argument of the unlimited bisection of the straight line, and of the impossibility of making a line longer or a volume bigger by adding one point to it. Although Plato did not solve the difficulties raised by the Eleatic, he objected to the Pythagorean conception of the point and to the Democritean notion of the atom because of their appeal to sense experience. He would not even think of a point in its own right, for he considered the genus of points as a "geometrical fiction." He would speak of a point as the beginning or the principle of a line, and he would use the term "indivisible lines" in the same sense.[7] This led most of the early commentators to assert that Plato did believe in the possibility of atomic magnitudes.

The controversy which developed around the Platonic in-

5 *Epinomis* 990C.
6 Diels, *Vors.,* 47 B 4, III, p. 438.
7 *Met.* 992ª 22.

divisibles is based mainly on their alleged confusion with the points, but Milhaud thinks[8] this dispute is due to a mis-understanding. He points out that the Aristotelian passage (quoted above) is the only one where the name of Plato is connected with the notion of indivisible lines; in all his other references to such lines, Aristotle seems to have in view the elementary triangles of *Timaeus,* for which Xenocrates may have substituted elementary lines for similar cosmological pur-poses. If there were to be a dispute about the indivisibles, it should rather have concerned these triangles or whatever ele-mentary magnitudes the Platonists wished to use for the con-struction of the universe. In this respect, Aristotle was right in criticizing the generation of the bodies by means of ele-mentary triangles,[9] although Plato was well aware of the hypo-thetical character of his cosmogony, which he considered as more likely than certain.

Points and indivisible lines, according to Milhaud, were never conceived by Plato as being identical. In fact, the Aris-totelian text already mentioned[10] implies a radical opposition between them. As regards the point, there is no difficulty in accepting it as a principle rather than an element of the line. It was unnecessary for Plato to consider the indivisible lines in the more recent sense of the Democritean atoms, as the minimum of insecable magnitudes. The word for "point" al-ready existed in the Greek vocabulary in the sense of something which is neither actually divided nor composed of actually separate parts, but it did not imply that a magnitude which was not divided was necessarily indivisible. Plato probably used it in that original sense, as it appeared in the only passage of the dialogues[11] where it is referred to explicitly. Consequently, Plato would consider indivisible lines as undivided lines, magnitudes which are not reduced to a sum of smaller parts,

[8] Aristote et les Mathématiques," *Archiv für Geschichte der Philosophie* (1903), p. 386 *sq.*
[9] Cf. *De Caelo* iii, chap. 8.
[10] *Met.* 992ᵃ 20.
[11] *Sophist* 229*D*

a conception which agrees fully with his own idea of the point. As principle of a line, the point cannot be a static notion. According to Aristotle, the Platonists taught that "a moving line generates a surface, and a moving point a line."[12] Hence, a line is not made of points added together, but is generated by the fluxion of a point; however short is a line, it cannot be divided into elements other than lines—it is a continuum. More generally, the continuum would be produced by the flowing of some undetermined element rather than by the actual juxtaposition of actual indivisibles. This would be true of numbers and of geometrical magnitudes, on account of the parallelism emphasized by Plato between numbers and figures.

As the generation of the continuum, both numerical and geometrical, must begin with some element, the principles of numbers and lines have to be something; they cannot be nothing. But the notion of the infinitesimal involved in these remarks need not be an actual indivisible or the actual and final result of a continued subdivision. It should be considered rather as the undivided genetic element of a magnitude capable of being made as small as we please, or as the "intensive" infinitesimal of the nineteenth century idealists. It is therefore difficult to accept the opinion that the Platonic conception of the point as principle of a line implies the idea of beginning the series of numbers with zero instead of with one. The Greeks had no conception of zero as a number.

Similarly, it is difficult to maintain[13] that the Platonic doctrines involve the first clear conception of the infinitesimal, or even that Plato "was thinking out the solution of problems that lead directly to the discovery of the calculus."[14] Nothing in his writings suggests that Plato could supply either a sensory interpretation or a proper definition of the intuitive infinitesimal conceived by the discoverers of the calculus. The

12 *De Anima* 409a 5.

13 Edmund Hoppe, "Zur Geschichte der infinitesimal Rechnung bis Leibniz und Newton," *Jahresbericht, Deutsche Mathematiker-Vereinigung,* XXXVII (1928), 152.

14 J. Marvin, *The History of European Philosophy* (New York, 1938), p. 142

modern logical notion of the infinitesimal depending on the derivative and the limit was out of the conceptual range of the Greeks; they had no general concept of number, and consequently of a continuous algebraic variable leading to the concept of limit.[15]

The intuitions of the infinitesimal and the continuum, vaguely indicated by Plato, were developed by his early successors in the direction of the indivisibles or fixed infinitesimals which are unacceptable to modern analysis. Menocrates taught the existence of indivisibles and established for them a definite doctrine, which prompted critical refutation of the Peripatetic tract *On Indivisible Lines*. Aristotle had already pointed out[16] that indivisible lines must have extremities which cannot be points, and that definition of a point as the extremity of a line is unscientific. Modern mathematics has upheld Aristotle in his vigorous opposition to infinitesimal line segments, as it is impossible to offer a logical elaboration and a satisfactory definition of such indivisibles. Although this notion played an important part in the early development of the calculus, it was definitely abandoned when modern analysis formalized its foundations.

It has been suggested that both the Platonists and the Peripatetics had misunderstood Plato, and that only Archimedes picked up the train of his thought about the indivisibles. But if Plato did not express his intuitions clearly enough to stimulate his disciples to investigate them further, Archimedes nowhere mentions his indebtedness to Plato in connection with his infinitesimal methods.[17] Although certain portions of the work of Euclid and of Archimedes may have a Platonic character, these 2 mathematicians cannot be credited with the actual elaboration of the scientific intuitions of the founder of the Academy.

The progress of science requires a combination of intuitions

[15] See Carl B. Boyer, *The Concepts of the Calculus* (New York, 1949), pp. 26-30.
[16] *Topica* 141b 21.
[17] *The Method of Archimedes*, p. 17 (ed. Heath).

with a proper technique to test their value. As such a technique was not developed by the Greeks, it is wiser to say that Plato tried to bridge the gap between arithmetic and geometry with his concept of number and his effort to axiomatize arithmetic. It may be added that "if Plato made an attempt to arithmetize mathematics in this sense, he was the last of the ancients to do so, and the problem remained for modern mathematical analysis to solve."[18] These remarks do not preclude a discussion of these Platonic anticipations in the light of the available sources.

18 Boyer, *op. cit.*, p. 27.

CHAPTER 14

The Arithmetical Continuum

The extension of the Pythagorean notion of number covering
the irrationals as well as the integers was a necessary condition of the arithmetization of the universe and of knowledge.
The generation of the arithmetical continuum, which is involved in such a task, is discussed by Plato mainly in *Philebus*,
which leads to his final views on forms and numbers.

In this dialogue, which recounts the Pythagorean opposites,
the limit and the infinite, the one and the many, the ideas are
termed units or monads, and the elements of things are given
as the limit and the infinite[1] in Pythagorean fashion. This
conception underlies Plato's fundamental doctrine. According
to Aristotle and Hermodorus,[2] Plato named the limit and the
unlimited as the two basic elements of the ideas and of all
existing things. The limit as the one represents unity and is
the form-giving or active element. The unlimited, which is the
infinite or the many, represents a formless matter and is the
form-receiving element. Ideas, numbers, and sensible things
are generated by the combination of the limit and the un-

[1] *Philebus 24A*.
[2] Simplicius *Commentary on Aristotle's Physics*, fol. 54b and 56b.

limited from the infinite and through the limit. In this sense the elements of numbers are the elements of things. These views may be related to the doctrine of *the same* and *the other* mentioned in the *Sophist* and in *Timaeus* (35*A*), where being is described as a blend of the same and of the other.

The operation of the limit shaping the infinite requires further elucidation, especially as it produces the lines, surfaces, and solids,³ as well as the numbers. The limit by itself is sterile, for it cannot explain how number one repeats itself and produces other numbers, just as it cannot explain how one point by itself may move to produce a line. In other words, with the limit alone we cannot show how mathematical operations are possible, how mathematics can be extended to the sensible world, and how the general problem of the one and the many can be solved. Even the participation of the mathematical numbers in the ideal numbers or number-forms cannot account for the various arithmetical operations. The forms of numbers are operationally impotent by themselves, for they cannot produce the union of the idea of 2 with the number one or the limit; without the help of another principle, we are left with the idea of 2 or twoness *and* the number one uncombined and unintegrated.

The other principle of generation needed to account for the real and the apparent is the *dyad,* which is a principle of plurality, movement, change, and becoming. In the physical world, the function of the dyad is to produce the plurality and spatiality of phenomena. By identifying extension with the stuff of sensible things, the cosmogony of *Timaeus* reduces to the dyad the solid and corporeal nature of the universe. In the world of ideas, the dyad accounts for their multiplicity and colors their relation with a continuity resembling that of numbers. With the help of the dyad, the mind glides without breaks from one idea to another. In the logical field, as indicated in the *Sophist,* the function of the dyad and its limitation by the one tend to give a mathematical color to the

³ Aristotle *Met.* xii. 9.

process of definition. "By the segregation of more specific within more general ideas, we close in upon the specific form by bracketing it, as it were, more and more narrowly until we have excluded from it everything that is not its proper essence; just as we approximate to our irrational numbers by a progressive reduction of the values that are greater and smaller than the one in question."[4] The essence of a thing is thus reached and expressed by a process similar to a mathematical division reaching by approximation the value of a surd.

More specifically, the dyad is the principle of numerical multiplicity and geometrical extension. It produces all the even numbers by multiplication, and all the odd numbers by the function of the limit, which stops, equalizes, and stabilizes the propensity of the dyad to multiply.[5] Furthermore, the combination of the one with the dyad generates not only the rational numbers but also the irrationals. Construction of the arithmetical continuum requires primarily a clear understanding of Plato's conception of the infinite: he considers it as an undetermined dyad and gives it the strange name of the "great-and-small." This dyad involves a double function of multiplication and division, but without an upper or lower limit in keeping with its indefinite nature. Moreover, it has many species, such as long and short, broad and narrow, high and low, more and less.

The dyad is undetermined because it is not any being in particular. That is probably why Aristotle identified it with not-being.[6] The following fragment of Hermodorus throws some light on this identification:

> Those things which are spoken of as having the relation of great to small, all have the "more and less," so that they can go on to infinity in the direction of the "still greater" and the "still less." In the same way, the broader and narrower, the heavier and

---

4 B. A. G. Fuller, *A History of Greek Philosophy* (New York, 1945), II, p. 391.
5 Cf. Aristotle *Met.* 999ᵃ 9, 1002ᵃ 15, and 1080ᵇ 11.
6 *Phys.* 192ᵃ 6.

lighter, and everything spoken of in that way can go on to infinity. But what is spoken of as equal and at rest and attuned has not the "more or less" as their opposites have. There is always something more unequal than what is unequal, something more in motion than what moves, something more out of tune than what is out of tune. Hence, that which is of this nature is inconstant, formless and infinite, and may be called not-being by negation of being.[7]

In this sense, the indefinite continuum of the more-and-less is not "nothing" but, rather, not anything in particular.

It remains to explain why the indefinite is a duality, an undetermined ratio which connotes a formless multiplicity, and why this duality is a great-and-small. The available references to Plato's views on this matter give neither the whole of his thought nor the reasons for his dissatisfaction with the Pythagorean conception of number. Some writers, like Burnet, Milhaud, and Stenzel, have suggested that the great-and-small is somehow connected with the irrationals, especially as it may help to obtain their values by successive approximations to a limit. But this view is considered by Taylor, Rey, and Toeplitz as too general and conservative to be fully satisfactory. To be sure, certain series converge to a limit smaller than the unit (like $1, 1/2, 1/4 \ldots 1/2n$), and certain others (like $1, 1 + 1/2, 1 + 1/4 \ldots 1 + 1/2n$) converge to a limit greater than the unit.[8] In both cases the series converge in a simple sense which does not justify the Platonic notion of the great-and-small. Hence the assumption that Plato must have thought of a specific way of constructing infinite converging series.

Working from this view, A. E. Taylor[9] suggested an interpretation of Plato's probable method by using the famous

7 Simplicius Commentary on Aristotle's Physics, in Diels, Vors., p. 247.
8 As n increases without limit.
9 Mind, t.35, pp. 419-440 (1926) and t.36, pp. 12-33 (1927). These articles are reproduced in his Philosophical Studies (London, 1952), to which our quotations refer. Against the general opinion, Taylor regards the Epinomis as a genuine Platonic writing. The authenticity of this work, however, does not affect the interest of this interpretation, inasmuch as the Epinomis is undoubtedly of strict Platonic inspiration.

passage in the *Epinomis* about the generation of numbers, and various other considerations of the Platonic dialogues and of later commentators. This passage[10] begins with a description of the various branches of mathematics. Pride of place is given to the study of numbers in themselves, to their generation, and to their influence on the nature of things. Then comes geometry, which helps to represent irrational numbers, and stereometry, which allows the construction of magnitudes with irrational cube roots. Here we have obvious references to the duplication of the square and of the cube, paramount problems in the sixth and fifth centuries respectively. But Taylor sees in them far-reaching implications concerning the Platonic theory of irrationals.

The origin of this theory he traces to the discovery of the *side* and *diagonal* numbers which form increasing approximations to $\sqrt{2}$ in an endless series. In fact, Plato seems to allude to a rule[11] for making approximations to $\sqrt{2}$ when he speaks of 7 as the "rational diameter of 5," meaning obviously that $\sqrt{2}$ is equal to 7/5 approximately. Theon of Smyrna gives a rule for finding an unending succession of rational diameters, which yields increasingly accurate rational approximations of $\sqrt{2}$ corresponding to solutions of $y^2 = 2x^2 + 1$ in modern notation. According to this rule, 2 columns of integers are formed, corresponding to the sides and the diagonals respectively. The unit is the first term in either column. The rest of the sides are formed by adding together the nth side and the nth diagonal to form the $(n + 1)^{th}$ side. As regards the diagonals, the $(n + 1)^{th}$ diagonal is obtained by adding the nth diagonal to twice the nth side.[12] Proclus has preserved a geometrical demonstration of this rule which depends on the identity

$$(a + b)^2 + b^2 = 2(a/2)^2 + 2(a/2 + b)^2$$

as given by Euclid.[13] As this second book of Euclid is con-

10 *Epinomis* 990C-991B.
11 *Republic* 546C.
12 *Expositio*, p. 43 *sq*. (ed. Hiller).
13 *Elements* ii. 10.

sidered to be early Pythagorean in character, Taylor thinks[14] that the rule was probably known to Plato and his friends.

The implications of this rule account for its philosophical interest. The ratios obtained by means of the sides and diagonals are identical with the successive convergents of $\sqrt{2}$ formed by expressing the irrational as an unending continued fraction. Hence the construction of the convergents of a given irrational pins it down betwen 2 values which approximate to it from both sides at once. In fact, each convergent is a nearer approximation to the required value than the one before it ($17/12$ is nearer to $\sqrt{2}$ than $7/5$). Moreover, the convergents are alternatively a little less and a little more than the value to which they approximate (thus 7 and 5 are solutions of $y^2 = 2x^2 - 1$, while 17 and 12 satisfy $y^2 = 2x^2 + 1$). Furthermore, the decreasing interval betwen 2 successive convergents can be made less than any fraction by taking a sufficiently large number of convergents, so that the difference between the last convergent considered and the given irrational is even smaller. But it is impossible to get rid of this difference, because there is not actually a last convergent. Finally this method, which has proved successful for the evaluation of the surd $\sqrt{2}$ in the case of doubling the square, should be applicable to the solution of other quadratic surds; *Epinomis* implies that it is the business of geometry to discover similar series for all quadratic surds.

From these considerations, Taylor concludes that the substitution of a dyad for the single infinite is due to the necessity of providing a means of checking the interval within which falls the error of an approximation. Moreover, this dyad is a great-and-small, because it is the limit to which one series of value, all too large, tends to decrease, and also the limit to which another series, all too small, tends to increase. As it is impossible to find an identical value for two successive convergents in the case of an irrational, there is always an unequality or tension between the great and the small; or, again, an

---

[14] Taylor, *Philosophical Studies*, p. 105.

unrationalized matter in the irrational number. It is the function of the formal element of number, the one, to equalize the great and the small, but it is not as successful for the irrationals as it is for the rational numbers, where the tension between the great and the small vanishes.

The specific function of the one to equalize the great and the small, which is expressly ascribed to Plato by Aristotle,[15] is indeed a Platonic conception. In a passage of the *Statesman* referring to the science of measure or *metretic,* we are told that the great and the small must not only be appraised by their reciprocal relation, but also by reference to the just measure. What is great is not so with reference to the small only, but also with reference to the just measure; the same is true for the small.[16] Hence there are two kinds of metretic: one considers the great and the small with reference to the just measure; the other considers them simply with reference to one another. The former may be assimilated to dialectic while the latter is identified with mathematics. In spite of this distinction, metretic does introduce the idea of a common limit between the great and the small, which can be applied to the problem of the generation of numbers. This application is the more permissible when we consider that this problem is not exclusively mathematical and that dialectic has some bearing on the foundations of mathematics.

If Plato did think of such a method of rationalizing the irrationals by means of the one and the dyad, he should be credited with the first discovery, although in incomplete form, of the *real number* conceived as the common limit of 2 infinite convergent series. In this connection, Taylor remarks that the Platonic theory must have been inspired by the same desire for pure rationality which has led to the arithmetization of mathematics in modern times.

The object aimed at, in both cases, is to get rid of the dualism between so-called continuous and discrete magnitudes. The ap-

15 *Met.* 1081ª 24.
16 *Statesman* 283D.

parent mystery which hangs about the "irrationals" is to be dispelled by showing how they can be derived, by a logical process which is transparently rational at every step, from the integers and the "rational" fractions or ratio of integers to integers. It is precisely the same process, carried further, which we see in modern times in the arithmetical theory of the continuum, or in Cantor's further elaboration of an arithmetic of the "transfinite." In all these cases, the motive for the construction is to get rid of an apparent mystery by the discovery in the seemingly unintelligible of the principle of order, of which the integer-series is the perfect and ideal embodiment.[17]

The analogy should not be pushed too far, especially as the knowledge of the Greeks about the surds of a higher order cannot be accepted without qualifications. The study of the solids initiated by the Pythagoreans and developed by Democritus and Plato became an important science with Theaetetus and Eudoxus, who dealt with problems involving cubic roots. Hence, the demand for a method of approximating cubic roots from the sides of the great and of the small alternately, as in the case of quadratic surds, must have been suggested by the growth of stereometry in the Academy. The simplest illustration of the general problem involved was offered by the duplication of the cube, which is reducible to the construction of a series of approximations to the real value of $\sqrt{2}$ from its 2 sides alternately.

The actual construction of these convergents requires algebraical methods unknown to the Greeks, while the absence of an efficient numerical symbolism and an operational system of position increased the difficulties of their arithmetical manipulations. Greek mathematics has not even detailed examples of the extraction of a cube root by means of the expansion of $(a + b)^3$, a process corresponding to the method for square roots elaborated by Theon of Alexandria.[18] Hence,

<hr>

[17] Taylor, *Philosophical Studies*, p. 120.

[18] *Commentary on Ptolemy's Syntaxis* 469.16-473.8 (ed. Rome). The extraction of the cube root of 100 given by Heron in his *Metrics* (iii. 20) is a description of an empirical method with no reference to a generalized formula.

no arithmetical evaluation of cube roots could be worked out by the Academy, even though Plato may have speculated on the analogy offered by the numerical treatment of quadratic surds.

The earliest attempt is the evaluation given by Archimedes.[19] All the other solutions offered are geometrical or empirical; even the author of *Epinomis* admits that the numbers with irrational cube roots, although "made unlike, are likened by that other art . . . called stereometry." Moreover, there is no indication that Plato considered irrational or even rational roots of orders higher than the third. He leaned too much on his spatial intuition to imagine any theories of numbers entirely independent of geometry, or to conceive a general and formal method for the generation of the arithmetical continuum. At best, *Epinomis* hints at a program of research more comprehensive than the current techniques could allow.

The generation of the irrationals does not cover all the aspects of the problem of number. So far, the integers and their order have figured as given in the construction of the continuum. There remains to consider how the determination of the dyad by the one affects the generation of the integers themselves. Plato must have presented his problem in this perspective, for Aristotle criticizes it in this form, although it is harder to detect the elements of matter and form within the integers series.

The available texts and relevant commentaries are more confusing than helpful. Nevertheless, *Epinomis* offers a characteristic passage concerning the integers.

First the double operates on the number 1 by simple multiplication so as to give 2, and a second double yields the square; by further doubling we reach the solid and tangible, the process having gone from 1 to 8. Then comes the application of the double to give the mean which is as much greater than the less as it is less than the greater, and the other mean is that which

[19] *The Measurement of the Circle* iii.

exceeds and is exceeded by the same part of the extremes; between 6 and 12 come both the sesquialter (9) and the sesquitertius (8) ; turning between these two, to one side or the other, this power (9) furnished men with concord and symmetry for the purpose of rhythm and harmony in their pastimes, and has been given to the blessed dance of the Muses.[20]

Whether this text is corrupt or unrevised by its real author, its purpose is clear. Successive multiplication of 1 by 2 gives the geometric progression 1,2,4,8, representing respectively a point, a line, a square, and a cube. Then comes a reference to the arithmetic mean, which is equidistant from 2 given terms, and to the harmonic mean, which exceeds one term and is exceeded by the other by the same fraction of each term. By reducing fractions, this gives the numbers 9 and 8 respectively. It may be observed that 8 was already given as the cube of 2 and that no indication is given about the generation of the other integers. A more important remark is that Plato favors distinctly the process of duplication in the generation of numbers.

This is also the case with the construction of the world-soul. Here Plato uses 2 basic geometric series—(1,2,4,8) and (1,3,9,27); then, by filling the intervals between these numbers with arithmetic and harmonic means, he gets a series of 34 terms.[21] This construction may be intended to represent the notes of a musical scale having a compass of 4 octaves and a major sixth, but it is more probable that it has to do with Plato's religious background and with his doctrine of numbers.

It is likely that Plato thought of constructing the arithmetical continuum with one single process when he discarded addition, which yields the integers in a simple and direct way, but cannot supply the irrationals, which are far more numer-

20 *Epinomis* 990E—Ivor Thomas, *Greek Mathematical Texts* (London, 1939), I, p. 403.
21 *Timaeus* 35B-36B. Cf. R. G. Bury, *The Symposium of Plato* (Cambridge, 1932), pp. 66-71; A. E. Taylor, *A Commentary on Plato's Timaeus* (Oxford, 1928), pp. 130-136; F. M. Cornford, *Plato's Cosmology: The Timaeus of Plato,* translated with a running commentary (Cambridge, 1937), pp. 67 *ff.*

ous than the rational numbers. The generation of all numbers could be achieved by a proper combination of the one
with the dyad, which already accounted in principle for the
irrationals. This may have originated in observing that in
Zeno's process of unending bisection of a given length, the
sum of the segments thus obtained is none other than the
finite line itself. Similarly, any real number could be conceived
as the sum of an unending series of rational or irrational
numbers. But Plato did not have the technical means of
elaborating this process, which is necessarily more complex
than the additive method of the Pythagoreans adopted later
by the Peripatetics.

Taylor believes that Plato's method of obtaining the integers involves not only the combination of the one and the
dyad, but also the operation of a particular aspect of the dyad,
the reciprocal functions of doubling and halving which yield
the simplest numerical ratios. Beginning with the unit, successive duplications produce the first even numbers in geometric progression. The first odd numbers are obtained by
halving the sum of 2 successive even numbers. This process
assimilates any odd number to the arithmetic mean between 2
successive even numbers, according to the identity

$$2\,n + 1 = \frac{1}{2}\,[2\,n + 2\,(n + 1)]$$

The indefinite repetition of these operations yields all the
integers, although they are not obtained in their natural order.
This is the case of the first 10 integers derived in the following
order: first 1, then 2 (double of 1), then 4 (double of 2),
then 8 (double of 4), then 3 (arithmetic mean between 2 and
4), then 6 (double of 3), then 5 (arithmetic mean between 4
and 6), then 7 (arithmetic mean between 8 and 6), then 10
(double of 5), and finally 9 (arithmetic mean between 8 and
10). In fact, "the powers of 2 have to precede the other integers of the decad; and further, no odd number $2n + 1$ can
appear until $2n$ and $2n + 2$ have already been obtained. A
number $2n + 1$ will always follow after $2n + 2$. Hence, Aris-

totle's criticism concerning these features of the doctrine are justified."[22]

According to Taylor, this procedure involves a double confusion: that of the integers with the rational real numbers, and that of the integers 1 and 2 with the one and the dyad. Consequently, the function of duplication is assigned to the undetermined dyad, although it belongs really to the integer 2 or auto-dyad. It is difficult to agree fully with these views. In the first place, if such an elegant interpretation of the Platonic construction of the integers with the one and the dyad can be given, there is no reason why it should not be extended to fractions as well. These could be obtained by using the process of halving and also by taking the arithmetic mean of successive rational numbers, one greater and one smaller than the resulting fraction. These numbers could be 2 integers, an integer and a fraction, or two fractions. The indefinite repetition of these operations would yield all the rational real numbers.

As regards the function of duplication, it can be rightly assigned to the dyad rather than to the auto-dyad. Plato could not confuse the 2 in itself with the dyad. The expandable and contractile nature of the latter cannot be identified with the changeless and absolute character of the former without obliterating one of the most remarkable Platonic intuitions and introducing confusion into a theory otherwise relatively clear.[23] The distinction between the auto-dyad and the dyad becomes more significant if the first is identified with *twoness* and the second with *twiceness*.[24] If twoness is the actual essence of the mathematical number 2, twiceness is the ability of any mathematical number to proceed from itself to another number and to be integrated into measures and formulas. Hence, twiceness is neither a limit, nor a measure, nor a mag-

22 Taylor, *Philosophical Studies,* p. 149.
23 This confusion of the dyad with 2 may account for some of Aristotle's criticisms of the Platonic conceptions.
24 J. Cook Wilson, "On the Platonist Doctrine," *Classical Review,* 18 (1904), 247-260.

nitude, nor a quantitative determinant of any kind. By its agency and its various functions (greater, less, doubling, halving), as well as by its combination with the one, twiceness produces all the real numbers.

This interpretation brings the dyad of *Philebus* into the mathematical fold and is accepted by most modern historians. As Rey remarks,[25] there is a real distinction between the dyad and the auto-dyad. The latter is the 2 in itself, unmovable, changeless, independent of becoming. On the other hand, the dyad is an operational process (hence a becoming) for the creation of the indefinite succession of all possible real numbers, rational and irrational. Like the Pythagorean limit, the one limits this operation each time and thereby determines a definite number at the expense of a numerical matter, the undetermined dyad which represents the becoming of all possible numbers. This limitation unifies in a certain way the converging function of the dyad, by causing it to yield one rational or irrational number; this may account for the substitution of the Platonic for the Pythagorean limit.

These remarks have their analogical counterpart in the generation of the geometrical magnitudes: the undetermined character of the formless space favors the generation of any ideal magnitude, whether rational or irrational, by means of a double series of greater and smaller magnitudes which oscillate about it, until the limit or the one ultimately equalizes them and produces thereby the required magnitude. This is a possible reason for the Platonic confusion between numbers and magnitude which Aristotle persistently distinguishes. But the results obtained by the combination of the one and the dyad are not identical; otherwise the numbers (and magnitudes) would be alike. While the operations involved are identical, the results are analogical but different. Hence, the one and the dyad alone account for every one and all numbers (and magnitudes); the auto-dyad need not appear in the generation of the arithmetical continuum.

25 A. Rey, *La Maturité de la Pensée Scientifique en Grèce* (1903), p. 344.

The Platonic method of deriving the integers suggests 2 practical remarks. One is that addition is not avoided in the process described, for the arithmetic mean, which yields the odd numbers, requires the addition of 2 successive even numbers before halving their sum. This indirect way of obtaining the odd numbers does not justify technically rejection of the additive process. The other remark concerns the order of the operations involved in the generation of the integers, which seems quite arbitrary in the Platonic construction. The sequence of the first 10 integers involves 3 duplications to begin with, then one mean, then one duplication, then 2 means, then one duplication, and finally one mean. There is no reason why 3 should not be formed before 8, and 7 after 10, and there are no indications about the integers after the decad. The Platonic sequence of the first 10 integers thus makes it impossible to formulate a general rule of order for the operation yielding the integers, and consequently a law concerning their succession. Such a law could be expressed by taking alternately the double and the arithmetic mean, beginning from the first even number. But this is not the method implied in *Epinomis,* which complicates the whole procedure by assigning a function to the other mathematical means in the generation of the integers.

Whatever the actual technical details of Plato's method, its purpose is to reconcile the incalculable with the calculable, to integrate all types of numbers and magnitudes into one single genus, and thereby to make possible to all the application of the same operational methods. This attempted unification of the various species of quantity involves an artificial generation of the integers, a possible construction of the irrationals by means of series, and a closer assimilation of numbers and geometrical magnitudes. This interpretation of Platonism allows us to ascribe to Plato a remote vision of later developments. But neither Plato's writings nor those of his successors contain any such references. Even Books V, VI, and X of Euclid's *Elements* cannot be considered as an elaboration of the Platonic views about arithmetic and geometry. On the other hand, the Greeks had no means of establishing a theory of series with its attendant notions of limits and infinitesimals. The construction of the integers has little or no practical value, but it involves 2 important principles: one is the necessity of a strict derivation of the integers from more fundamental notions, and the other is that multiplication is logically independent of addition. Plato may have perceived both of them, but he had no means of developing them or discussing them in their mathematical setting. Hence, he could not attempt the analysis of number and of its properties by means of purely logical elements, as modern mathematical logic tries to do. Instead, Plato proposed to justify number with the help of ontological arguments involving references to an ideal world of forms. This endeavor, which was rightly criticized by Aristotle, leads to consideration of the ultimate Platonic doctrine concerning the identification of forms and numbers. It remains to discuss the various aspects of this controversial problem, which brings unity into the several stages of the Platonic philosophy.

CHAPTER 15

Forms and Numbers

The most characteristic theories of Plato were elaborated toward the end of his life. Even the philosophy of the sciences presented in the *Republic* was completely transformed later. The Pythagorean influence in the Platonic doctrines grew stronger as the founder of the Academy grew older. But although Plato's last vision was the complete identification of forms with numbers, it is difficult to interpret with certainty this central doctrine of his philosophy; Plato has not left a written exposition of his ultimate teaching to the inner circle of his students. That is why, after his death, so many versions were current of his lecture on "The Good," which was believed to contain the most explicit account of his philosophy.

Perhaps Plato had no desire to leave behind any formal statement of his views, because he probably thought they would sound absurd to the public, although men of keen intelligence would find them admirable and inspired. This opinion is supported by this remarkable testimony of Aristoxenus describing the feelings of those who attended Plato's lecture on "The Good":

Everyone went there expecting that he would be put in the way of getting one or other of the things accounted good in human life, such as riches or health or strength or any extraordinary gift of fortune. But when they found that Plato's arguments were of mathematics and numbers and geometry and astronomy, and that in the end he declared the One to be the Good, they were altogether taken by surprise. The result was that some of them scoffed at the thing, while others found great fault with it.[1]

Many who had followed Plato's teaching and once held his doctrines to be incredible considered them afterwards the most credible, while what they had held most credible appeared to them the opposite. Plato explained this change of attitude by the frequent repetition of his doctrines, which became refined like gold after many years of labor. Therefore, "the greatest safeguard is to avoid writing and to learn by heart; for it is impossible that what is written down should not get divulged. For this reason, I myself have never yet written anything on these subjects; and no treatise of Plato exists or will ever exist."[2] The same cautious remarks are found in another Epistle where Plato says that "every serious man in dealing with really serious subjects carefully avoids writing, lest thereby he may possibly cast them as a prey to the envy and stupidity of the public."[3]

These thoughts were probably inspired by the difficulty of explaining in words the final vision of the good, which is the last effort of the mind ascending towards reality. Plato admitted that after the name, the definition, the essence, and the knowledge of that essence, it is necessary to see the thing itself if one is to explain it. But here neither receptivity nor memory will ever produce knowledge in him who has no affinity with the object, since it does not begin to germinate in unfavorable states of mind.

---

[1] *Elements of Harmony* ii. 122. 3-16 (ed. Macran).
[2] *Epistles* ii. 314*A-C*.
[3] *Epistles* vii. 344*C*.

One must learn at the same time both what is false and what is true of the whole of existence through the most diligent and prolonged investigation. It is by the examination of each of these objects (names and definitions, vision and sense-perception), comparing one with another, proving them by suitable proofs and employing questions and answers void of envy,—it is by such means and even then with difficulty that the light of intelligence and reason bursts out illuminating each object in the mind of him who uses every effort of which mankind is capable.[4]

A reconstruction of Plato's ultimate views can be attempted by using his own dialogues, Aristotle's references to them, and some brief excerpts from later commentators. Perhaps one may doubt at times the accuracy of Aristotle's interpretation of his master, although he may quote him rightly, for Aristotle was anxious to push forward his own ideas, thus giving a polemical character to his references. Moreover, his criticism of Platonism in *Metaphysics* seems to be subsidiary to his standing polemic against Xenocrates, the contemporary head of the Academy.

It is difficult to believe that Aristotle misunderstood Plato altogether; not only do his works remain the best source for Plato's later views, but also these "unwritten doctrines" must have been very definite to Aristotle, who knows of no other Platonic philosophy than the one identifying forms and numbers. He neither mentions an earlier Platonism, where forms were not identified with numbers, nor does he give any grounds for considering the philosophy of Plato as "a senile aberration." On the contrary, he complains that his contemporaries considered mathematics and philosophy to be identical and replaced philosophy by mathematics.[5] This attitude may account for the obvious difficulties found in the 2 last books, *M* and *N* of *Metaphysics,* dealing expressly with the objects of mathematics. Yet in the first book of *Metaphysics,* Plato's philosophy is carefully stated and compared with Pythagoreanism, which inspired it considerably. We have explained the

4 *Epistles* vii. 344*A-C.*
5 *Met.* 992ᵃ 30-32.

connection between the 2 systems as a consequence of Plato's endeavor to correct the failure of the Pythagorean mathematical philosophy.

There are 2 main points of difference between Pythagoreanism and Platonism which Aristotle mentions specifically. One is the exact relation between numbers and things. While the Pythagoreans identified numbers and natural things, Plato thought of them as being distinct, the objects of mathematics being different from both forms and perceptible things and being intermediate between them. The other point concerns the elements of numbers: to the limit (form) and the infinite (matter) of the Pythagoreans, Plato substituted the One and the Undetermined Dyad. These distinctions are made clear in the following passage, where Plato is credited with the view that "besides perceptible things and forms, there are the objects of mathematics occupying an intermediate position. These differ from perceptible things in being eternal and unchangeable; for many forms in being are alike, while the form itself is unique in each case. Since the forms were the causes of all other things, he thought their elements were the elements of all things. As principles, the great-and-small was matter and the One was essential reality: from the great-and-small by participation in the One come the Numbers."[6]

The "separation" between numbers and natural things was due to the use of the dialectical method[7] and to the impulse given by Socrates[8] to this kind of reasoning. In discussing the views of the Pythagoreans, Socrates would have shown that ethical inquiries required certain forms which were not numbers, although they would be separate from the things of perception, just as the numbers were. Furthermore, if forms and things were identical, the Socratic definition of what is permanent could not be applied to the Heraclitean flux of things. Hence, form must be distinct from the perpetual objects; this accounts for the introduction of the forms.

6 *Met.* 987b 14.
7 *Met.* 987b 29 and *Phaedo* 99E.
8 *Met.* 1086b 3.

With Socrates, this distinction seems to be more logical than real; in the second part of *Phaedo* the forms are certainly *in* things, and Aristotle's interpretation of the Socratic doctrine confirms this view.[9] But for Plato, forms and things are really separate; that is why Aristotle commends Socrates for his restraint and complains of the Platonic separation of forms and things. Yet Aristotle did not stress the difference between participation and imitation. He considered this difference as purely verbal, probably because both imitation and participation make numbers the principles of the reality of all things. Although we are not told what imitation or participation of things in forms could be, the difference between them is of great importance because participation implies the immanence of the forms in the things.

With regard to the difference between perceptual and mathematical objects, the diagrams of the mathematician are shown in *Phaedo* to be only a rough image of what he really means. The geometer makes use of visible figures without thinking of them "but of those things they are a likeness of, pursuing his inquiry for the sake of the square as such and the diagonal as such, and not for the sake of their images as drawn."[10] In other words, "geometry is not the business of making diagrams, but the discovery of realities."[11] As regards arithmetic, it is not the study of things numbered, but of number.[12] The statement "2 and 2 is 4" is not about pairs of visible and tangible things, but about the numbers 2 and 4 in their essence. In short, the science of figures and numbers as such should be distinguished from "the mathematics of the many," which is applied to sensible objects.

Mathematics is thus divorced from experience; its propositions do not necessarily refer to the external world, and their truth is indifferent to the passage of events. Mathematics deals

9 *Met.* 1078b 30.
10 *Republic* vi. 510D.
11 *Euthydemus* 290E.
12 *Republic* 525D.

with "what always is and not with what comes to be and passes away."[13] Hence, perceptual and mathematical objects are different, and because numerical and geometrical beings have an existence of their own and cannot be actually immanent in the particular symbols and diagrams of the mathematician, the stronger is the distinction between mathematical objects and sensible things in general. Plato could not have ignored the many arguments in favor of this distinction. Aristotle's refutation of this immanence in Book *M*,2 of *Metaphysics* is really directed against the dissenting Platonists who followed a more orthodox Pythagoreanism. Nevertheless, the Platonic conception that the forms of things are themselves numbers lends itself to criticism. Aristotle raised the further question (Book *M*,7) whether the units making up the number which is the form of man or horse are the same as those found in the form of animal, and whether those of the form of man are the same as those of the form of horse.

Let us now turn to Plato's distinction between numbers and the mathematical objects considered as intermediate between forms and things. We are told that the mathematical objects are many, although eternal and immovable, whereas each form is one and unique. In fact, the mathematician deals with circles of different sizes and in varying positions; he speaks of various kinds of triangles; and he handles numbers with different values. Mathematical reasoning has to do with many circles, many triangles, and many numbers. But the circle as such is one only; so is the triangle, and so is each type of number. The interesting point is that whereas there is one form of a circle or of a triangle, there is not one single form of number. In a significant passage, Aristotle says that as the Platonists "did not posit ideas of classes within which they recognize priority and posteriority, they did not maintain the existence of an idea embracing all numbers."[14] For Platonism there is one idea of each thing, one of man-himself and

13 *Republic* 527B.
14 *Ethica Nicom.* 1096a 15.

another one of animal-itself, but the similar and undifferentiated numbers are infinitely many, so that any particular number 3 is no more man-himself than any other 3.[15]

These 2 passages imply that mathematical numbers are undifferentiated, as there are several of the same denomination, each one being composed of undifferentiated units, so that there cannot be a simple form corresponding to number in general. In other words, the generation of the numerical continuum by the combination of the One and the dyad entails that mathematical numbers must fail continually to achieve a perfect form.

> For it is in the nature of the continuum that numbers themselves shall be always in the making and never quite made, and shall approximate but never quite attain or keep their forms. Thus, the number two is never completely and unreservedly given over to twoness and nothing else. It is a passage, a transition, a looking backward and forward through a perspective of infinite gradations towards one and towards three. It can never be caught in the act of being wholly and merely an example of twoness.[16]

On the strength of this interpretation, Fuller suggests that Plato had perhaps found a mathematical solution of the problem of evil and a scientific explanation of the continual failure of the sensible things to enact their forms perfectly. If numbers, the most adequate measure of quantity, are too changing to yield any simple number-form, then the sensible world, which requires quantitative existence, must be doomed to imperfection.

Without some corresponding forms, however, even mathematical numbers would be impossible. By themselves, these numbers cannot explain how and why the One and the dyad are directed towards their construction. Hence it must be asked whether these numbers are somehow preformed in the mind, and whether they have an existential ground beyond them-

---

15 *Met.* 1081ª 9.
16 B. A. G. Fuller, *A History of Greek Philosophy* (New York, 1945), II, p. 392.

selves and the 2 principles of their generation. Plato solves the question by justifying the existence and function of the mathematical numbers through their participation in the ideal numbers which exist beyond them in a substantial world of reality. This solution readily entails not only a distinction between numbers and mathematical objects, but also a difference in their mode of existence.[17]

From Aristotle's polemic in *Metaphysics*, it appears that the numbers which Plato declared to be forms are just the integers and nothing else. These ideal numbers or number-forms are not obtained through an operation. At least the first 10 of them exist separately as forms, so that the first 10 mathematical numbers participate in the monad, the auto-dyad, and so on, up to the decad. For example, although there are many pairs of things and although there may be as many 2's as there are pairs, as Aristotle says, there is only one 2 in itself, or auto-dyad. Each one of these ideal numbers is a unity by itself and does not contain any units. In other words, the number-forms are not collections of units of which they are the cardinal numbers.

Hence, the ideal numbers are not subject to any operations, although they may be given in a certain order. They cannot be added and they are not obtained by addition. "There must be a first 2 and a first 3, and the numbers must not be addible to one another."[18] This peculiar character may be explained by the continuity of the series of the mathematical numbers: the addition of integers does not yield what is intermediate between 1 and 2, or 2 and 3, like the fractions and the irra-

---

17 It appears that Enriques confuses numbers and mathematical objects when he writes: "It is impossible to attach any meaning to the Platonic ideas if we do not regard them as having the same kind of existence as the one predicated of mathematical forms and relations in nature"— Federigo Enriques, *History of Logic* (New York, 1929), p. 13. In this particular work, Enriques refers to the *Republic* only and does not offer a serious interpretation of the Platonic views.

18 *Met.* 1083ᵃ 30. The ideal numbers are such that all their units are different in species: thus, one of the units in 2 is prior to the other and therefore to 2, and it comes next after the original 1. Similarly, between 2 and 3 there will be the first unit in 3, and so on.

tionals. Yet Plato does not think of the continuum of the real numbers, but of the integer-series, which is not a continuum and which admits the additive process. Hence, the ground for the non-addibility of the Platonic integers must be sought elsewhere.

A more adequate explanation is that each number possesses an internal structure particular to it and independent of any combination of homogeneous units. In other words, ideal numbers cannot be added because when we say "2 and 2 is 4" we mean that 2 units of a given kind added to 2 units of the same kind are equal to 4 units of that kind; we do not mean that the number 2 added to the number 2 is the number 4. The number 2 does not consist of 2 units, nor does the number 4 consist of 4 units. Each number has a specific nature as a universal; it is one and unique. The universal we call "two" somehow partakes in the number 2 without being identical with it, as there is one number 2 only, or rather one auto-dyad. The relation between the numbers themselves cannot be expressed by any additive formula; it is somehow the relation of equality, and not of addition, which suits them.

In fact, the ideal numbers are neither addible nor capable of mathematical manipulation, because they are not mathematical entities at all. As they are the logical essences or natures of these entities, they are in logical relation between themselves, they may be subsumed, and they may participate in one another. For Plato, they seem to be essentially expressions determining the most general type of relations and denoting higher and lower degrees of generality and value. Particularly in *Timaeus*, the ideal numbers appear to be the principles of the eternal model of the universe. In other words, the ideal numbers are the forms of quantity, but they are not quantitative in themselves: they are qualitative essences, such as oneness, twoness, threeness, just like humanity or virtue. An example will make this point clear: geometrical squares and circles may have relations of juxtaposition, congruence, intersection, inclusion, and exclusion, but not the ideas of squareness and circularity, which constitute the ontological ground of squares and circles. Similarly, although we can manipulate numbered objects as well as mathematical numbers, the ideal numbers as such are not capable of any mathematical operations. Although the ideal form of number 2 is twoness, it cannot be said that twoness and twoness make fourness. From this point of view, the ideal numbers are not mathematically larger or smaller than one another.

Although abstract and substantial in themselves, the ideal numbers make the various mathematical operations possible. The results of mathematical operations are not justified by the operations themselves, but by the participation of these results in the ideal forms. For example, the ideal numbers make counting possible, for they enable the addible mathematical numbers to do the counting and the concrete objects to be counted. It is usually thought that 2 is obtained by adding one to one, as though a number could be changed by a juxtaposition; and that by dividing the number one we get 2, as if division could multiply.[19] In fact, unity can be neither increased nor divided because it has no parts and is identical with itself. When one is added to one, it is not addition which is the cause of 2, but participation in duality, or twoness.[20] In short, arithmetical operations and geometrical constructions[21] are not causes in the ideal science of mathematics, but they are permissible on account of the number-forms.

These mathematical processes are carried out by numerical symbols or geometrical diagrams which are particular in a sense, while the number-forms themselves are general. Arithmetical and geometrical operations do not concern *the* 2 or *the* triangle, but *any* number 2 and *any* triangular figure. In other words, mathematical processes do not concern forms but their specifications in numbers and figures. From this point of view, the mathematical numbers mediate not only between the ideal numbers and the concrete objects, but also between the ideal numbers and the other forms, since the latter are many and can be counted separately. This mediation would bring into greater relief the ontological and epistomological impor-

19 *Phaedo* 96E-97A.
20 *Phaedo* 101C.
21 *Republic* 527A.

tance of the ideal numbers as the ground for the existence and the understanding of everything.

The question arises whether a distinction exists between the ideal numbers or number-forms and the forms or ideas in general. Granted that ideas and numbers are separate from both mathematical numbers and sensible things, and also that the ideal numbers are substances having an existence of their own, it is natural to ask what is the ontological relation between numbers and forms. Three alternatives may be considered: either both numbers and forms are on the same level, or numbers are posterior to the forms, or numbers are prior to the forms. There are many objections of a metaphysical nature to the first view, while the second alternative is definitely unacceptable, as it almost entails the identification of the ideal numbers with the mathematical numbers. We are thus left with the third alternative,[22] that numbers are prior to the forms.

The key to Plato's final views on forms and numbers should be found in a theory concerning the series of the first 10 integers; these occupy the highest position in his doctrines and condition the relation between the forms to which they are prior.

> The numbers are the models of the ideas; they are the types of the relations which may be established between them. The idea is not something simply by itself; its simplicity is relative and not absolute. The ideas are many, but they can form a unity thus becoming patterns of the constitution of numbers. As regards the mathematical numbers, they appear to be intermediate between the ideal and the sensible realms; and their function is to introduce quantity into the sensible world.[23]

---

22 L. Robin, *La Théorie Platonicienne des Idées et des Nombres* (Paris, 1933). This is also the opinion of Theophrastus, who must have heard of Plato's unwritten doctrines from Aristotle, his master. In his *Plato's Theory of Ideas* (New York, 1951), W. D. Ross rallies himself to Robin's interpretation (*ibid.*, p. 218, n. 1), and submits (*ibid.*, p. 220) that Plato simply assigned numbers to ideas without identifying them.

23 Robin made this statement during the public examination of his thesis, *La Théorie Platonicienne des Idées et des Nombres* [*Revue de Metaphysique* (Paris, 1908), Appendice].

It thus seems that the forms should be considered somehow as formulas in order to fulfill the requirements of absolute determination.

To get at the real nature of a thing, we must get the thing's measure in mathematical terms. Until we have found its formula, we have not found its form. Now, Limit is just the principle of formulation. It sums up the concepts and processes of mathematics which enable us to weigh and measure and arrive at exact results. Without it, the forms could not be distinguished, nay could not exist; for without precision and measurableness, the Universe would have no articulate structure and would offer no handhold to reason and science. . . . Plato has found at last the least common denominator of the whole formal side of Nature. The ideas of number are the limits and determinants of every form.[24]

24 Fuller, *op. cit.*, p. 161.

CHAPTER 16

The Mathematical Universe

The most fundamental and original phase of Platonism is the recognition of the forms, their independent existence, and their normative character. But as the real and substantial ideas share our interest with our universe of appearance and physical change, there must be an intimate relation between these 2 worlds for the latter to be intelligible. Hence Plato's doctrine that the forms themselves account ultimately for the sensible world, and that the whole of existence is conditioned by the good.

It is in *Timaeus,* one of his last writings, that Plato describes in mathematical terms the relations between numbers and things. Unfolding a majestic vision, this dialogue recounts the creation of the world-soul, the universe, the elementary bodies, and the soul and body of man, with their attendant psychological, biological, and medical details. In the physical use of mathematics, the Demiurge is inspired by harmony and beauty because he is good himself (29E) and because the good is the source of all proportion and truth. This exposition takes the characters of a myth because Plato cannot offer more than likely conjectures (29C-E) in such a vast enterprise. In fact,

144

Plato considers it as combining "likelihood with necessity." It is likely, because he can prove neither his physical explanations nor the genetic relations between the mathematical and the natural objects. And it is necessary insofar as his mathematical constructions are implied logically in the consequences of his initial assumptions.[1]

The mythical form of *Timaeus* illustrates the hypothetical character of its doctrines, which were rightly criticized by Aristotle[2] and others. What invites distrust in them is, of course, their arbitrary use of mathematical relations. But their inspiration is most remarkable, as they attempt to put the world into equations. By describing how the proper combination of the numerical relations of the elementary figures could account for the physical world, Plato thought he could rationalize it in mathematical terms. He goes further by envisioning the good as the ultimate reality which justifies the structure of the world.

The Platonic creation of the world was conditioned arbitrarily by an ideal model of geometrical and arithmetical relations which the Demiurge had before him and which he made manifest in the realm of becoming. For example, the spherical form given to the universe is an imitation of the model of geometrical perfection (32*B*), and the account of the recurrence of time points to the model of eternity (37*D*). That is why the chaos out of which the Demiurge brought the world to order (30*A*) does not lack intelligibility completely, although it is without a final cause (47*E*-48*A*). This intelligibility implies a mechanical and geometrical necessity, as in the Democritean cosmology, which Plato gradually unfolds by making use of the irrationals.

The first object created by the Demiurge is the world-soul (34*C-D*), which envelops everything and constitutes the heavens. Just as the soul is the principle of motion,[3] similarly

---

1 Cf. F. M. Cornford, *Plato's Cosmology: The Timaeus of Plato*, translated with a running commentary (Cambridge, 1937), p. 212, n. 3.

2 *De Caelo* iii. 8.

3 *Phaedrus* 245*C* and *Laws* 894*D*.

the world-soul must be anterior to the body it animates in orderly fashion. Moreover, this creation must exemplify all the arithmetical and geometrical relations which are to be realized in the world (35*A*-36*D*) because the world-soul must act according to regular and fixed laws. The soul is composed of an indivisible essence and of a divisible essence in bodies (35*A*). To combine these two essences, the Demiurge thus mixes the same (corresponding to the limit) and the other (corresponding to the infinite), for all mixtures are composed of the limit and the infinite. Three substances are thus mixed with a greater proportion of the indivisible essence, which remains nearer to the outer part of the sphere; 2 successive combinations are used in order to make the mixture as intimate as possible.

This mixture of the world-soul is then divided into 7 parts proportional to the numbers (1, 2, 4, 8 and 1, 3, 9, 27) forming 2 geometrical progressions. The Demiurge combines them into one progression (1, 2, 3, 4, 9, 8, 27) where the order of 2 terms is inverted for no apparent reason. The intervals between these numbers are then filled with an elaborate series of proportional means, in the construction of which Plato uses the arithmetic, the geometric, and the harmonic means.[4] This construction also seems to use musical analogies, emphasizing the harmonious qualities of the soul. But the final series obtained is much longer than the usual musical scale, as if Plato meant to show that the world-soul contains all the possible scales, and that it can produce infinitely richer harmonies than our imperfect musical instruments.

Finally, as the world-soul moves the universe, it must exemplify astronomical as well as musical and numerical relations. So the Demiurge manipulates his creation further, by dividing the combination already obtained into 2 branches crossing at an acute angle, and by bending them into circles inclined on one another, like the equator and the ecliptic, and surrounded by a uniform motion. The movements of the exterior and

4 Albert Rivaud, *Notice sur la traduction du Timée* (Paris, 1925), pp. 42-45.

interior circles are identified respectively with the motion of the substance of the same and of the substance of the other. The circle of the same is one and rotates from east to west (motion of the planets), while the circle of the other is divided into 7 and rotates from west to east. When the Demiurge thus created the world-soul, he placed inside it all that is corporeal and tuned the soul and the body into harmony by making their centers coincide.

The construction of the physical world takes into account the blind necessity inherent in the original chaos. The ground of this necessity is not in the elements of the chaos but (52B) in the receptacle, which plays an important part in Greek physics.[5] This mysterious notion was invented by the Pythagoreans, who endowed it with numerical potentialities as the field bearing the monads and the intervals between them. It assumed later many names and functions: Plato calls it a matrix as well as an imprint; it is a place as well as a noncorporeal matter; it is assimilated to the dyad as well as to the indefinite. In other words, it is the indeterminate source of becoming, the non-qualitative field in which generation develops and is nursed, the natural recipient of all impressions, the neutral element out of which all beings are formed, the stuff underlying all things. It is the principle of deficiency, of matter, and of potency, as well as the field where all determinations develop.[6] Consequently, the receptacle is an entity inaccessible to sensation or thought. It ceases to be itself when anything definite happens to it. It is not a substance, but its contrary. As Leucippus would say, it is and it is not, it is being and non-being.

In the Platonic doctrines, the function of the receptacle is logical in *Philebus* (240) and in the *Laws* (x 89C), and cosmological in *Timaeus*. It makes participation logically possible and accounts for the possibility of mathematical relations. At the same time, it is the primary condition of becoming, of the

[5] Albert Rivaud, *Le problème du Devenir* (Paris, 1925), pp. 277-362.
[6] The receptacle is not extension, as Zeller suggests. It is less determined than extension and the void.

combination of the forms,[7] and of their introduction into the world. As the receptacle of the physical elements of the universe, it is undetermined both mechanically and geometrically, for it has no uniformity in motion (52E) and no fixed magnitude (50C-D), although it has all motions and all magnitudes. Disposition of the elements in the receptacle depends on their blind reaction to the disorderly shaking of the receptacle; as in a sieve (52B), they tend to combine according to their affinities and similarities.

In the process of world-building, various determinations are introduced in this chaos. Relations of magnitudes are established by the use of elementary triangles and polyhedra (53C). Both kinds of elementary triangles, the isosceles and the scalene right-angled triangles, involve irrationals in the relations between their sides. As we have explained previously, the cube is formed by putting together triangles of the first type, and the 4 other solids are constructed in similar fashion with the second type of triangle. At this stage, fire is identified with the tetrahedron, air with the octahedron, water with the icosahedron, and earth with the cube. These conceptions help to explain the transmutations of physical bodies—one corpuscle of water contains as many triangles as 2 corpuscles of air plus one of fire, and one corpuscle of air contains as many triangles as 2 corpuscles of fire (53C-57C). Other determinations, mostly mechanical, are gradually introduced until the whole universe becomes intelligible.

With the 4 natural elements, the Demiurge created the body of the world. He began with 2 of them, fire and earth, and soon used a third to link them together according to a geometrical proportion. For "of all bonds, the best is that which makes itself and the terms it connects a unity in the fullest sense; and it is of the nature of a continued geometrical proportion to effect this most perfectly" (31C). But 3 terms cannot produce a solid; hence it is necessary to use a fourth body and to bind them together by 2 combined proportions, with

[7] Aristotle *Phys.* 209b.

fire and earth as the 2 extremes, air and water being the 2 middle terms. As in the case of the world-soul and of the human soul,[8] beauty and perfection are imparted to the work of the Demiurge by geometrical proportion, the most beautiful link in itself, which induces the most complete unity between the things it connects. In making the world according to these proportions, the Demiurge exhausted the whole of the 4 natural elements, so that nothing is left outside the universe; but he used the dodecahedron in shaping it[9] into the form of a sphere, which is the most perfect figure and makes the world self-sufficing and imperishable.

This remarkable but mythical cosmogony proves conclusively that Plato's last studies were stimulated and dominated by the notion of mixture which was already implied in the Pythagorean doctrines. This notion recurs in fact throughout his teaching. From the schoolroom exercises on division mentioned in the earlier dialogues *(Statesman* 258C-267C and *Sophist* (218D-231C) to the comprehensive creation in *Timaeus,* Plato attempts to master the art and the rules of mixing. The dialectical process itself, with its attendant operations of division and composition, is a method of producing mixtures. Its results are illustrated in *Philebus.* This operation involves the introduction into any data of a number of fixed intervals characterized by numerical relations. Knowledge of the number and nature of these intervals yields science.[10]

A mixture is not an arbitrary fusion of unspecified things, but a fixed combination of the One and the dyad under their various aspects; it is produced by the introduction of a determined numerical ratio formed with these opposites. As the

8 The immortal element of the human soul is shaped according to the same mathematical principles as the world-soul (43D); it also has a spherical form, as well as the 2 circles of the same and of the other. But the motions of these circles are perturbed by the effects of nutrition and sensations.

9 Plato seems to use the dodecahedron (55C) for the sole purpose mentioned, for he gives no other details of its action and makes no reference to it when describing earlier (31B-34C) the composition of the world.

10 *Philebus* 18B.

One and the dyad are the ultimate elements common to forms and things, the form numbers as well as the sensible things are mixtures. Hence Plato was led to consider the process of mixing as a becoming which has being for its result, and the mixture itself as a being, or rather as a being which has become one. From this point of view, as Burnet suggests, the physical object may be considered just as real in a way as any other mixture. "In other words, the mature philosophy of Plato found reality, whether intelligible or sensible, in the combination of matter and form and not in either separately."[11]

There is a difference between the mixing which produces forms and the one which causes the emergence of things. The former is direct and immediate, while the latter is indirect and mediate because the One and the dyad produce physical objects according to the mathematical ideas which are between the forms and the things. Hence, the creation of the universe is a likely description of the introduction of the forms into the material world, through the instrumentality of mathematical proportions. There is a necessary relation between the forms and the external world exhibited by the orderly organization of the universe, because the forms alone bring order into an otherwise chaotic flux of unordered qualities. The cosmogony of *Timaeus* is thus supported by an explanation of the nature of the forms, which Plato had neglected after the difficulties raised in *Parmenides* concerning participation. For the same reason, the material things are not simply in a state of flux as suggested in *Theaetetus*; they present an established scale of mixtures as parts of an ordered cosmos shaped into a most beautiful mixture according to fixed relations.

Determination of the details of this mixture is a rational process because the forms of the mathematical and physical objects are identical, as both types have the One and the dyad as constituents. The identity of the forms is further illustrated by the close parallelism between the generation of the numeri-

---

11 J. Burnet, *Early Greek Philosophy* (London, 1914), p. 331. This quotation involves an important analogy with the Aristotelian hylemorphism.

cal continuum and the development of the natural processes. This continuum, which brings together arithmetic and geometry, makes them glide into the sensible world. As they ultimately determine geometrical structure, the real numbers mediately determine the physical attributes of things. The elusive character of change finds its counterpart in the hopeless striving of the irrational towards the rational.

The changing sensible things will never attain their changeless forms, just as neither the form of the irrational will ever attain the form of a rational number, nor the mathematical number its corresponding ideal form.

If we are to equate forms with numbers, as Aristotle assumes that Plato did, and also to say with the *Epinomis* that irrational roots are numbers and therefore forms, the relation Phaedo assumes of sensible things to forms must also exist among the forms themselves. The irrational is a form but it is always trying, and never quite succeeding in the attempt, to exhibit the form of a rational. (The amending decimal tries its hardest to recur.) This is, in principle, why the elements of the forms are the elements of all things.[12]

The identification of the forms with numbers means that the "manifold" of nature is only accessible to scientific knowledge, insofar as we can correlate its variety with definite numerical functions of "arguments." The "arguments" have then themselves to be correlated with numerical functions of "arguments" of a higher degree. If the process could be carried through without remainder, the sensible world would be finally resolved into combinations of numbers and so into the transparently intelligible. This would be the complete "rationalization" of nature. The process cannot in fact be completed because nature is always a "becoming," always unfinished; in other words, because there is real contingency. Our business in science is always to carry the process one step further. We can never completely arithmetize nature, but it is our duty to continue steadily arithmetizing her. "And still beyond the sea there is more sea"; but the mariner is never to arrest his vessel. The "surd" never quite "comes out" but we can carry the evalua-

12 A. E. Taylor, *Philosophical Studies* (London, 1952), p. 115.

tion a place further, and we must; if we will not, we become "ageometretes." [13]

As mathematical relations cannot explain everything by themselves, the final elaboration of the Platonic doctrine on mixtures offers elements which add color and warmth to its rationality. Going beyond the binary division of the *Sophist* as required in the processes of logical combinations, *Timaeus* determines the number of elements of each mixture by external means, such as musical and stereometric conditions. To be sure, the earlier dialogues involve a relation of logical necessity between the same and the other. But the limit and the infinite do not imply one another and do not necessarily require one another, nor does their combination explain itself. In order to account for it, we must use a fourth type of entity, different from the limit and the infinite as well as from their mixture—the cause of the mixture.

For the logical necessity of the *Sophist,* the cosmology of *Timaeus* substitutes considerations of harmony, beauty, and goodness. In this process Plato refines and resets the crude conceptions of the Pythagoreans, where the combination of the limit and the infinite ultimately produces health and even harmony. Instead, Plato uses harmony as a casual condition of the mixture of the One and the dyad, considered as the ultimate elements of every class of being. The idea of the good, which is dominant in the *Republic,* reappears here under a mathematical guise. The good is what determines all relations and mixtures; as these are essentially numerical, the good must be identified with the One in order to preserve its unity and its activity, as well as with measure, which causes proportion and harmony. Unable to define the good in its unity, Plato describes it under its 3 fundamental aspects: beauty, symmetry, and truth. In the world of forms as well as in the physical universe, any one of these channels leads to the vision of the unconditioned. All explanations cease at the threshold of the ultimate, for there is total fulfillment in the intuition of the good.

[13] *Ibid.,* p. 150.

Part III

THE MATHEMATICAL THOUGHT OF ARISTOTLE

The golden age of Greek speculation reached new heights with Aristotle (384-322 B.C.), the son of a physician, who rose to be the tutor of Alexander the Great and the founder of many branches of knowledge. His time is particularly important in the cultural and political history of the ancient world. The Academy was flourishing under the leadership of Plato and later of Speusippus and Xenocrates, his successors. Aristotle entered the Academy as a youth and remained there for 20 years, until Plato's death (348 B.C.). After several years of experimental studies and travel, during which he had Alexander the Great as his pupil, Aristotle opened his own school (*ca.* 334 B.C.) in the gardens of the Lyceum in Athens.

At that time, the various sciences were diligently investigated by members of the Academy and later of the Lyceum. Mathematics was graced by Eudoxus, his pupil Menaechmus and his brother Dinostratus, Theudius, Leodamas, Philippus, Leon, Hermotimus of Colophon, Speusippus, who wrote on prime, linear, and polygonal numbers, Xenocrates, who is credited with a history of geometry in 5 books and a theory of indivisible lines, and Eudemus of Rhodes (*ca.* 320 B.C.), a pupil of

Aristotle, who wrote a most valuable summary of the early history of mathematics. Astronomy boasted of the names of Heraclides of Pontus (*ca.* 388-315 B.C.) and of Callippus (*ca.* 370-330 B.C.), who improved the Eudoxian theories; the natural scientist named Lysistratus and 2 disciples of Aristotle: the naturalist Theophrastus and the physicist Aristoxenus, who wrote primarily on music.

The towering figure of the second half of the fourth century is Aristotle himself, whose works are an encyclopedia of the learning of the ancient world. He made great progress in philosophy and biology, but was less successful in physics and astronomy. The integration of his views on the positive sciences into his philosophy helped him to establish his method of demonstration, develop his theory of the infinite, and attempt the first construction of qualitative mechanics. With these contributions to knowledge, Aristotle secured for himself a conspicuous place in the history of mathematical philosophy. If their technical value has been unduly discounted by the controversy between classical and mathematical logic and by later developments in applied mathematics, the fact remains that Greek mathematics did take a different turn with the Aristotelian doctrines.

There is little doubt that Aristotle was considerably influenced by mathematics. As a youth, he turned his mind towards empirical investigations, and developed remarkable speculative powers while a student at the Academy. During the 20 years he spent there, he had to master and practice mathematics, which occupied such a prominent position in the Platonic program of studies. Indeed, Plato's fundamental interest in mathematics as an educational instrument and as an essential constituent of his philosophy could not but leave a deep and lasting impression on his pupil, who was known as "the mind of the school." To be sure, Aristotle was so familiar with the results and discussions of Greek mathematics in his time that his early writings display a strong Platonic influence.

In this respect, the chronology of Aristotle's works shows a remarkable evolution in his outlook and method. Although he did not share his master's apparent neglect of observation, Aristotle thought that empirical conclusions have a value only when they can be subordinated to reasoning. This attitude is displayed in *Physica, De Caelo, De Generatione et Corruptione,* and in the first and other books of *Metaphysics,* which were written about the time Aristotle spent with Hermias at Assos in the Troad (347-345 B.C.). In these early works, Aristotle discusses questions having mathematical implications, such as the question of change, the problem of the infinite, the nature of number and figures, and the application of mathematics to the concrete world. Their dogmatic or deductive character, in spite of their stress on observational methods and results, bears witness to the influence of the Platonic conception of mathematics on Aristotle's thought. In his later works, the founder of the Lyceum acknowledged more openly the value of experience and induction in the promotion of knowledge, and he established a science of pure thought distinct from mathematics and nature.

His works also prove his direct grasp of the mathematical topics which his colleagues and contemporaries liked to discuss. In fact, he was acquainted with the method of Eudoxus, whose terminology he often uses; he mentioned frequently the scientific views of Democritus in order to refute them; he criticized at some length the arguments of Zeno; and he developed a theory of the infinite and of continuity. He is even credited with treatises on the Pythagoreans and on the philosophy of Archytas, although these writings have not come down to us.

With this mathematical background and his interest in natural science and the major fields of knowledge, Aristotle worked out a refutation of Plato's mathematical philosophy and opposed its mystical interpretation through his successors at the Academy. Mathematics continued to a large extent to inspire Aristotle in his own constructive work. Like his master, Aristotle borrowed freely from the exact sciences and used mathematical illustrations whenever they helped him emphasize his views.

CHAPTER 17

The Organization of Knowledge

Faithful to the Socratic tradition, Aristotle considered the conceptual rationalization of the universe as the fundamental problem of philosophy. For him, knowledge is not conditioned exclusively by mathematics. Science as such has a much wider extension than any particular field of study, for it concerns what is necessary and eternal as well as communicable by teaching. It is "the true disposition by virtue of which we demonstrate."[1] The diverse manifestations of what is necessary and eternal led Aristotle to classify the special sciences according to their particular subject matter. He distinguishes among theoretical, practical, and productive sciences. The theoretical sciences deal with knowledge for its own sake; the practical refer to knowledge as a guide to conduct; and the productive consider knowledge for the making of useful or beautiful things. The theoretical sciences are subdivided into physics, mathematics, and theology, which covered the field later known as metaphysics. Physics has to do with changeable things which have a separate existence; mathematics is con-

[1] *Ethica Nicom.* 1139b 31.

cerned with unchangeable things which have no separate existence; metaphysics deals with things which are unchangeable and which exist separately.

It follows that the science of numbers and figures has only a restricted function, and that the conceptual rationalization of the universe cannot be obtained by the progressive mathematization of our knowledge. In this respect, Aristotle offers good reasons in criticizing Plato, who was fascinated by the necessity of mathematical relations, and his doctrine that ideas are the only true realities. For one thing, Plato was unable to show how number and magnitude generate qualities. His mythical descriptions in *Timaeus* do not actually explain how quality can be reduced to quantity. Indeed, he was unable to establish mathematics as a universal method of knowledge; in spite of his profound intuitions of the characteristics of that science, he left its positive elements hanging in the air. The identification of forms and numbers does not provide a clear and definite method of increasing our knowledge of the universe. In fact, Plato neither established definitely the principles which could account for being, nor determined in a compelling and decisive way which things are represented by ideas and the nature of the ideas themselves. He did not even prove how the good or being is actually connected with or differs from the numbers.

The Platonic doctrine of the soul offers a striking example of the difficulties involved in the identification of forms and numbers. In *Timaeus* we are shown how the substance of the soul is fashioned out of the elements so as to respond to harmony and to move accordingly. We are told also how the Demiurge bent the straight line into a single circle which he divided into 2 circles united at 2 common points, and how he subdivided one of these into 7 circles. In recounting these details, Aristotle remarks that the movements of the soul are thus identified with the local movements of the heavens, although "it is a mistake to say that the soul is a spatial magnitude."[2] He also points out that the soul cannot be a self-

2 *De Anima* 407ᵃ 4.

moving number, because what is without parts or internal differences cannot move at all, so that if the unit both originates motion and is capable of being moved, it must contain differences, which is impossible. Further, assuming that the number of the soul is somewhere and has position, its motion must be linear, for a unit having position is a point, and a moving point generates a line. If from a magnitude another magnitude or a unit is subtracted, the remainder is a different magnitude; yet "plants and many animals when divided continue to live."[3]

When Plato assumes that the ideal numbers and the sensible things are related through the arithmetical numbers, the relation between these numbers and the sensible things, or between the arithmetical numbers and the ideal numbers, should similarly entail a series of intermediate terms. Speaking of those who posit the ideas as causes in seeking to explain the world, Aristotle observes that they add an equal number of causes, just as if a man about to count things thought he would be unable to do it while they were few, but tried to count them after adding to their number. "In trying to explain things around us, these thinkers proceeded from them to the forms. For to each thing there answers an entity having the same name and existing apart from the substances. In the case of all other groups also, there is one over many, whether the many are in this world or are eternal."[4] This famous argument of the "third man" is also referred to in Parmenides, and was used most effectively by Aristotle against the Platonic doctrines.

The logical weakness of Plato's doctrine and the mystical speculations of his immediate successors prompted Aristotle to seek a new interpretation of the world. In shaping his views, he dismissed the numbers and ideas from the eternal world where Plato had placed them, and reduced mathematics to a mere elaboration of the category of quantity. At the same time, he went further than Plato's precept of "saving the

3 De Anima 409ᵃ 8.
4 Met. 990ᵇ 5 to 990ᵇ 10; also 1038ᵇ 34.

appearances" by turning his attention to the external world, which he considered as the most immediate object of investigation. This accounts for Aristotle's elaborate work in physics, astronomy, and especially biology.

He remained loyal to the main objective of the Socratic method, which is the apprehension of the universal on which science rests. He thus maintains with Plato that the result of this operation is the concept which determines the intimate nature of a thing with all its distinctive marks.[5] The concept represents what is equally identical in all individuals, and not an enumeration of the multiplicity it denotes. It stands for the universal without which no particular has meaning. It expresses the essence of a thing as determined by the common but exclusive attributes shared by all things belonging to the same class. This is emphasized by the process of division, which separates a group into its kinds according to their real differences and not according to their quantitative disparity. Division helps to state correctly the relations of concepts and to combine the unity of a class with the multiplicity involved in its denotation.

While Plato and Aristotle agree about the logical nature and importance of the universal, Aristotle stressed the importance of sensible perception in obtaining knowledge of this world. Starting with experience, he endeavored to reach its ultimate elements by using the analytical method. He thus found in the things themselves the very forms which Plato had placed in an independent world of ideas not realized under the moon. For Aristotle, forms are immanent in things and are manifested through the particular things they cause. The empirical universal thus provides the means to understand being as such. This eternal, incorporeal, and motionless cause of all forms and movement in the world became the essential subject of the *first philosophy*, the most fundamental of all sciences. Between the individual objects of experience and being as such, Aristotle visualized the world as a hierarchy

5 *Theaetetus* 208D; *Statesman* 285A.

of substances, with the immaterial forms as its highest elements.

Because the forms embedded in the individuals are what they are, necessity pervades their relations. Knowledge emerges when the mind perceives universals and their necessary or contingent connections. These perceptions are expressed in words combined in sentences and developed according to some fundamental patterns manifesting the very necessity involved in their elements. Because breathing is essential to a living organism, it must be assumed of necessity in any argument about living organisms; this necessity attached to the very essence of the concepts will affect the sequence and form of any sentences about them. This simple Socratic intuition dominated Plato's thought to such an extent that he built up a separate world of ideas and declared the realm of change to be a world of appearance, but as Aristotle was greatly interested in the wonders of nature this same intuition led him to organize a general method of exposition and demonstration for his investigations.

In the field of natural science, Aristotle was engrossed by his detailed studies of animals and other concrete objects. While allowing full reality to individuals, he also recognized an accidental reality to the universals which make science possible. The establishment of connections between universals on the pattern of the actual relations in or between the individuals embodying them led to their arrangement according to species and genera which implies the idea of class. Any argument concerning biology should therefore exhibit the permanent qualities and relations which follow of necessity from the analysis and synthesis of the universal concepts involved.

In the field of physics Aristotle considered as real the various individual objects under investigation. This distinction between matter and form, which has its parallel in the distinction between the particular and the universal, helped him to systematize the substantialist physics of the Greeks. He taught that the ultimate material element of the world, which corresponds to the indefinite of the pre-Socratics and to the receptacle of the Platonists, is primary matter. This undetermined and chaotic substratum is organized by the forms which introduce definite attributes into matter. The hot, the cold, the wet, and the dry are the 4 fundamental qualities which inform the primary matter. United in opposite and contrasted pairs, these qualities constitute the 4 elements—fire (hot and dry), air (hot and wet), water (cold and wet), and earth (cold and dry). The combination of these elements into varying proportions produces the different kinds of matter and the many substances of increasing complexity. Each of these results is at the same time actual for itself and a potency with regard to its next transformations caused by the intervention of new forms.

The transformation of substances is made possible by the opposition of contrary qualities, and involves the important notion of motion, which assumes a most general character in the Aristotelian system. Insofar as it stresses the qualitative description of change rather than the quantitative interpretation of a continuous state of change, motion is defined as the fulfillment of what exists potentially, or as "the fulfillment of the movable as movable."[6] There are 4 kinds of motion: local movement, affecting positional changes; generation and destruction, concerning living organisms; increase and decrease, accounting for quantitative variations; and alteration, which substitutes forms or superimposes one form on another. Most fundamental is alteration, which causes the intrinsic qualitative mutations of substances by the opposition of contrary forms. Yet local motion is the condition of all types of motion, because it carries a subject considered as a potency to where it will be actualized by a new form.

Motion cannot account by itself for its results; the rationalization of experience further requires the combined operation of 4 causes. The material cause furnishes the stuff of a subject tending towards its fulfillment; the formal cause satisfies this tendency imparting to the subject its actual character; the final cause actuates the subject toward its specific form; and

6 *Phys.* 201ᵃ-202ᵃ.

the efficient cause moves the subject in its process of completion. The Aristotelian doctrines concerning the elements, motion, and causality apply fully to the sublunary world only. Aristotle believed the heavenly bodies to be made of *aether*, a simple and incorruptible substance different from the 4 elements. He taught further that, as prime mover of the universe, God is beyond change or causation.

From the Ionians to the Socratics, generations of thinkers had attempted to explain the composition and transformation of substances by the operation of different ultimate elements. For the most part, these explanations gave no more than a verbal account of change and opened the door to relativism. The scientific conceptualism of Aristotle enabled him to explain the composition and transformation of substances by the mutation of opposite qualities and their participation in certain forms, and this process was made rationally manifest by the adequate relations established between the concepts expressing these forms.

The mutual relations of mathematical concepts are conditioned similarly by the necessity involved in their essence. For Plato, their necessity results from their participation in the ideas. In *Meno,* Socrates proved the duplication of the square to a slave by rearranging its elements so as to make their connections perceptible more readily to his untrained listener. For Aristotle, "necessity in mathematics is somehow similar to necessity in things produced through the operations of nature. Since a straight line is what it is, the angles of a triangle must necessarily equal two right angles."[7] The conclusiveness of mathematical reasoning thus reflects the parallelism between thought and being, which is confirmed by the derivation or construction of the mathematical concepts from empirical perceptions.

[7] *Phys.* 200ᵃ 15.

CHAPTER 18

Nature and Constructibility
of Mathematics

In the second book of *Physics*, Aristotle discusses the nature of mathematics by comparing its object with that of physics. At first, it may seem that these sciences deal with the same objects because physical bodies involve solids, planes, lines, and points connected by certain propositions. While physics considers figures and numbers as limits or qualities of movable bodies, mathematics deals with them in abstraction from matter and motion. Physics studies the mathematical and general properties of the bodies as immersed in sensible (or local) matter, but mathematics deals with the general properties of the elementary constituents of the bodies divested of their sensible matter and left only with their intelligible (imaginable) matter. This notion[1] covers nothing more than the spatial extension of bodies and their numerical attributes. As Aristotle puts it,[2] mathematics is to physics as "curved" is to "snub": these 2 adjectives refer to concavity, but while the latter qualifies a nose, the former may refer to any physical object.

1 Cf. *Met.* 1036ᵃ 9.
2 *Met.* 1025ᵇ 30.

These views entail a fundamental distinction between the Platonic and the Aristotelian doctrines. It is maintained by Aristotle that extension and number, though necessarily involved in the sensible world, are not the stuff out of which things are made; Plato treated the formless space as the material element or substratum out of which the sensible things are produced by the penetration into it of shapes which are like the numbers.[3] Furthermore, Aristotle separates from sensible matter the notions which do not require it actually, while Plato abstracts from matter not only mathematical objects but also entities involving matter in their very nature. Finally, figures and numbers are not identified by Aristotle as they are by Plato; although both are aspects of quantity, they are the objects of different sciences. Geometry deals with figures, that is, with quantity continuous or extended; arithmetic deals with numbers, that is, with quantity discrete and unextended. Aristotle even goes so far as to maintain[4] that the specific postulates of either of them cannot be applied to both.

Mathematical objects are obtained by the same process used in the apprehension of the universals.

The mathematician deals with abstractions, for before his investigation he eliminates all the sensible qualities, weight and lightness, hardness and its opposite, heat and cold and the other sensible contraries. He keeps only the quantitative and the continuous in one, in two, or in three dimensions and the attributes of these as quantitative and continuous, for he does not consider them in any other respect. He examines their relative positions, their commensurabilities and incommensurabilities or their ratios.[5]

To be sure, "when the mind thinks the objects of mathematics, it thinks as separate elements which do not exist separately. In every case, when the mind is actively thinking, it is the object it thinks."[6] It even seems that the universal notions of mathematics are elicited and known by induction.

---

3 *Timaeus* 50C-52A.
4 *An. Post.* 75a 35-b 17.
5 *Met.* 1061a 28.
6 *De Anima* 431b 15.

"It is possible to familiarize the pupil with the so-called mathematical abstractions through induction only, because the proper mathematical character of each subject-genus furnishes it with certain properties which can be treated as separate, even though they do not exist separately."[7]

Having no separate existence, mathematical objects are not independent of and prior to experience. As they are abstractions suggested by physical objects, they cannot exist on their own and they are not a cause of motion and rest. Such views obviously entail a strong dependence upon sensible and logical evidence, as well as a distrust for extrapolation beyond the powers of sensory perception. They may lead to the belief that mathematical objects are characteristics of natural things which have been separated from their material context. For example, "geometry investigates physical lines, but not as physical."[8] Yet if the objects of mathematics do not belong to sense experience, they have an adjectival existence as they qualify substances. Moreover, the figures or symbols used in demonstrations are employed for illustration only, without being part of the inference. In short, the relation between mathematical objects and sensible things is one of rational rather than of factual separateness.

Aristotle's conception of the status of mathematical objects is in line with his fundamental criticism of Plato's doctrines. Although both place them in an intermediate position, Plato considers them as a distinct class of objects between ideas and particulars, while Aristotle denies them a separate existence. They are intermediate for the latter insofar as the mind places them between the sensible things out of which they are abstracted and the generic essence of the things, which is reached by a further mental operation. In other words, Aristotle denies that mathematical objects are real substances, but he considers them as substantives in order to incorporate them as subjects in the various propositions of mathematics.

The mind apprehends geometrical objects by applying its

---

[7] *An. Post.* 81b 1.
[8] *Phys.* 194a 10.

power of abstraction to actual bodies, until the only qualities left are the quantitative and the continuous with their attributes. By removing their secondary qualities and their capacity for motion, the mind leaves them with their shape and size. At this stage, bodies are considered merely as three-dimensional solids. We can think further of plane sections of solids and of linear sections of surfaces, although neither solids, surfaces, nor lines exist separately.[9] An additional operation is needed to obtain pure geometrical forms capable of definition, for a particular solid, surface, or line is embedded in a particular extension which must be abstracted in order to reach the universal form.[10] Only then do individual differences vanish and universals alone shine forth. Aristotle does not identify lines, planes, and solids with the numbers 2, 3, and 4 as the Platonists do,[11] for the geometrical objects would then lose their continuity, which is their essential characteristic.

For Aristotle, the opposition between continuity and discontinuity accounts for the distinction between figures and numbers. While Plato conceives number as a combination of the limit and the infinite, Aristotle shares the more conservative view of number as a collection of units, a discontinuous plurality. The notion of unit is obtained by abstraction and is justified by the ontological character of the unity of being. Numbers are obtained by adding one unit to another and then adding one unit to the preceding number,[12] so that numbers are nothing beyond the units of which they are essentially formed. Instead of the synthetic and dynamic conception of number given by Plato, we have now the notion of a whole formed of partitive elements juxtaposed in succession. Hence, Aristotle thinks of number as an integral and discontinuous quantity.[13] He does not follow the Platonic view of conceiving it as continuous and almost geometrical. Stressing the cardinal

9 *Met.* 1060b 12.
10 *Met.* 1035b 33-1036a 12.
11 *Met.* 1090b 20. Cf. *De Anima* 404b 18.
12 *Met.* 1080a 30.
13 *An. Post.* 76b 10.

as against the ordinal aspect of number, he criticizes the Platonists for counting 1, 2, 3, and so on, without adding successively one unit of the preceding number.[14]

Another difference between Plato's and Aristotle's conceptions of number is the latter's dissociation of number from the idea of ratio. Referring to the Platonic doctrine that numbers are the principles of sensible qualities, Aristotle criticizes the view that numbers should be employed to define the essence of flesh and bones by asserting that these substances may be composed of 3 parts of fire and 2 parts of earth. He justifies his criticism with the remark that such definitions do not involve numbers, but their ratios. For him, a number is a collection of parts of fire, or of earth, or of units. Hence, it cannot determine the essence of a substance which results from the ratio of the elements involved.[15] Moreover, a number is not a particular case of the more general notions of ratio, relation, or function; number and relation belong to 2 different categories of being.

These essential distinctions between mathematics and physics and between figures and numbers are particular elaborations of the Peripatetic philosophy. They have far-reaching consequences insofar as they stress what we called the *qualitative aspect* of mathematics. Many mathematical notions are defined qualitatively in the Aristotelian treatises. In *Physics*,[16] the notions of contact, contiguity, and continuity are defined in a positive way without any reference to number or measure. In *Metaphysics* we read that "a circle is a figure of a certain quality because it has no angles, which implies that a differentia of essence is a quality. This is one sense in which quality is called a differentia of essence; another sense is that in which immovable mathematical objects are qualities: thus numbers have a certain quality, for example numbers which are composite and not of one dimension only."[17] Although such pas-

14 *Met.* 1082b 28.
15 *Met.* 1092b 14-23.
16 *Phys.* 226b 21-227a 20.
17 *Met.* 1020a 35 *sq.*

sages have been diversely interpreted by various commentators, the attitude of mind they reveal is technically justified by the mathematical theories known to Aristotle's contemporaries.

To be sure, the Greeks could have grouped together in a separate qualitative system (in opposition to a metrical system) a mass of mathematical properties they had discovered, especially in the field of geometry. They were more interested, however, in systematizing their geometrical and other discoveries by combining qualitative and quantitative considerations. Subsequent generations of mathematicians continued to use this fertile method, which reached its highest fulfillment with the modern analytical and infinitesimal methods. Their success was such that even capital projective discoveries by Ceva, Pascal, and Desargues were kept in the background until Poncelet laid the foundations of projective geometry. Meanwhile, the Aristotelian attitude proved equally close to fact by stressing the distinction between number and magnitude and by implying that mathematics has a qualitative as well as a quantitative aspect. Indeed, a deep qualitative strain runs right through the development of the exact sciences and links this Aristotelian point of view with what we may call *qualitative mathematics,* namely projective geometry, axiomatics, topology, theory of sets, modern algebra, and mathematical logic.

Another basic feature of modern mathematics, its constructibility, is also found in the Aristotelian conception of the exact sciences. Most commentators would scarcely agree at first with such a view. If they acknowledge that modern mathematicians indeed construct their concepts, they would think that Aristotle derives them from experience by abstraction. If one looks closer into the matter, one finds that Aristotle combines abstraction and construction in order to give to mathematical objects their being, necessity, coherence, and applicability to natural phenomena. For one thing, only the most general mathematical concepts, such as volume, surface, and line or number, are mentioned as results of abstraction. To these would have been added more technical concepts such as squares, triangles, pyramids, cylinders, or polygonal numbers, if abstraction alone were involved in their generation. Consequently, although Aristotle asserts rightly that mathematical notions in general result from an abstraction from sensible data, this statement should not be understood to mean that all mathematical objects as such are obtained from experience by abstraction exclusively.

Mathematical practices of the Academy and the Lyceum obviously manifested the constructibility of mathematics; this is the case with the invention of the higher curves, and particularly with the loci obtained by mechanical means. As regards Aristotle himself, several texts in his works prove that he knew and accepted this fact as a matter of course. None of the ancient texts referring to Greek mathematics hint or assert that figures or numbers were ever obtained by simple abstraction. On the contrary, such mathematical elements were *imagined,* or *invented,* or *constructed,* by assigning to lines and surfaces abstracted from experience particular conditions required for the solution of specific problems. The constructibility of mathematical notions is confirmed by the canonicity of the proof by ruler and compass. Moreover, the treatment of the infinite obviously required construction processes rather than abstraction exclusively. Finally, the systematic exposition of mathematics clearly entails the factual construction.

The *Posterior Analytics* (I.2 and I.10), the definitions of the primitive notions of surface and line, as well as the technical concepts of straight line or triangle or any definite combination of lines and surfaces, are justifiable only with reference to a *hypothetical existence.* Furthermore, all concepts derived from the primitive notions *must be proved to exist.* The proof of existence and the imputation of hypothetical existence entail some construction, which may be a logical or a technical combination of elements.

> By demonstration we prove the existence of everything, save being itself. . . . That a thing exists is matter for demonstration; and this is the actual practice in the sciences. The geometer assumes what

is a triangle; but he proves that it exists. . . . In fact definitions do not include any proof that the thing defined may exist or must be the thing of which it is claimed to be the definition. Anyone may ask why it is so.[18]

The same view is expressed in other passages. "We must assume that a triangle means a certain thing, whereas we must know both what a unit means and that it exists."[19] We are also told that

> the things peculiar to the science, the existence of which must be assumed, are the things of which the science investigates the essential attributes, namely arithmetic with reference to units and geometry with reference to points and lines. With regard to their essential properties, only the meaning of each term employed is assumed: thus arithmetic assumes the answer to the question what is odd or even, a square or a cube; and geometry to the question what is the irrational, or deflection or verging. The existence of such things is proved by the common principles and by what has already been demonstrated.[20]

The usual means of strengthening a demonstration was a construction. This practice in Greek mathematics was known to Aristotle, who never said that abstraction alone suffices to establish mathematical truths. On the contrary, he asserted that "even if it had been possible to perceive by sense that the angles of a triangle are equal to two right angles, nevertheless we should have looked for a demonstration without which we should not have possessed knowledge of the fact as some assert."[21] To obtain an explicit mathematical truth, Aristotle explicitly requires a demonstration and not simply abstraction.

The relation between demonstration and mathematical constructibility is implied in these 3 texts. One is given in *Physics*

18 *An. Post.* 92b 12.
19 *An. Post.* 76b 5.
20 *An. Post.* 76b 5.
21 *An. Post.* 87b 35.

(II.9), where Aristotle acknowledges a similarity (not an identity) between necessity in mathematics and the necessity governing natural phenomena. "If the straight line has such-and-such a character, then of necessity the angles of a triangle are together equal to two right angles, but it does not follow that given the latter [assertion], the former is necessarily true. We can only say that if the triangle has not the property in question, the straight line as we understand it does not exist."[22] The second text comes from *De Caelo* (I.12), where Aristotle discusses mathematical truth with reference to an hypothesis. "If certain assumptions are made, it is impossible for a triangle to have its angles together equal to two right angles, or for a diagonal to be incommensurable."[23] These remarks are corroborated and expanded in the third text, taken from *Eudemian Ethics* (II.6), where Aristotle insists on the relativity of certain principles, and in particular of mathematical hypotheses.

Immovable principles such as those of mathematics do not possess absolute authority although they are admitted to have similar force. For even in mathematics, if a given principle were changed, almost all the propositions proved by it would be altered; but if one of these is destroyed by another, they will not all be changed mathematically, save by the destruction of the hypothesis and the proof using it. Now ... if a triangle has its angles together equal to two right angles, it necessarily follows that a square has its angles together equal to four right angles. Here the fact that the triangle has two right angles is the cause of the other proposition. So that if the triangle changes in this respect, so must the square. Assuming the sum of the angles to equal three right angles for the triangle, then it will be six for the square; if four, then eight. On the other hand, if the triangle does not change but has the said property, so must the square have the corresponding property. The *Analytics* make clear the necessity of the inference.[24]

22 *Phys.* 200ᵃ 15.
23 *De Caelo* 281ᵇ 3.
24 *Eud. Ethica* 1222ᵇ 23 *sq.*

These texts taken together point to the necessity involved in the inferential process, as well as to the hypothetical and relative character of mathematical principles. The incidental reference to this character and the significant examples given as illustrations add their weight to the constructibility of mathematics, for if mathematical notions were the exact results of abstraction alone, there could be no relativity in their meaning.[25] Furthermore, there are no mathematical objects to which abstractions could be applied simply. As there are no squares, no cylinders, no actual polygonal numbers in nature, the mind cannot separate their essence from empirical data. Although we perceive things having certain familiar mathematical forms, their actual forms are never identical with their mathematical definitions. Consequently, mathematical objects and truths involve a basic process of construction as the prerequisite and unavoidable operation which gives them being, necessity, and a proper position in the orderly exposition of a systematic science.

If Aristotle had been opposed to construction, which was a current practice with the mathematicians of his time, he would undoubtedly have said so clearly. On the contrary, his doctrines imply this process as a matter of course. The flowering of these doctrines and their most convincing illustration came with Euclid, who always constructs the notions required before using them in a demonstration, although he may define them previously in accordance with the Aristotelian theory of proof. For example, the *Elements* use straight lines at right angles to one another only after the construction (I.11, 12) of a perpendicular to a straight line. Similarly, the square which is defined in Def. I.22 is used only after its construction (I.46). The same remark holds true for all the specific notions of geometry.

---

[25] We might draw attention to the unconscious prophecy entailed in Aristotle's view on the relativity of some properties of the triangle, but he could not foresee the possibility of a non-Euclidian geometry, even as a convenient illustration of his doctrine.

CHAPTER 19

The Mathematical Infinite

The Aristotelian opposition between the continuous and the
discrete in mathematics is an aspect of the rationalization of
the irrational, which remains as basic a problem for Aristotle
as it was for Plato. If the mathematical solution of the latter
is rejected, something else must take its place. Beyond mathematics, Aristotle reaches for an answer to this riddle with his
doctrine of the infinite, which reconciles the discrete and the
continuous in the depths of ontology proper.

This theory is developed in *Physics* through the analysis of
motion, which involves matter, space, time, and number. The
interpretation of these fundamental notions involves some
major arguments in favor of the qualitative aspects of mathematics. As regards the infinite proper, Aristotle finds that the
perpetuity of matter and motion, the divisibility of magnitudes, the possibility of forming larger numbers by addition,
and the analysis of time with increasing and decreasing elements point to the infinite as a common constituent of these
notions. Just as Aristotle's theory of motion is based on the
distinction between act and potency, so his views on the
infinite take the same distinction into account.

Experience reveals that change is an essential character of the universe—certain things have definite attributes actually, while others are in the process of displaying them gradually. The difference between being and becoming calls for the distinction between act and potency. The process of becoming is called motion, which Aristotle defines as "the fulfillment of what exists potentially, insofar as it exists potentially."[1] Motion is considered here in its most general aspect, covering both change of place and growth. The mathematical importance of Aristotle's discussion of the infinite is due to his showing it to be a potency, something which is always becoming without ever reaching a final form.

He argued against an actual infinite with regard to extension and number, for such a notion involves a contradiction in terms. An actually infinite extension would require the factual existence of a body having no outer boundary or limit whatsoever, but, whatever its greatness, any physical body must be bound by surface and limited by the other existing bodies, or else there would not be room for any other body.[2] Most of the reasons against the existence of an infinite physical body, however, are based on the Aristotelian theory of the "natural places" of the 4 elements, which makes them rather inconclusive.

Similarly, Aristotle maintained that it is impossible to think of the whole material universe as having an actually infinite extension. This view, which was held by Melissus the Eleatic, cannot be proved. Although the enormous expanse of the material world exceeds anything we can really picture in our mind, it does not necessarily follow that this actual extension has no actual end. On the other hand, if no single body is actually infinite in extent, then all bodies must be finite; no matter how large each might be, their sum could not reach an actually infinite extension unless there is an actually infinite number of them. Such a number could neither be counted nor completely traversed in thought; if it could, then more units

1 *Phys.* 201ᵃ 10.
2 *Phys.* 204ᵇ 1-206ᵃ 8.

could be added to it by the very same process of counting, with the result that it would not be actually infinite.

Among the many reasons adduced by Aristotle against the actual infinity of the universe, the so-called geometrical proof is particularly interesting.[3] This argument requires an unlimited straight line in a plane and an infinite radius rotating about a point exterior to the line. If the radius touches the line at any point, its motion will keep it always in contact with the line, thus making a complete rotation impossible. If the radius does not touch the line, then it must never meet it, although it may complete its rotation in a definite period of time; otherwise we revert to the first alternative. According to Milhaud,[4] this argument has many analogies with those of Zeno and implies a confusion of the proper functions of the concepts involved. If rotation and angular variation are independent of the length of the lines considered, this distinction is effective only in the formal realm of mathematics. As Aristotle deals with actual infinite lengths, the validity of his argument is not necessarily impaired.

Assuming that there cannot be an actual infinite with regard to extension and number, there must be some kind of an infinite if change is possible, if magnitudes are addible or divisible into magnitudes, and if intervals of time with a beginning and an end can be conceived. Aristotle solved this difficulty by considering the infinite as a potency and by restricting the use of the term "infinite" to indicate a potency only. The infinite exists "potentially and by way of exhaustion. . . . Its potential existence is akin to that of matter, but it is not capable of separate existence like a finite being."[5] The Aristotelian pure matter does not exist separately, but only as a constituent of things composed of matter and form. Similarly, the infinite is never realized by itself permanently and fully, but only progressively and partially. Having no per-

3 *De Caelo* 272a and b.
4 G. Milhaud, "Aristote et Mathématiques," *Archiv für Geschichte der Philosophie,* XVI (1903), 368ff.
5 *Phys.* 206b 10.

manent actuality, "it consists in a process of becoming, like time."[6] The difference among the actual infinite, the potential infinite, and a finite being is this: the actual infinite cannot be added to, and therefore it cannot be of a mathematical nature if it exists; it is possible to add to the potential infinite and to a finite being, although the latter only may and does exist actually.

The infinite changes endlessly into something else, that something being itself always finite and different. Hence, the infinite exists by one part of it after another coming into being, just as the progressive emergence of the parts of a day or of a game makes that day or that game. When made actual, these parts remain, as in the case of magnitudes, or disappear, as in the case of time. But whatever be their different manifestations, it is their unbroken succession which accounts for the infinite. As against the view commonly held, Aristotle maintains that the infinite is not that which has nothing beyond it, but that which has always something outside it.[7] Therefore, the infinite cannot be identified with a complete, a whole, an all-inclusive entity. If it were exhausted and complete, the infinite would have a limit, which is a contradiction in terms.

In discussing the views on the infinite held by his predecessors, Aristotle refutes the opinion shared by the Pythagoreans and the Platonists that there is an infinite which is neither a plurality nor an extension.[8] Hence, the preliminary distinction he draws between the infinite with respect to addition which cannot be exhausted by adding part to part, and the infinite with respect to division which is reducible in size without limit.[9] Number is infinite in the first sense, and extension in the second, while time is infinite in both senses. This distinction entails a fundamental difference in the relation of numbers and of figures to the infinite. "Every assigned mag-

6 *Phys.* 207b 14.
7 *Phys.* 207a 1.
8 *Phys.* 204a 8.
9 *Phys.* 204a 6.

nitude is surpassed in the direction of smallness, while in the opposite direction there is no infinite magnitude. . . . On the other hand, as number is a plurality of units, it must stop at the indivisible. . . . But with respect to size, it is always possible to think of a larger number."[10]

Although capable of infinite addition, number has a fixed limit which prevents it from being an actual infinite. This limit is the unit, beyond which there is no number. Hence the conception of the zero did not occur to Aristotle, but neither did he consider the integer 1 as a number. For him, "the smallest number in the strict sense of the word 'number' is two."[11] The unit is the "generator of numbers" which are obtained by the successive addition of the unit to itself. Even the fractions and the approximations to irrationals are expressed with integers. This is why Aristotle agrees with the Pythagoreans that a number is a collection of units.[12] If there is a smallest number, the unit, there cannot be a greatest one, for it is always possible to add units to any number which might be considered as the greatest.

With regard to an increasing magnitude, the spatial infinite is prevented from being an actual infinite by a limit, which is the heaven. There cannot be an extension greater than the universe, for it would reach beyond the heaven.[13] Aristotle assumes a finite material universe, a world limited by the sphere of stars. As there is no void, no fluid, not even a space beyond it, our imagination cannot add anything actual to this limit. Consequently, we cannot add endlessly to magnitude; what is more, even as a potential infinite, extension has an upper limit which cannot be exceeded by successive additions of magnitudes.

The indefinite divisibility of extension allows the process of division to yield results continuously without exhausting it. Hence, the addition of the parts thus obtained is also a

10 *Phys.* 207b 3-11.
11 *Phys.* 220a 26.
12 *Phys.* 207b 6.
13 *Phys.* 207b 20.

continuous process which cannot reproduce completely the original magnitude. If we consider a finite magnitude divided into equal and definite parts, their addition will exhaust the finite magnitude, according to the fundamental principle of exhaustion[14] with which Aristotle was acquainted.

Spatial magnitude is thus infinite in divisibility, although it cannot be increased infinitely. This is because each step of a division produces an actual result—there is something actual in the divisibility of the infinite, just as there is something real in the indefinite flux as such. As the infinite is never exhausted, there is no entelechy to it—infinite extension is a potency. It follows that the actual division of extension never yields a magnitude which may be considered as the smallest possible. For this reason, Aristotle rejects the notion of indivisible lines[15] which had become a characteristic doctrine of the Academy.

The Peripatetic tract *On Indivisible Lines* represents fairly well Aristotle's views on this matter, although he may not have been its author.[16] It is directed against the theory of atomic magnitudes as developed by Xenocrates in particular.[17] The tract begins with the arguments in favor of the indivisible lines, as Xenocrates would have conceived them. It then refutes each of them by showing their incompatibility with the principles assumed or proved in mathematics. For example, it is argued that a line cannot be made up of points or of indivisible lines, and that if an indivisible line has any points on it or at its ends, then it must be divisible. The conclusion states that the assumption of indivisible lines "conflicts with practically everything in mathematics."[18] Elsewhere[19] Aristotle

14 *Phys.* 266b 1.
15 *Phys.* 206a 17.
16 It is thought that Aristotle did not write this tract because many expressions in its text have no parallel in his genuine works. Simplicius ascribed the tract to Theophratus, whose doctrines it resembles closely. Strato is also mentioned as a probable author.
17 Aristotle does not refer to Xenocrates specifically in the various passages of *Physics, De Caelo,* and *Metaphysics* dealing with indivisible lines.
18 *De Lin. Insec.* 970a 17.
19 *Topica* 141b 21.

remarked that indivisible lines must have extremities and cannot be points. His vigorous opposition to indivisibles has been fully sanctioned by modern mathematics.

On the other hand, the concept of an actual quantitative infinity could not be employed in mathematics, as it involves contradictory elements. An infinite quantity in mathematics means only a quantity greater than any definite quantity which may be assigned. As such a quantity is indefinitely large but not actually infinite, it does not require the existence of bodies with an extension or a number corresponding to it—existing beings are definite in size and number, whereas the mathematical infinite is always indefinite. Here Aristotle points out that, when mathematicians speak of infinite magnitudes, they do not need them actually and do not use them as such—they simply require the finite to be as great as they please. "They postulate only that the finite straight line may be produced as far as they wish. . . . For the purpose of proof, it will make no difference to them to have such an infinite instead, while its existence will be in the sphere of real magnitudes." [20]

These remarks readily agree with the practice of the Greek mathematicians. The Eudoxian method of exhaustion assumes in the proof that bisection can be continued as far as one may wish, but not to infinity. Conversely, when mathematicians consider large magnitudes, they reduce them by proportion to magnitudes they can handle more easily and which do not exceed the maximum extension of the universe. In both cases, these geometrical fictions cannot suggest any real connection between the mathematical infinite and the maximum magnitude of the universe.

The Aristotelian theory of the infinite leads naturally to his doctrine of the continuous, which is an essential characteristic of motion. This notion is analyzed in the sixth book of *Physics* after the discussion of place, time, and change in the 2 preceding books. Aristotle based his definition of the continuous on the intuitive notion of a magnitude made up

[20] *Phys.* 207b 30-32.

of 2 consecutive or contiguous parts kept together by the fusion of their boundaries into one and the same limit.[21] Hence, the continuum is "that which is divisible into divisibles that are infinitely divisible."[22]

With these premises, Aristotle argues convincingly that every continuum must be divisible infinitely, and that the infinite divisibility of extension, motion, and time imply each other, with the infinite divisibility of motion as middle term between the other 2.

> The firmness with which he rejects any suggestion that a line can be divided without remainder into points, a period of time into moments, or a movement into infinitesimal jerks—and this at a time when thinkers of repute believed in all these things—seems to indicate that he had a more mathematical turn of mind than he is usually credited with. So far as we know, he was the first thinker who clearly stated the infinite divisibility of all continua.[23]

There are some obvious difficulties in these Aristotelian doctrines. If the potential infinite is divisible and addible endlessly, it should be so without restriction as to figure or number. The endless division of number may never logically give anything beyond the idea of the unit. The limitation of the increase of potential extension scarcely seems to be warranted by the arguments offered, although this limitation may be true for the actual universe. Again, if the greatest physical body is finite, why should there not be a minimum finite body? Aristotle argues that atoms are incompatible with mathematical processes,[24] but so is the idea of a maximum physical body. Moreover, if mathematicians reduce magnitudes in some required proportion to keep them within the bounds of a maximum actual extension, they should also be able to enlarge them in proportion without transgressing the bounds of a minimum actual extension.

21 *Phys.* 227a 10 and 231a 24.
22 *Phys.* 232b 24.
23 W. D. Ross, *Aristotle's Physics* (Oxford, 1936), p. 70.
24 *De Caelo* 303a 20.

On the other hand, it seems difficult to prove or believe that the infinitely numerous parts of a spatial whole are only potentially existent in it. It cannot be validly demonstrated that the points in a line are brought into existence either by the act of dividing it, the act of counting points in it, or the act of drawing to it a tangent or a secant. "All these processes alike must be held to imply the pre-existence of points, and thus the existence of an actual infinity of points in a line; and similarly we must believe in the actual existence of an infinite number of lines in a plane and of planes in a solid, not brought successively and partially into existence but coexistent from the start."[25]

The irreducible distinction between the continuity of motion and the discreteness of number could not induce the Greeks to establish a rigorous mathematical analysis. Implying the impossibility of an instantaneous velocity (ds/dt) and of an instantaneous rate of change, which are fundamental concepts of the calculus, Aristotle tried to disprove by reduction ad absurdum that motion is the traversal of indivisible minima of distance in indivisible minima of time,[26] and he asserted that "nothing can be in motion in a present . . . nor can anything be at rest in a present."[27] With mathematics seen as a pattern of the sensible world, with the limitations of sensory perception, and with his qualitative conception of change, Aristotle could not go beyond the recognition of average velocities ($\Delta s/\Delta t$). Such intuitive conceptions helped him to answer Zeno's arguments, which have been preserved in his own writings.

In referring to the *Dichotomy* and the *Achilles*, he points out that both proofs rest on the fact that "a division of the distance in a certain way causes the failure to arrive at the end."[28] He does not answer the difficulty involved by asserting that the *Dichotomy* falsely assumes the impossibility of

25 Ross, *op. cit.*, Introduction, p. 53.
26 *Phys.* 233b 18-30 and 239b 5-10.
27 *Phys.* 234a 24-33.
28 *Phys.* 239b 18.

traversing or touching each of an infinite number of points in a finite time.[29] The question is not whether the length-series and the time-series are exhausted simultaneously, but how either of these logically inexhaustible series can be exhausted.

Similarly, Aristotle appeals to sensory perception rather than to a logical construction when he tries to solve the paradoxes of the *Arrow* and the *Stadium* by denying the assumption of indivisible instants (or magnitudes) and, consequently, of instantaneous velocity.[30] Of course, he could not give the modern answer in terms of the derivative and the converging infinite series. Yet, the notion of convergence does not answer the metaphysical implications of Zeno's arguments, for it does not indicate satisfactorily the actual relation between the infinite series and its limit. Hence, it would be difficult to improve on Aristotle's discussion of the paradoxes if they are to be answered in terms of continuity considered as irreducible to discreteness.

A clear demonstration of the difficulties implied by the paradoxes required more precise definitions than Aristotle could furnish for the subtle notions of continuity, the infinite, and instantaneous velocity.

Such definitions were to be given in the nineteenth century in terms of the concepts of the calculus; and modern analysis has, upon the basis of these, clearly dissented from the Aristotelian pronouncements in this field. The views of Aristotle are not on this account to be regarded—as is all too frequently and un-critically maintained—as gross misconceptions which for two thousand years retarded the advancement of science and mathematics. They were rather matured judgments on the subject, which furnished a satisfactory working basis for later investigations which were to result in the science of dynamics and in the mathematical continuum.[31]

29 *Phys.* 233ᵃ 17-22.
30 *Phys.* 239ᵇ 5 *sq.*
31 Carl B. Boyer, *The Concepts of the Calculus* (New York, 1949), p. 44.

Some important considerations follow from these doctrines. Because of the irreducible quality of the infinite, the continuum cannot be made of indivisible parts and numbers cannot generate a continuum, as there is no contact between them.[32] Hence, the discreteness of number rules out the possibility of arithmetizing the continuum. Owing to the restricted arithmetical techniques available at the time, no adequate and effective arguments could be found in favor of the Platonic mathematical intuitions. The primacy of arithmetic maintained by such younger Pythagoreans as Archytas, and expanded by Plato into a mathematical doctrine, expressed an attitude of mind and a pious hope rather than a technical interpretation of current mathematical knowledge.

In these circumstances, Aristotle cannot be blamed for refusing to accept the Platonic conception of number, and for reconsidering the relations between arithmetic and geometry in the light of the current mathematical techniques and his own epistemology. His scientific perspicacity in these matters is proved by the perennial success of his views on the infinite and the continuous, which held the ground until the last century, when the continuum was defined more precisely in terms of the new concepts of number and separation of classes. Although it is difficult to agree with Cantor that the Aristotelian views on infinity and continuity may be considered as an introduction to the calculus,[33] it must be conceded that the Aristotelian definition of motion as the striving of a body to become actually what it is potentially, helped to elaborate the notions of velocity and acceleration in terms of an *impetus* and of a *conatus,* which developed later into the notion of the derivative. In conclusion, it may be said that the Aristotelian views on the infinite did inspire the manner and form of several generations of mathematicians, and did provide a starting point for the speculations which led gradually to the rise of the calculus.

[32] *Met.* 1075[b] and 1085[a].

[33] Moritz Cantor, "Origines du calcul infinitesimal," *Logique et Histoire des Sciences* (Paris, 1901), III, p. 6.

CHAPTER 20

Geometridal Discussions

The many mathematical references contained in Aristotle's works are supplied as illustrations to specific philosophical doctrines. They need not prove that Aristotle was technically interested in mathematical research, but they do witness his knowledge and understanding of the scientific controversies of his time. In fact, his discussions of Hippocrates, Antiphon, Bryson, Zeno, Democritus, Eudoxus and the Pythagorean and the Platonic doctrines in particular are of singular importance, for they throw much light on the principles of mathematics as they were accepted then, as well as on the influence of his own views on subsequent mathematical developments. As technical achievements they cannot claim a great importance, but most critics unduly minimize Aristotle's mathematical ability on the grounds that his mathematical examples are of an elementary character, some of his arguments are open to criticism, and he was against the prevalent conceptions of the Academy.

Aristotle had good reason to turn to elementary mathematics for his current supply of technical illustrations. The establishment of his theory of demonstration on a previous analysis of the method of mathematics could be made only with reference to a body of knowledge properly systematized. Elementary mathematics alone fulfilled such a condition at the time, with the textbooks of Hippocrates, Theudius, and Leon, which were used both in the Academy and in the Lyceum. Hence, Aristotle referred more readily to the elementary rather than to the advanced mathematical theories, which were only beginning to take shape. This circumstance is particularly interesting for the history of mathematics, and Heath himself acknowledges that "the works of Aristotle are of the greatest importance"[1] in this respect.

The Aristotelian treatises contain several definitions and the proof of many theorems which Euclid later incorporated into his *Elements*. We find in them the equivalent of Euclid's first 6 definitions, with the exception of that of the straight line, for which Plato's definition is given. Similar figures are defined as in the *Elements,* and the same terminology of proportions is often used by both. Some terms like *inflected* lines and *verging* lines[2] were current in Aristotle's time and abandoned later. In a striking passage,[3] Aristotle points out that the theory of parallels involved a vicious circle; but as he gives no examples of geometrical or mechanical postulates, Euclid was probably the first to solve this difficulty by formulating the famous postulate upon which he based his own system.

We need not elaborate on the theorems found in Aristotle's works as they are not necessarily due to him, but we must point out that, in spite of his logical theory of demonstration, Aristotle has not always given rigorous and final proofs of the mathematical propositions he mentions. Many of them involve more complex assumptions than the propositions to be proved. But, after all, Aristotle was less concerned with mathematical research than with formulation of his logical and physical theories, and with their illustration by means of the best

---

[1] Thomas L. Heath, *A History of Greek Mathematics* (Oxford, 1921), I, p. 335.

[2] *An. Post.* 76b 9.

[3] *An. Priora* 65a 5.

mathematical examples given in the current manuals. His purpose was not to improve their proofs or their arrangement. This task was left to Euclid, whose results can be assessed by comparing his definitions and proofs with those found in the Aristotelian works.

The Aristotelian corpus contains many demonstrations different from those of the *Elements*. Two remarkable examples of such proofs concern the equality of the angles at the base of an isosceles triangle where mixed angles are used,[4] and the angle in a semicircle which must be a right angle.[5] The former is given to illustrate the rule that the 2 premises of every syllogism must have between them an affirmative and a universal proposition. The latter proof is given by Aristotle in 2 stages: he shows first that it is true for an inscribed isosceles triangle with the diameter as its base, for the median of the given angle bisects it and forms 2 right-angled isosceles triangles; the proof is completed by using the equality of the angles in the same segment. The demonstration of Euclid (*Elements* III, 31) is more direct and general.

Some propositions given by Aristotle are not found in Euclid, such as the sum of the exterior angles of any polygon being equal to 4 right angles, and various properties of the circle concerning plane loci and isoperimetry. He also makes many references to the fundamental notions of solid geometry, especially in *De Caelo* (Book III), where he alludes to the construction of bodies out of planes. Here he mentions that the only 2 solids which can fill up space are the cube and the pyramid,[6] but he does not make clear what kind of pyramid has that property, for that is not true of a regular tetrahedron. This statement remains ambiguous, although several commentators since the Renaissance have tried to explain it satisfactorily.

With regard to higher mathematics, Aristotle was interested mainly in the implications of the methods of quadratures and

---

[4] *An. Priora* 41b 13.
[5] *An. Post.* 94a 30.
[6] *De Caelo* 306b 7.

in the corresponding problem of the infinite. He does not make any reference to the higher curves known then, not even to the conic sections discovered by Menaechmus, his contemporary. He refers to a type of spiral as one of the figures such that no part of it will coincide with any other part,[7] and we find in the *Problems* a question about the shape of the curve of a cylindrical roll which is cut by a plane and then unrolled: a right section gives a straight line, but an oblique section traces a crooked line.[8] Such statements do not indicate that Aristotle investigated them mathematically.

As many higher curves invented by the Greeks were used for rectifications and quadratures, the analysis of any of these processes could furnish Aristotle with an adequate basis for discussing their implications. The squaring of the lunes, the various attempts to square the circle, the general problem of the irrationals, and the method of exhaustion formed together a body of knowledge adequate for such a discussion. In the 4 passages where Aristotle mentions the squaring of the lunes and the attempts to square the circle, he considers the proposed solutions as instances of improper arguments.

In the first passage,[9] the Hippocratic quadrature of the sum of a circle and certain lunes is given as a bad example of *apagoge*. This type of reasoning consists of reducing a problem to another one capable of an easier proof. Let us consider 3 terms such that the relation between the first and the second is known, but not the relation between the first and the third. This connection between the extremes would be proved apagogically if it is shown that the middle and last terms are linked together by means of one or a definite number of intermediate terms. Aristotle applies these conditions to the following example: let *D* be the property of being capable of quadrature, *E* a square, and *Z* a circle; if there could be one intermediate term between *E* and *Z*, namely the addition of lunes to the circle so as to make it equal to the square, we

---

[7] *Phys.* 228b 24.
[8] *Probl.* 914a 25.
[9] *An. Priora* 69a 30.

would be very near to a proper solution. In other words, although D belongs to E, yet D cannot be an attribute of Z, as between E and Z no intermediate term can be found. According to Tannery, this passage involves a recognition of the quadrature of the lunes, but this interpretation scarcely agrees with Aristotle's logical illustration—no apagogical reasoning would be necessary if the identity of E and Z were accepted as proved in the manner described.

Bryson alone is mentioned in the second reference,[10] and his method of squaring the circle is criticized as being "eristic" because it involves principles not specifically geometrical. Hippocrates as well as Bryson are mentioned expressly in the third reference,[11] where the "fallacy" of their quadratures is denounced. Finally, in the last passage,[12] Aristotle asserts that arguments concerning quadratures must be refuted with the distinction between the proofs which may be called geometrical and those which are not. Antiphon's method is given as an example of the latter, while the former concerns specifically the proofs by the segments, an obvious reference to the method of squaring the lunes by a series of circular segments corresponding to the 2 arcs of a lune.

Some may wonder why Aristotle did not accept the solutions of Hippocrates, which rank among the most remarkable discoveries of Greek mathematics. According to Alexander, as quoted by Simplicius,[13] it seems that Hippocrates confused the lunes of an interior arc of 60 degrees with those of 90 degrees when he applied to the former the quadrature established for the latter. It is hard to believe that Hippocrates could have made such an obvious mistake. If such a paralogism were known at the time, Tannery suggests[14] that the name of Hippocrates may have been connected accidentally with it by some careless copyist. Whatever be the case, there is no

10 *An. Post.* 75ᵇ 40.
11 *Soph. Elenchi* 171ᵇ 15.
12 *Phys.* 185ᵃ 14.
13 *Commentary on Aristotle's Physics*, p. 327.
14 Paul Tannery, *La Géométrie Grecque* (Paris, 1887), chap. VIII.

doubt that Aristotle's criticism is directed against the Hippocratic quadratures of lunes.

The reason for Aristotle's stand in this matter may be that rectilinear and curvilinear boundaries are of a different nature, so that conclusions reached about either of them should not be logically applied to the other. For example, in discussing the inequality of a rectilinear and a curvilinear motion with respect to velocities,[15] Aristotle considers these motions as totally different and incomparable because, if the velocity of a moving object is greater on a straight line than on a curve, the former would be equal to a portion of the latter; he could not admit that the straight line and the circle can be compared. Similar motives may partly account for Aristotle's rejection of the validity of the quadratures attributed to Antiphon and Bryson. In claiming that it is not "the geometer's business" to refute Antiphon's quadrature, and that Bryson's proof is eristic, Aristotle implies that the principles they infringed are logical rather than strictly mathematical.

As regards Antiphon, his method consisted of inscribing a regular polygon in a circle and doubling continually the number of its sides until a polygon is reached with sides so small as to "coincide" with the circumference of the circle. This asserted "coincidence" of the rectilineal and circular segments probably prompted the formal objections of Aristotle, for it involves principles the Sophists used in their current discussions. Ignoring the distinction between an abstract and a concrete geometrical construction, Protagoras maintained that a tangent actually touches a circumference in more than one point. This happens formally in Antiphon's quadrature, as Alexander pointed out, unless the increasing smallness of the rectilineal and circular segments causes them to lose their identity and to become points. Then, lines would actually be made up of points, a conclusion already refuted by Zeno's arguments. Moreover, the ultimate coincidence of the segments implies the divisibility of magnitudes without limit, as

[15] *Phys.* 248a 15.

Eudemus observed, so that the geometer can actually reach the infinitesimal. As Aristotle could not accept such arguments, he was entitled to reject Antiphon's quadrature, even though he may have realized its practical and historical importance.

As regards Bryson, he improved on the quadrature of his immediate predecessor by using both inscribed and circumscribed polygons and by assuming between them an intermediate polygon to which the circle would be ultimately equal.[16] As the circle is greater than all inscribed and less than all circumscribed polygons, he sought to relate the area of the circle to the intermediate figure obtained, probably by increasing the number of its sides. These constructions involve the following reasoning: things which are greater and less than the same things respectively are equal; both the circle and the intermediate polygon are respectively greater than the inscribed polygons and less than the circumscribed polygons; therefore, they are equal.

We do not know how the intermediate figure was constructed and whether it corresponded to the arithmetic or to the geometric mean of the inscribed and the circumscribed polygons. We are told by Themistius[17] that Bryson considered the circle to be greater than all inscribed and less than all circumscribed polygons, while the assumed principle (expressed in the major premise) was declared to be true but not specifically geometrical. The eristic character of this argument is obvious, for the assumed principle, without specification, is not true generally. Taking an example quoted by Alexander, the numbers 8 and 9 are both less than 10 and greater than 7 without being equal. Hence, when applied to geometrical magnitudes with or without a common measure, the major of the above syllogism requires some specification in order to connect with the minor unambiguously.

Although the quadratures of Antiphon and Bryson were considered by Aristotle as founded on different principles,

16 Cf. Alexander *Commentary on the Sophistic Elenchi* 306b 24 *sq.* (ed. Brandis).
17 *Commentary on the Posterior Analytics* 211b 19 (ed. Brandis).

they could have certain characteristics in common. The interpretation of Bryson's method given by Themistius suggests a continuous duplication of the sides of both the inscribed and the circumscribed polygons, with the assumption that this process, carried far enough, would yield an inscribed and a circumscribed polygon differing so little in area that any intermediate figure described between them would equal the original circle. This would be a technical improvement of Antiphon's method, which involved only an inscribed figure, but it would also open Bryson's quadrature to the same objections Aristotle leveled against Antiphon, in addition to the specific refutation already mentioned.

To be sure, Aristotle's criticism of the early methods of quadrature involves a rather rigid conception of the mutual relations of arithmetic and geometry and of the working methods of mathematics. It respects his strict requirements for a good demonstration; after all, Aristotle was right in refuting these early quadratures in their given terms, even though he may have known their later improvements through the Eudoxian method of exhaustion.[18] Hence, it is fair to assume that Aristotle was not necessarily against the practical use of the systematic quadratures developed by his contemporaries, especially as he does not mention them in his critical references to the older methods.

Furthermore, it is not improbable that Aristotle's critical and constructive views on the infinite, coupled with the development of the method of exhaustion, led to the remarkable improvements of the Alexandrian period. In fact, Euclid used Antiphon's construction and improved his proof with the remark that by doubling the sides of the inscribed polygon long enough, the small segments left over will be together less than any assigned area.[19] This almost amounts to considering

[18] The principle of this method is expressed in *Physics* (266ᵇ 2) as follows: "If I continually add to a finite magnitude, I shall exceed every assigned magnitude; and similarly, if I subtract, I shall fall short [of my assigned magnitude]."

[19] *Elements* xii. 2.

the circle as the *limit* of the inscribed polygon when the number of its sides increases indefinitely. On the other hand, Archimedes followed Bryson's method by compressing into one, as it were, 2 polygons inscribed and circumscribed about the curvilinear figure to be measured. In this manner, he proved that the value of π stands between 3 10/70 and 3 10/71, the lower limit equalling the perimeter of the inscribed polygon of 96 sides constructed by doubling the sides of an inscribed equilateral triangle.[20]

Aristotle was right in maintaining, against the prevalent opinion of his contemporaries, that the circle could not be squared exactly. Neither the theory of the higher curves known in his time, nor the approximate solutions worked out later by Archimedes, nor even the development of the calculus, shattered the truth of his view. On this point, the promptings of his logical acumen are still upheld by modern mathematics.

---

[20] *The Measurement of a Circle*, prop. 3, in *The Works of Archimedes* (New York, 1897), (ed. Heath), p. 93.

CHAPTER 21

The Origin of Logic

The idea of necessity, which Plato attempted to impose in his own way on the world of being, was transmuted by Aristotle into concrete things, and into the realm of thought. In endeavoring to systematize the conditions of this parallelism, which the Eleatics had already noticed, Aristotle opened the way to the establishment of logic as a new science. His statement[1] that the subjects treated in the *Topics* had never before received any scientific discussion does not mean that a ready-made science of logic came out of his mind; but even though many elements of his system are found in earlier writers, it would be unfair to consider Aristotle as a mere compiler or systematizer of what had been worked out before in this field.[2] In fact, no formal logical system can be found in the works of his predecessors, although their discussions about mathematics and language manifest an active interest in the problem of the structure of a deductive science.

Plato was aware of the postulational character of mathe-

[1] *Soph. Elenchi* 183b 34-36.
[2] Cf. Federigo Enriques, *The Historical Development of Logic* (New York, 1929), p. 4.

matics, which was not real knowledge for him as long as its assumptions were left unexamined.[3] Although he considered the possibility and the necessity of a higher and more rigorous science, he was only able to describe the aims of dialectic[4] without establishing it as an independent system. Thinking and reasoning are so natural to our mind that it seemed unnecessary to express in cold rules these activities of what man enjoys as a natural gift. Hence, Plato went no further than urging the gradual mathematization of knowledge as the practical means for rationalizing the real world.[5] If he gave in his writings important logical hints used later by Aristotle, these cannot supply by themselves a science of pure thought. As Zeller says, "though we cannot but recognize in Plato essential elements of the Aristotelian logic, it would be a mistake to force these out of their original connection in order to construct from them a Platonic logic on a later model."[6]

The supreme science which the Platonic dialectic could not establish took shape in the Aristotelian *Analytics*, developed in the logical works forming the Organon. This system dominated Western thought to our day, although its influence on Aristotle's successors is less exclusive than is commonly believed. In its spirit and presentation, it was an entirely new science. Indeed, the Stagirite alone was responsible for the systematization of the powerful implications of the critical work of the mathematicians and philosophers about the nature and structure of mathematics and language. Moreover, as a result of his own reflections about biology, he integrated into that logical systematization some of the characteristics and fundamental factors of natural science. These multiple elements of the Organon can be revealed by analyzing the scientific aspects of the Aristotelian doctrines.

[3] *Republic* vii. 533*B*.
[4] *Philebus* 57*E*-59*D*.
[5] The reduction of pure mathematics to absolute deduction remained but an aspiration in Plato's philosophy. After 2,000 years, the same ideal has been adopted and worked out more technically by the founders of mathematical logic.
[6] E. Zeller, *Plato and the Older Academy* (London, 1876), p. 210.

Of all the sciences then known to the Greeks, mathematics alone showed a sufficient degree of abstraction, accuracy, and systematization to yield a system of relations involving necessity. Because of these characteristics, the Pythagoreans and the Platonists had used it extensively in their doctrines. The rational necessity of mathematics became more prominent when treatises on its elements began to be written, and theories like the irrationals were carefully investigated and elaborated by various thinkers. As a member of the Academy, Aristotle must have been impressed from the first by the formal perfection of mathematics.

An interesting passage in the *Posterior Analytics* indicates that mathematics was currently considered the practical organon of the thinking mind. Discussing the difference between fact and reasoned fact, Aristotle says:

> The business of the empirical observers is to know the fact and of the mathematicians to know the reasoned fact. For the latter possess demonstrations giving the causes, while they are often ignorant of the fact; just as we have often a clear insight into a universal, though we are ignorant of some of its particular instances through lack of observation. These connections have a perceptible existence, though they are manifestations of forms. For the mathematical sciences concern forms: they do not demonstrate properties of a substratum, even though geometrical objects are predicable as properties of a perceptible substratum; for it is not as thus predicable that the mathematician demonstrates their properties.[7]

The mathematical inspiration of the Organon is noticeable in its terminology. In the *Prior Analytics,* Aristotle uses the words scheme or pattern for the figure of a syllogism, distance for the proposition, and boundary for the term. He may have represented geometrically each figure of the syllogism by using lines for propositions and points for terms.[8] Perhaps Aristotle thought of the premises in the different figures somewhat on

[7] *An. Post.* 79a 2-10.
[8] W. D. Ross, *Aristotle* (London, 1930), p. 33.

the analogy of the various proportions, but the compelling force of a mathematical argument had to be sought beyond its structural presentation. Relations alone could not justify the necessity of a conclusion, for they are accidents by themselves and indifferent as such to a determined result. This necessity had to be rooted in something more fundamental and substantial than relations, such as in their very terms and ultimately in the objects of the external world which account for them.

The basic importance of terms is implied in the reasons Aristotle gives for the logical superiority of mathematics over dialectic. A mathematical argument is rarely weakened by formal fallacies because its middle term can be seen with an "intellectual vision," while in dialectic the ambiguity may escape detection. It is usually in the middle term of an argument that the ambiguity lies, since the major is predicated of the whole of the middle and the middle of the whole of the minor.[9] Moreover, mathematics always takes definitions rather than accidents for its premises, while such is not always the case with dialectic.[10] Indeed, it is the Aristotelian theory of the universal which explains the necessity involved in formal arguments.

Although both Plato and Aristotle recognized the scientific value of the concept, their metaphysical standpoints are different. Whereas Plato justifies the universals through their participation in the world of ideas, Aristotle finds their roots in the concrete world. The Aristotelian universals abide basically in the individual objects of experience, but they exist formally in the mind. Yet, their essence and properties are independent from the mind; they are conditioned by the very reality of the particulars in which they reside. Hence, the analysis of concrete things brings to light the relative necessity of the characters of the universals and the logical importance of the notions of species and genus embodying them.

9 An. Post. 77b 27-33.
10 An. Post. 78a 10.

Moreover, the necessity involved in the universals determines the processes of the mind as well as the ultimate laws of thought.[11] Thus, judgments are really explicitations of the analysis of universals—as they are not arbitrary constructions of the mind, they are ultimately justified by the factual relations of the particulars embodying the universals concerned. On the other hand, the principles of identity, contradiction, and excluded middle express the relations resulting from the confrontation of being with itself; as such they are perceived by an intellectual intuition which is immediate in its operations and results.

The necessity involved in the universals and in the laws of thought is enshrined in the fundamental forms of language, which is the only means of communicating knowledge. All the sciences, whether theoretical or practical, have to be expressed in language. It is natural, therefore, that the analysis of language should also contribute to the establishment of a science of pure thought. This expectation is more justified when one takes into account the confusion which the Sophists had introduced into the realm of thought by their abuse of rhetoric and their deliberate use of fallacious arguments.

With their quick wit and ready tongues, the Greeks in general were fond of playing with words. It appears that Heraclitus was aware of the importance of linguistic expression, and that his followers and those of Anaxagoras had developed into arbitrary etymologies the belief that everything has its natural name from which its essence can be known. It was the controversies of the Sophists which led to a closer study of the forms of speech and their relation to thought. The subtlety of some of their arguments, like the double dilemma marking the dispute between Protagoras and his pupil Euathlus, indicates the depth of their linguistic analysis and accounts for the errors resulting from its improper application. An example of such confusion is the anti-mathematical discussion

[11] Cf. J. Chevalier, *La Notion du Nécessaire chez Aristote* (Paris, 1915).

broached by the Sophist Protagoras[12] and Antiphon,[13] who defended the empirical character of geometrical concepts.

The inquiries of the Eleatics at that time, and their controversy with the Sophists, dealt openly with linguistics, but they reached deeper into substantial reality. As Zeno's arguments could not be solved by rhetoric, mathematicians ignored them and developd their methods in spite of the alleged logical blind alley into which they seemed to lead.[14] There ought to be no essential discrepancy between language and mathematics, as both are reasonable. In fact, the analogy between the form of mathematics and the structure of language pointed to a deeper element of certainty common to both, the concept. Since the discovery of this common factor by Socrates, Greek thought was dominated by the philosophy of the concept, and the problem of the relation of language and thought could expect a more constructive solution.

The first steps were taken by Platò in acknowledging the close affinity between speech and thought.[15] For him, language is not an arbitrary production of man, and names must provide us with a picture of the essence of the things they represent. A picture never reproduces completely its real subject, so that makers of words may make mistakes affecting the whole language. This may explain the arbitrary morphology of certain words, and why most of them do not entail the same view of the world. Hence, attention must be given to the things themselves rather than to names, while acknowledging the superiority of dialectic which passes judgment on the correctness of words. Incidentally, although Plato claimed that philosophy is independent of philology, few literary productions can match the beauty of his dialogues. Thus at the time of Aristotle, the Greek language had already achieved its literary perfection and most of the poets and writers had given

12 Aristotle *Met.* 998a 1-6.

13 Simplicius *Commentary on Aristotle's Physics* (Diels, *Vors.*, B. 13).

14 It seems that Democritus also investigated the problem of verbal expression (Diogenes Laertius, ix. 48), and that Anthisthenes the Cynic wrote on names and language.

15 Cf. *Cratylus* 385D-390E and 422C-440E.

their best. For over 100 years, Greek was being improved and analyzed in its grammatical, linguistic, and logical aspects. As the founder of the Lyceum had then all the required elements for writing his 2 didactic treatises on *Rhetoric* and on *Poetics,* there is little doubt that his linguistic interests helped him in the elaboration of his logical doctrines.

The structure of a Greek sentence is always centered grammatically and logically on the subject. The orientation of the various elements of a proposition is always towards the subject. From its central position, the subject keeps together the attributes, and it conditions the proposition as the expression of one or more of its various properties. In fact, a proposition unfolds the internal structure of the subject, for the predicate sheds more light on the subject by manifesting its attributes. In the Aristotelian terminology, the words proposition, affirmation, and negation, in Greek, are obviously related to light, and they illustrate the parallelism between the world of experience and the operations of the mind. Truth emerges from this illumination, which manifests the ontological relation of certain attributes to the subject under consideration. This ontological participation becomes a logical subsumption in the operational development of an argument, as expressed by a series of transformations from one proposition into another. Such a sequence has its parallel in the hierarchy of predicates, which exemplifies the structural order of the universe.

The linguistic transformations characterizing the processes of thought are not tautological elaborations of sets of notions and postulates arbitrarily stated as primitive. They result from the analysis and synthesis of concepts which allow the mutual predicability of their elements. The verb *to be* manifests these operations and the generation of each subsequent proposition from the preceding . data. Consequently, the Greeks could scarcely think of a calculus of unanalyzed propositions as does modern symbolic logic. The propositional operations visualized by Aristotle had to be explicit so as to display the paramount importance of the universal. For Aristotle, this operational explicitation of the processes of thought was confirmed by every branch of knowledge. The statements used by the practical and productive sciences express transformations of materials or of given situations, with the purpose of exhibiting their participation to the good and the useful. Biological statements are transformations illustrating the hierarchical connections of the organisms. Physical explanations are transformations tending to show how any object of experience embodies the elements. Mathematical operations are transformations exhibiting the various implications of the terms involved. Metaphysical statements also involve transformations, insofar as they illuminate more and more the complex denotation of being and its various manifestations according to their causal development.

In every science, therefore, all thought processes tend to make plain the mutual relations of concepts and their successive participation in the various aspects of being, according to their degree of universality. Hence, all patterns of thinking as such must be fundamentally identical when considered independently of the subject matter. From this angle, even demonstrative and persuasive reasoning are alike, although the former deals with necessary sequences while the latter involves contingent elements. In fact, reasoning consists of a series of propositions obeying the principle of contradiction individually and collectively. Each one of them expresses the attribution to a subject of a compatible property which is either necessary or contingent. In the same argument, these propositions are linked together because of the relations between their terms. This technique is performed in the dialectical method, which leaves to thought its alertness and its freedom of movement. It becomes fully articulate and conscious in the Aristotelian theory of the syllogism. This explains why the syllogism was not used formally by pre-Aristotelian mathematicians and why it was generally adopted by mathematical writers since its discovery.

The description and codification of the processes of thought must not obscure or destroy their dynamic character. Unless thought displays its dynamism, it becomes tautological, unprogressive, and liable to error. Thought must go forward or perish. By considering it as static in its various stages, the Sophists opened the road to metaphysical relativism. In their time, no theory could check their abuse of loose meanings dressed in strict grammatical forms. Heracliteanism favored that instability of meanings, while Eleaticism could do no more than point out the contradictions resulting from it. With the philosophy of the concept, however, Aristotle was able to preserve the dynamic quality of thought and to account for all mutations, predications, relations, and propositional connections. Moreover, Aristotle did not consider the science of logic as a study of words, but as a study of the thought signified by words, and more particularly as the analysis of thought with reference to its success or failure in attaining truth, and not with regard to its natural history. Logic is concerned with thought as apprehending, and not as constituting, the nature of things.

These are the differences between logic and grammar, psychology and metaphysics. Yet logic is not a substantive science, but a part of a general propaedeutic to the study of any science which indicates what kinds of propositions require proof and what sorts of proofs should be required for them.[16] In spite of its formalism, the Aristotelian logic has thus a dynamic and progressive character. Hence, it would be unfair to suggest that it marked a return to the static view of reasoning. On the contrary, it emphasized and improved the value of the Socratic and the Platonic methods of reasoning by making explicit their underlying logical structure.

This discussion indicates that the science of pure thought has its origin in the explicitation of the mechanism of mathematical reasoning and of the structure of language, coupled with the analysis of the necessary relations between universals considered in intension as concepts and in extension as classes. Aristotle called it *analytic*[17] insofar as it studies the methods of demonstration by which are derived the conditions of the

16 *Ethica Nicom.* 1094b 23.
17 *Rhetorica* 1359b 10.

structure of science. He does not seem to use the term *logic* generally, although it occurred in a lost work of Democritus.[18] It is said also[19] that Aristotle applied the term *logic* to those methods which do not start from principles and therefore have no demonstrative value. It appears from the *Topics* and the *Sophistici Elenchi* that he reserved the Eleatico-Platonic name of *dialectic* for the art of debating about the probable. The word *logic* was used in the sense of dialectic in the time of Cicero. The Stoics called *logic* the study of questions of discourse, rhetoric, grammar, and logic proper, while the Epicureans used the Democritean word *canonic* to denote rules of method. The term *logic* was first used in the sense of logic proper by Alexander of Aphrodisias, who applied to it the word *organon* or instrument. The collection of Aristotle's logical works has been referred to as the Organon since the sixth century.

Aristotle gave the name of *analytic* to the science of pure thought because it deals primarily with the analysis of arguments into the figures of the syllogism,[20] presumably because this operation presupposes the analysis of the syllogism into propositions and of the proposition into terms. The elementary theory of the term and of the proposition is established in the first 2 treatises, the *Categories* and *On Interpretation,* which may be considered as an introduction to the Aristotelian Organon. Here, the doctrine of the predicable is particularly significant, for it shows the biological interests of Aristotle by stressing the function of the genus and the species and by marking a distinction between the proprium and the accident. Further, it emphasizes the necessity of an ordered universe with its notion of the definition. The maximum explicitation of a concept is obtained by identifying it with the combination of its 2 essential attributes chosen among the hierarchy of possible predicates. Finally, it provides a basis for the class

18 Diels, *Vors.,* A 33, B. 10.
19 Carl Prantl, *Geschichte der Logik* (Leipzig, 1855), I, pp. 116 and 336.
20 *An. Priora* 47ª 1-5.

relations required by the syllogism, and it offers an adequate approach to the modern calculus of classes.

Whatever be the special conditions of scientific knowledge, the mind must be sure of the validity of each step it takes, and this coherence is secured when the rules of the syllogism and demonstration are observed. These basic doctrines of the Aristotelian logic are contained in the *Prior Analytics* and the *Posterior Analytics*. The last 2 treatises of the Organon, the *Topics* and the *Sophistici Elenchi*, analyze the arguments which may be syllogistically correct without satisfying one or more of the conditions of scientific thought. In other words, they refer to the art of arguing where it is aimed at the probable.

CHAPTER 22

The Value of Syllogism

The central doctrine of the syllogism is expounded in the *Prior Analytics*. It has been said that, in spite of its name, this treatise was actually written after the *Posterior Analytics*, but the grounds for such a contention are not conclusive. Discussing this problem, Ross adduces fresh evidence in favor of the traditional view that the *Prior Analytics* is earlier.[1] He shows that there are more references in the *Posterior* to the *Prior* than the other way around; he submits that the doctrines of the *Posterior* presuppose those of the *Prior*, but not conversely; and he refutes the view that the *Posterior Analytics* belong to an early stage of Aristotle's development in which he was predominantly under Plato's influence.

The discovery of the syllogism is entirely due to Aristotle. The Platonic method of division foreshadowed the Aristotelian process of reasoning from the universal to the particular, yet it did not exhibit the syllogistic link of this progression. Aristotle stated clearly this difference in the 2 methods[2] when

1 W. D. Ross, "The Discovery of the Syllogism," *Philosophical Review* (May 1939), pp. 251-272.
2 *An. Priora* 46a 32, and *An. Post.* 9b 11.

he called the division a powerless or sick syllogism because its conclusion is not necessary. He explains this defect by the fact that each progressive step of the Platonic division postulates an option between 2 opposite terms, so that the minor term which conditions the conclusion is chosen and accepted without demonstration. On the other hand, the syllogism is "an argument in which, certain things being admitted, something other than these follows of necessity from their essence without requiring any other elements."[3] This seems to be a considerable improvement of the Platonic method, provided an adequate explanation is given on the subsumption of the minor term under the middle term.

The best illustration of the function and structure of the syllogism is offered by the principle of the first figure, the *dictum de omni et nullo,* which is the basic rule of the various types of syllogisms, as they are always reducible to the first figure. This principle states that "when three terms are so related to one another that the last is included in the middle as in the whole, and the middle is or is not included in the first as in a whole, there is necessarily a perfect syllogism connecting the extremes."[4] This statement entails that the terms of the syllogism be predominantly considered in extension, although their intension is fully operative. This is in keeping with the Aristotelian theory of the universal and of the proposition, which accepts the Socratic conception of the essence or universal as the fundamental element of demonstration.[5] The syllogism is justified partly by the formal conditions of its structure and necessarily by the quiddity of its terms. It manifests the grounds of the attribution of this predicate to that subject by means of the middle term, which links the 2 extremes together. In other words, the syllogism facilitates the shining forth of a given subject by bringing into relief its various attributes. At the same time, it helps the explicitation of that subject by making clear its relations with other subjects.

3 *An. Priora* 24b 18.
4 *An. Priora* 25b 32.
5 *Met.* 1078b 24.

In case the attribution of a predicate to a subject seems to be remote, an adequate number of middle terms may be called upon to manifest the chain of causal relations linking together the 2 elements of the final conclusion. Even then, such a complex argument (the sorites) can be reduced to a sequence of formal syllogisms. Hence, as the ultimate pattern of the discursive explicitation of a given subject, the syllogism requires 3 terms only. Moreover, the order of the syllogistic progression is irreversible, because the causal relation among its terms exemplifies the real order of the substantial world. For these reasons, the Aristotelian logic, unlike the modern symbolic logic, cannot countenance any rules permitting the indefinite substitution or mutation of the terms or propositions of an argument without the strongest qualifications.

Thus the basic form of discursive thought is the syllogism. Presumably, Aristotle believed in the congruence of mathematical reasoning with his syllogistic doctrine, for he reduced to the syllogism all the various kinds of arguments.[6] For example, he did not treat the hypothetical proposition and syllogism as separate logical types. He recognized 2 kinds of conditional arguments: the *reductio ad impossibile*, which assumes that a proposition from whose opposite a false conclusion follows is itself true, and the hypothetical argument, involving the idea of contingency. He also mentioned the process of reduction proper, which is more appropriate to mathematics, although it can be properly used in all the sciences, including ethics.[7] This method consists of working back from a given problem to a simpler one whose solution leads to the demonstration of the first, and so on until a problem is reached which can be solved by the knowledge already at hand. The last step in this analysis is the first to be presented in practice. Aristotle realized that the process of reduction, as opposed to deductive exposition, corresponds to the analytical method of investigation and to the method of deliberation in ethics.[8]

6 *An. Priora* 46a 3.
7 *An. Priora* 69a 20-25.
8 *Ethica Nicom.* 1112b 20.

Many criticisms have been leveled against the Aristotelian theory of deduction throughout history. The Stoics, the Epicurians, and the Sceptics, developing the principles of the Democritean epistemology, took up positions incompatible with the Aristotelian ontologism. Stressing the importance of sensation and the purely formal character of thought, they introduced relativism into the realm of logic and robbed the syllogism of its value and purpose. By exposing the relative elements contained in the criteria of truth, they directed their attacks against the Socratic rationalism, which asserts that we can reach something of the nature of things in themselves. The Sceptics denounced the Aristotelian theory of demonstration on the grounds that it leads to an infinite regression and communicates to the understanding the uncertainty of sensation from which all concepts are derived.[9]

Although Aristotle laid down the basic principles of logic, he did not analyze all the intricate details of the inferential processes and of the various logical problems connected with the science of thought. In particular, he did not develop a logic of relations which would offer a pattern closer to the structure of mathematics proper for lack of an adequate symbolism, and because the idea of relation was for him just another kind of a predicate amenable to the fundamental subject-predicate form. Hence, it should be possible to derive a logic of relations, as well as the various other calculi of modern logic, from the implications of the categorical proposition. This derivation is made possible by stressing certain details of the standard forms of propositions and their operational use.

The categorical proposition usually symbolized by *S-is-P* is the simplest expression of a judgment. Hypothetical and disjunctive propositions are really compound propositions, insofar as they are formed by simple categorical propositions having between them relations indicated by specific conjunctions. The possibility of transforming these compound propositions from one into the other, as when a hypothetical is

9 For an elaboration of the views contained in this chapter, see T. Greenwood, *Les Fondements de la Logique Symbolique*, 2 vols. (Paris, 1938).

reduced to a disjunctive, implies some general rules justifying these reductions. In elementary logic, these operations are explained by a direct analysis of the meaning of the propositional forms involved, but it is possible to establish these rules in a formal way illustrating their operational character.

These technical transformations may also be justified by stressing some distinctions used in the elementary doctrine of propositions. It has been observed that many technical considerations apply to categorical propositions when they are taken as parts of compound propositions without any reference to their quality and quantity. This happens in the analysis of such expressions as *If A, then C*. Other principles concerning categorical propositions refer more specifically to their quality and quantity, as in the doctrine of opposition applied to categoricals and hypotheticals. Another set of rules displays the particular relation between *S* and *P* considered as classes when their extension is emphasized. Finally, propositions involving relations as such require some supplementary principles to justify their treatment. These remarks show that any simple categorical proposition can be considered from 4 aspects.

In the first place, the proposition *S-is-P* can be considered as a single whole, a logical unit which is not split into its component elements. Such propositions can be represented by the letters *p, q, r*, and so on. An expression such as *If A, then C* will be read *If P, then q;* special symbols can replace the conjunctions used in such expressions and any relations postulated between them. With these elements, it is possible to establish a calculus of propositions dealing with the formal relations between propositions considered as single units.

Second, the proposition *S-is-P* can be interpreted as the simple attribution of a quality to a single subject. The letters ϕ, χ, ψ can be used to represent the qualities, and the letters *x, y, z* to represent the individual subjects. An expression such as ϕx is called a propositional function, that is, a form which becomes a proposition when a definite value is substituted for the *variable x*, representing the undetermined individual. Special symbols for quantifying the subject can be applied to this expression in order to obtain the standard forms of categorical propositions. With these elements, it is possible to establish a calculus of propositional functions dealing with all formal relations between expressions containing variables linked up with fixed but unspecified qualities. As a propositional function expresses the form of a proposition, the initial postulates and definitions of the calculus of propositions are applicable analogically to the calculus of propositional functions. As the latter may be quantified, some special principles must be added to those of the calculus of propositions. The theory of descriptions, which is a part of the calculus of propositional functions, is also used to derive the calculus of classes from that of propositional functions. The calculus of classes, which developed historically before the calculus of propositional functions, can stand on its own.

Third, the proposition *S-is-P* may be considered as expressing a relation of membership or inclusion between an individual or a class *S* and another class *P*. In order to indicate that a categorical proposition involves a class relationship, we can use the letters *a, b, c* for classes; *x, y, z* for individuals; and special symbols for the relations involved, such as the symbol ⊂ representing the relation of inclusion. The notion of a class may be derived from that of a universal, and more particularly from an analysis of the doctrine of the predicables. A class is a universal viewed in extension—it thus stands for like entities sharing the essence of that universal. A calculus of classes may be organized to deal with such notions, insofar as they can be combined by the 2 fundamental relations of class membership (for individuals) and class inclusion (for classes only), as well as by some other notions and operations derived from them. The 2 fundamental class relationships are reducible to the subject predicate form: thus *a* ⊂ *b* may be read *a—is—included in b,* and the relation *included in,* which is part of the predicate, can be transferred to the copula in order to facilitate operations with classes.

This leads to some basic developments concerning relations and their calculus. The proposition *S-is-P* may represent generally a relation between *S* and a term *T* contained in the predicate *P*, which would be the combination of a relation *R* and the term *T*. In other words, as a relation in a category, it should be treated as a predicate and not as a verbal copula. Nevertheless, such a predicate can be split into its component elements, the relation itself and the term related to the subject; then, by explicit convention, the relation proper can be transferred to the copula itself. Thus the expression *S-is-P* may be analyzed first into *S-is-RT*; then it may be turned into *S-is-T* by transferring the relation *R* into the copula; and finally the new copula *is R* may be represented by specific operators. This procedure allows the symbolization of relations and the development of a calculus simplifying the otherwise cumbrous expressions involved in the traditional treatment of propositions containing relations as predicates. In such a calculus, the letters *R, S, T* can be used as symbols of relations, and the letters *x, y, z* as symbols of the various terms related. Such expressions as *xRy, xSz* stand for categorical propositions containing 2 terms linked up by a relation. Moreover, if we define a relation between 2 terms as the class of couples with a specified connection between these terms, a relation becomes a class of classes and therefore a proper subject for the calculus of classes. In fact, the calculus of relations develops on the same lines as the calculus of classes, although additional notions belong specifically to the former, thus increasing its complexity and interest.

It follows that a categorical proposition of the form *S-is-P* can be represented by one or more of 4 types of expressions, such as p, ϕx, $a \subset b$, or xRy, according to its particular structure. Hence, these 4 types of expressions can be reduced to the standard subject-predicate form, which is really the ground of their ontological justification. In fact, it appears that the

$\overleftarrow{relation\ of\ inherence}$ expressed by the form *S-is-P* centered upon the subject is more fundamental than any other type of relation between the terms of a proposition. This fundamental relation of inherence centered upon the subject should not be identified exclusively with the class relations which are so prominent in Aristotelian logic. This confusion, which should not be attributed to Aristotle, is the source of many misunderstandings. In fact, the classical form *S-is-P* is not a particular aspect of a more general propositional form, but the very source and justification of the many developments in logical technique.

On these grounds, the various forms or types of reasoning can be readily reduced to the syllogistic pattern for the sole purpose of their justification. It is not suggested that the effective symbolism used by logistics should be abandoned for the verbal and structural patterns of the syllogism. Once their foundations have been clearly visualized in their proper ontological perspective, mathematics and symbolic logic can proceed along the lines best suited for their progress. The practical consequence of this view is to free symbolic logic from many serious objections leveled against it by non-positivistic schools of thought. To be sure, this new integration of symbolic logic entails a reinterpretation of its standard principles. Far from impairing the development of logistics, such a revaluation would assist the solution of current difficulties, most of which refer to the analysis of meanings rather than to symbolic or structural operations.

CHAPTER 23

The Structure of Mathematics

The views of Aristotle on the structure of mathematics as a science may be gathered mainly from the *Posterior Analytics*, which contains the most important passages relating to mathematics. Although this treatise deals generally with demonstrative science,[1] most of the illustrations used are mathematical and suggest that Aristotle was inspired by mathematics when laying down the conditions of science. If the "form" of mathematics exhibits all the characteristics of a science, its "matter" limits its object to numbers and figures or magnitude in general, which are derived and constructed by abstraction from empirical elements.

The importance of demonstration in the structure of mathematics is justified by the fact that proof gives a universal value to the knowledge it is applied to. The Pythagoreans raised the study of numbers and figures to the status of a science by showing the necessary connections between the propositions dealing with such objects. Plato improved the technique of mathematics by his analytical method and dialectical reasoning, while the mathematicians of the Academy and their con-

[1] *Analytica Posteriora* 24ª 11.

temporaries used this method and reasoning to produce wonderful results. Consequently, demonstration ought to be a subject of inquiry by itself. This is the aim of the *Posterior Analytics,* where Aristotle discusses the features of scientific reasoning in contradistinction to dialectical reasoning.

The relation of the *Prior Analytics,* which deals with the forms common to all reasoning, to the *Posterior Analytics* is that of syllogism to demonstration: "Syllogism should be discussed before demonstration because it is the more general. Demonstration is a sort of syllogism, but not every syllogism is a demonstration."[2] In fact, demonstration is scientific syllogism which yields true knowledge and not merely opinion.

Faithful to the general inspiration of his method, Aristotle does not describe a priori the characteristics of demonstration; he infers them from the nature of science. The *Posterior Analytics* may be divided into 5 principal parts. Aristotle gives first the condition to be fulfilled by the premises of any science (I. 1-6). He then infers the properties of any demonstration showing why subjects have certain characteristics (I. 7-34). He examines next demonstration by a means of defining properties (II. 1-10). Then he considers in greater detail various topics mentioned in the preceding sections (II. 11-18). Finally, he describes the origin of the immediate propositions from which demonstration begins (II. 19).

As demonstration must yield true knowledge, its premises must be true and indemonstrable, preceding and causing the conclusion. They must be true (while those of the syllogism need not be), otherwise the conclusion would not be necessarily true. They must be indemonstrable or immediate, otherwise they could not be first principles and ought to be demonstrated. "The necessity of this is obvious, for since we must know the prior premises from which demonstration is drawn, and since the regress must end in immediate truth, those truths must be indemonstrable."[3] The premises must be more intelligible than the conclusion and known before it so that we perceive its truth more clearly when we become aware of them.

2 *An. Post.* 25b 28.
8 *An. Post.* 72b 20.

Finally, they must be causes of the conclusion in the sense that the facts stated must determine the fact expressed in the conclusion, and also that our knowledge of the premises must be the cause of our knowledge of the conclusion.[4]

Aristotle draws an important distinction between formal and basic truth. The first is nothing more than self-consistency,[5] while basic truths involve existence which cannot be proved but must be assumed, as, for example, unity and magnitude.[6] Of the basic truths used in the demonstrative sciences, some are particular to each science and some are common to all. The former are used effectively by a specific science, "for a truth of this kind will have the same force even if not used generally, but applied by the geometer only to magnitudes or by the arithmetician only to numbers."[7] As examples of particular truths, Aristotle gives the definitions of line and straight for geometry, and those of odd and even for arithmetic.

Common truths, common things, common opinions, common axioms are the names given by Aristotle to the propositions which Euclid calls "common notions." An example of such truths often quoted by Aristotle is the equality of the differences when equals are taken from equals. Hence, Aristotle's explanation of these terms applies to Euclid's axioms, excluding those of a geometrical character, such as the assumption that 2 straight lines cannot enclose a space, the parallel-postulate, and the equality of all right angles. The proposition concerning the equality of things that coincide when applied to one another, which is a working definition of geometrical equality, implies a proof of superposition and the possibility of motion without deformation. Hence, it should be alien to mathematics, which deals only with things without motion.[8] Nevertheless, Euclid could not dispense with the use of superpositions, even if he disliked this method of proof.

4 *An. Post.* 71ᵇ 19-33.
5 *An. Priora* 47ᵃ 8.
6 *An. Post.* 76ᵃ 31-37.
7 *An. Post.* 76ᵃ 42.
8 *Phys.* 198ᵃ 17.

The most fundamental axioms are the basic truths which must be used in order to learn anything at all. They include the universal propositions known as the laws of thought, through which all sciences have common relations. There are other axioms, the ignorance of which does not constitute a total bar to progress.[9] Although Aristotle does not give any examples of them, he refers most probably to the particular axioms of each science; thus ignorance of the axioms of quantity is a bar to mathematical knowledge only. In speaking of axioms "such as the law of the excluded middle, the law that the subtraction of equals leaves equal remainders, and other axioms of the same kind,"[10] Aristotle seems to assimilate the laws of thought to strict mathematical axioms. This casual enumeration does not affect his main teaching about the function of axioms in demonstration.

The laws of thought are part of the prior knowledge required for the study of any special science. These regulative axioms cannot serve as premises for the proof of all conclusions; by themselves they lead to nothing because they refer only to being as being, while being manifests itself differently in the various sciences. In order to be possible, demonstration requires the common axioms as well as premises involving the genus and properties of the relevant science.[11] The only case in which the law of contradiction is expressly required as such in a demonstration is when a conclusion has to be stated in that form.[12] The proof thus lays down as its major premise that the major term is truly affirmed but falsely denied of the middle.

The basic truths appropriate to a particular science must refer to the same genus as that of the science, otherwise the conclusion could not be related to them as effect to cause. Consequently, it is not permissible to pass from one genus to another, even if the axioms which are premises of demonstra-

---

9 *An. Post.* 72ª 15.
10 *An. Post.* 77ª 29-32.
11 *An. Post.* 88ª 36-88ᵇ 4.
12 *An. Post.* 77ª 10.

tion be identical in 2 or more sciences, as in the case of sub-ordinate sciences. Hence, the basic truths of mathematics must be axioms referring to being, supplemented by the distinctive attribute of quantity.

Aristotle goes even further by drawing a distinction between geometrical and arithmetical truths. As the genera of these sciences are different, he disclaims any validity in the proof of geometrical truths by arithmetic.

> In the case of two different genera such as arithmetic and geometry, one cannot apply arithmetical demonstration to the properties of magnitudes unless these are numbers. . . . Arithmetical demonstration and each of the other sciences possess their own genera. So that if the demonstration is to pass from one field to another, the genus must be the same either absolutely or partially; otherwise transference is clearly impossible because the extreme and the middle terms must be drawn from the same genus. Unless predicated with this condition, these terms will not be essential but only accidents.[13]

For this reason, geometry cannot prove that opposites fall under one science, or that "the product of two cubes is a cube," meaning that the product of 2 cube numbers is a cube number.

As no science is concerned with proving anything beyond its own subject matter, geometry cannot demonstrate that lines have properties they do not possess as lines, by means of the fundamental truths of their particular genus. For example, it cannot prove the straight line to be the most beautiful line or the contrary of the circle, for these qualities do not belong to lines in virtue of their particular genus, but because of some property shared with other genera. Therefore, theorems of any one science cannot be demonstrated by means of another science, unless they are related as subordinate to superior, as optical theorems are related to geometry or harmonic theorems to arithmetic.

[13] *An. Post.* 75b 4-12.

This point is fully emphasized when Aristotle says that not all falsehoods are derived from a single set of principles, and that not all these principles are inferred from the same basic truths: "Many of them in fact have basic truths which differ generically and are not transferable; for example, units which are without position can not take the place of points which have position. The transferred terms could fit in only as middle terms or as major or minor terms; or else have some other terms between them and others outside them."[14] Hence, there are no general mathematical axioms, but only basic truths of arithmetic and basic truths of geometry. Although the expression of such particular basic truths might suggest the possibility of more general axioms, these could have no practical value, as their meaning would be ambiguous owing to their reference to different kinds of beings. This may explain Aristotle's rejection of Antiphon's and Bryson's methods of squaring the circle, which are based on principles applicable to geometry and to other subjects as well. Aristotle's distinction among the special axioms of the particular sciences is related to his classification of the sciences according to their specific object.

Besides the axioms, the other elements of demonstrations are definitions and hypotheses. Definitions explicitate the meaning of terms. They assume the existence of genera and their species connoted by the terms. The logical theory of definition is treated in the *Posterior Analytics,* especially in chapters 9, 12, and 13. The definition of a term is obtained by a gradual restriction of the extension of the assumed genus by means of successive differentiae, until the extension of the term itself is completely circumscribed.

Hypotheses, or postulates, as Euclid called them later, are propositions laid down without proof and used without demonstration.[15] They refer explicitly to the terms of each particular science and state various relations between them. If Aristotle assumes that hypotheses can be proved, he probably

14 *An. Post.* 88a 32-35.
15 *An. Post.* 76b 26.

means it with reference to knowledge as a whole, for they cannot be demonstrated within the particular science to which they belong; otherwise they could be eliminated as elements of demonstration. Hypotheses are only relative and mediate knowledge. In this sense, they differ from the axioms, which are immediately evident.

There are important distinctions between a definition and a hypothesis. When a proposition asserts the existence or the non-existence of a subject, it is a hypothesis; when it does not refer to existence, it is a definition.[16] To define what is a unit and to affirm its existence are 2 different things. Definitions require only to be understood, while hypotheses postulate facts on which the inferred propositions depend.[17] In arithmetic, the existence of the notions of unit and magnitude has to be assumed, while the existence of everything else has to be proved. In geometry, the only objects which must be assumed are points and lines; all the figures constructed from them and their properties have to be proved. This procedure, which implies the constructibility of mathematical notions, is adopted by Euclid, who admits as a proof of existence an actual construction based on accepted principles.

The particular assumptions used in geometrical constructions are conventional. It is not false to assume that the line which is drawn is a foot longer or straight, when it is actually neither. The geometer does not draw any conclusion from the actual line he mentions, but from what his diagram symbolizes.[18] In other words, the geometer argues only about what his diagrams represent, the figures themselves being mere illustrations. The meaning of "existence" with reference to mathematical objects is independent of their actual symbolical representation. Our knowledge of them is based on existential assumptions which are true by themselves or by construction. To be sure, "demonstration does not refer to external speech, but to the speech of the soul."[19]

16 *An. Post.* 72a 19.
17 *An. Post.* 76b 37.
18 *An. Post.* 77a 1. Cf. *An. Priora* 49b 35 and *Met.* 1089a 20.
19 *An. Post.* 76b 25.

These views are closely related to the teaching of the Academy, and especially to the methodological doctrines of the *Republic* and *Theaetetus*. Indeed, Aristotle's awareness of the self-evident nature of thought is similar to Plato's belief in the intrinsic sincerity of reason. "Thought is a conversation the soul holds with itself about the things it examines. . . . Not even in sleep did you ever venture to say to yourself that odd is even or anything of the kind."[20]

For Plato, self-evident principles are innate in the mind, which becomes aware of them through reminiscence, while Aristotle maintains that the knowledge of these principles is acquired primarily through sensation. The unity of experience existing in the soul allows the mind to apprehend similarities found in particulars and to perceive them as universal elements of thought.[21] With this intellectual vision, the understanding confirms the absolute truth of its fundamental principles. In turn, these are used as elements of demonstration: they give to the development and conclusion of a proof the necessity and the coherence which characterize the deductive sciences and make possible our knowledge in general.

---

[20] *Theaetetus* 189C-190.
[21] *An. Post.* 72ᵃ 30 *sq.*

CHAPTER 24

Plato and Aristotle

The progress of mathematics in the fourth century B.C. prompted attempts to organize its various fields and incorporate its principles in a wider philosophical synthesis. The alternative methods of arithmetic and geometry for the solution of problems called for a rationalization of the intimate relations between these 2 sciences. Emerging from the realm of the discontinuous, where it was enshrined by the Pythagoreans, the Platonic conception of number used more consciously the implications of its early fusion with spatial intuition in order to express the continuous character of geometrical notions. This mathematical synthesis was encouraged by the systematization of the theory of irrationals, the establishment of the doctrine of loci requiring the manipulation of various types of functions, and the elaboration of methods involving the infinite. The variety of the technical expressions of spatial intuition and the methodological application of the infinite allowed number to assume a more universal significance. The elaboration of the Platonic doctrines corresponds to this synthetic development of mathematics.

If this movement had developed further without hindrance,

Greek science and philosophy might have taken a different turn. The successful development of Plato's basic intuition might have given to mathematics a formal flexibility and an independence of sense perception which became essential in the later formulation of the concepts and methods of the calculus. Moreover, his creative cosmogony, with its insistence on mathematical relations, might have inspired the gradual establishment of a mathematical physics of an idealist type. That is why several modern commentators believe that recent views on the relations among logic, mathematics, and physics are foreshadowed in the Platonic doctrines.

In many cases, such enthusiastic opinions are coupled with adverse criticism against Aristotle, who is accused of having blocked the way to the early development of the calculus, experimental science, and quantitative physics. It is also said that Aristotle remained outside the synthetic movement in mathematical theory which was taking place in his days. As he was not technically a mathematician, some blame him for having misunderstood the progress of the mathematical views of his contemporaries, and for having failed to estimate the value of their discoveries.[1] It is even asserted[2] that the authority of Aristotle held back for 2,000 years the fruition of Plato's conception to arithmetize mathematics.

In this connection, Whitehead writes that Plato and Pythagoras stand nearer to modern science than does Aristotle.

The two former were mathematicians, whereas Aristotle was the son of a doctor, though, of course, he was not thereby ignorant of mathematics. The practical counsel to be derived from Pythagoras is to measure and thus to express quality in terms of numerically determined quantity. The biological sciences, then and until our own time, have been overwhelmingly classificatory. Accordingly, Aristotle by his logic throws the emphasis on classification; and the

[1] A. Rey, *La Maturité de la Pensée Scientifique en Grèce* (Paris, 1939), pp. 332 and 335.
[2] Otto Toeplitz, "Das Verhältnis von Mathematik und Ideenlehre bei Plato," *Quellen-Bund Studien zur Geschichte der Mathematik*, Part B (1931), I, pp. 10-11.

popularity of Aristotelian logic retarded the advance of the physical sciences throughout the Middle Ages. If only the Schoolmen had measured instead of classifying, how much they might have learned![3]

Similar opinions are expressed by other scholars without a proper interpretation of the historical facts available. Thus we are told that Aristotle's "dead hand" held back the advance of physical knowledge because the prestige of his work "did much to turn Greek and Medieval science into a search for absolutely certain premises and into the premature use of deductive methods."[4] It is asserted that Aristotelian logic accounts for the neglect of experience and the stagnation of science for nearly 2,000 years because "the whole theory of science was so interpreted, and the whole of logic was so constructed, as to lead up to the ideal of demonstrative science, which in its turn rested on a false analogy which assimilated it to the dialectics of proof."[5] An identical judgment is given by Jeans when he says that "nearly two thousand years were to pass before the deductive methods of Aristotle were discarded in favor of inductive methods, and then progress became rapid indeed. In the meantime, the dead hand of Aristotle lay heavy on physics."[6] Shifting his remarks to a higher level, Whittaker boldly asserts that "it was impossible to extract a true metaphysics from the false Aristotelian physics. The evil was aggravated by the medieval schoolmen."[7]

Such summary pronouncements are unduly unfair to Aristotle, who cannot be responsible for the misuse others made of his works. His successors had before them both the doc-

[3] A. N. Whitehead, *Science and the Modern World* (New York, 1941), pp. 42-43.

[4] W. Dampier-Whetham, *A History of Science and Its Relations with Philosophy and Religion*, 3rd ed. (New York, 1943), p. 39.

[5] This is the opinion of F. C. S. Schiller; see *Studies in the History and Method of Science* (ed. C. Singer) (London, 1917), p. 240.

[6] Sir James Jeans, *The Growth of Physical Science* (Cambridge, 1946), p. 52.

[7] Sir Edmund Whittaker, *A History of the Theories of Aether and Electricity* (London, 1951), p. 2.

trines of the Academy and those of the Lyceum. No authority forced them to choose between them save their reason, their interests, and the technical circumstances of scientific research. To be sure, in order to prove that Aristotle was averse to the scientific developments implied in the Platonic conceptions, it is necessary to show first that Greek mathematics and physics were actually capable of developing technically in those directions; but this cannot be proved. Plato did not suggest any practical and immediate means for such developments, and neither the mathematical symbolism and techniques of the Greeks, nor their physical conceptions and means of observation, encouraged a mathematical treatment of the Platonic intuitions. On the contrary, Plato's successors and the neo-Platonists insisted more on the mystical aspect of his doctrines than on their scientific implications.

Furthermore, the elaboration of the theory of forms and numbers was far from being logically satisfactory. This is shown by the progress of the Aristotelian polemic against the Academy. Again, the mathematical construction of the concrete world suggested more fundamental problems than it was capable of solving. In addition, Plato not only failed to give conclusive answers to the difficulties involved in the Pythagorean discoveries and the Eleatic paradoxes, but he also allowed his thought to be colored by Pythagorean and Democritean influences, with their emphasis on sense perception. Moreover, his disregard for observation and experiment may be considered from a scientific viewpoint as an unmitigated misfortune, for many scientists still believe that mathematics becomes sterilized by losing contact with the world's work.

In these circumstances, Aristotle had a reasonable excuse for showing his opposition to the Academy. Of course, he would agree with Plato that both mathematics and science are the result of deductions from clearly perceived first principles, but he would insist that experience and induction provide much of their material. He would agree that the method of analytical regression had to be followed by a synthetic progression, but, instead of centering this process upon the world of ideas, he would direct it towards concrete reality and thus stress the parallelism between existence and thought. Finally, Aristotle would argue that the ultimate notions obtained by this double discursive method need not be mathematical in character, for quantity is only an aspect of being.

Consequently, Aristotle had to reject the Platonic view that there is no necessary distinction between mathematics and science, because he had shown that the study of numbers and figures does not unfold the essence of mind and nature and does not force its results on both. Just as any other branch of knowledge requiring universals, mathematics involves notions which are idealized properties of sensible objects. These notions have not a separate existence like the Platonic ideas, but they can be isolated by abstraction to provide the matter of mathematical demonstration.

For Aristotle, mathematics covers just one aspect of being, the category of quantity; as such, it loses the all-pervading character it assumes in the Platonic system. This reaction against Plato's teaching placed mathematics in its right place in the universe of knowledge. It opened new perspectives in mathematical philosophy by stressing the rational rigor of mathematics as against its development by dialectical or intuitive speculation. Even though mathematical invention does not follow any rigid succession of particular rules, the rational value of its results can be estimated only by their integration in a deductive system.

Moreover, the Aristotelian doctrine of the structural character of demonstrative science and the empirical background of its elements preserved in Greek mathematics a reasonable and factual cast. This characterizes the work of Euclid in particular and of the mathematicians of the Hellenistic period in general. Although many of these scientists do show traces of Platonic influences, they used the Organon extensively in their research. And though this gave a practically static character to Greek mathematics, the Aristotelian view of science is far from being simply outdated. Of course it contrasts with the spirit of the calculus and modern analysis, which display a dynamic character with their attempt to rationalize change by describing it arithmetically. However, some trends in mathematical theory seem to revive the Aristotelian dualism between number and the logical factors of science, as well as the subordination of arithmetic to the qualitative requirements of science. This is particularly the case with the axiomatic development of projective geometry, the theory of groups, the topological systems, the elaboration of abstract algebras, and the dependence of quantum mechanics on the physical magnitudes of the empirical systems investigated.

In this respect, Weyl asserts that

> Western mathematics has followed less the Greek conceptions than ideas we inherited from India through the Arabs, by asserting the logical priority of number over geometry. Mathematicians have investigated the various types of magnitudes with the help of one and the same universal concept of number, elaborated in abstract fashion independently of any eventual application. It may be said, however, that we are now witnessing in mathematics a complete reversal of this perspective. It seems to us that, in the last resort, the more profound view of mathematics is the Greek conception, according to which every domain requires a specific and characteristic system of number.[8]

The critical analysis of quantum mechanics and of the intuitionist school of mathematics would thus show a direct filiation between the ontological and "naive" realism of Aristotle and the more recent theories or controversies about the nature and value of mathematics.

Turning to Aristotle's influence on the development of natural science, his distinction between mathematics and physics in a general sense involves a wider criterion of reality and truth than the one required by the Platonic cosmology. This criterion is not reasonableness in thought exclusively, but also consistency in experience. Hence, it would be unfair to suggest that the Aristotelian methodology hampered the

---

[8] H. Weyl, *Philosophy of Mathematics and Natural Science* (Princeton, N. J., 1940), p. 36.

progress of the physical sciences. Syllogistic logic as such is seldom used in experimental research, where the main objective is discovery and not final proof. Aristotle did not consider the syllogism as the essential method of discovery; on the contrary, his later works especially insisted on the valuable information provided by the use of strict observation and experiment. Surely, he cannot be blamed if his later followers neglected to take his advice. For that matter, it is fortunate that the natural sciences now agree with Aristotle's insistence upon experimentation rather than with Plato's disregard for empirical methods. The history of science might have taken a different turn if Aristotle's successors had used more universally his method of experimentation rather than his syllogistics and his *Physics,* which exhibited more Platonic influences in structure and outlook.

With regard to the alternative ways proposed by Plato and Aristotle for the unification of knowledge, either alternative was possible due to the Socratic conceptualism to which both Plato and Aristotle remained faithful. Plato tended to unify knowledge by extensive arithmetization at the expense of the claims of the concrete world and the apparent irrationality of change. Equally respectful of the requirements of thought and the empirical characteristics of actual existence, Aristotle sought the elements of this rational integration beyond the ontological results of the Platonic dialectic.

These essentially formal elements are centered upon the notion of class, which was used in Plato's rational doctrines and which gained more emphasis in Aristotle's biological and linguistic disquisitions. By taking as fundamental the notion of class instead of the idea of relation, which is more prominent in the Platonic system, Aristotle ordered the objects of knowledge according to an ontological hierarchy of genus and species. If this basic notion were to be enshrined in any classification of all living organisms and in all current linguistic expressions, the establishment of a science of pure thought needed further the structural support of a system of relations involving necessity.

The establishment of a universal Organon and of an ontology independent of mathematical requirements enabled Aristotle to account for the parallelism of thought and being, and also to outline the development of our knowledge without giving primacy to mathematics. To be sure, the Aristotelian logic does not cover explicitly all the problems of the science of thought, but it contains some of the basic intuitions which justify many of the remarkable developments now obtained by the combined efforts of philosophers, logicians, and mathematicians.

These fundamental intuitions may ultimately condition the solution of the difficulties offered by logic and mathematics, and facilitate the application of these formal techniques to the study of nature and other human interests. By making logic the methodological technique of thought, Aristotle was able to differentiate the various sciences; henceforth the conditions of their development and validation were to be found in logic alone. The scepter of the human intellect thus passed from mathematics to logic, which keeps it unchallenged. With Aristotle, philosophy became basically logical, and it retains that character even in the modern systems of mathematical philosophy.

Part IV

THE EUCLIDIAN SYNTHESIS

The philosophical and technical interpretation of Greek mathematics is dominated by the opposite views of Plato and Aristotle, which influenced even modern mathematical philosophy. Briefly, Plato teaches that mathematical objects are intermediate between the ideas and the sensible world. As such, they reflect the eternal relations of their own ideas and are separate from the external world; they are discovered and not invented; they are expressed in assertorical and not in problematical propositions. Aristotle also thinks that mathematical objects are intermediate between being and the sensible world, but they cannot be deduced from the analysis of being and have no separate existence. Indeed, they are abstracted from the sensible world, which accounts for their being applicable to it. Hence, Plato accounts mathematically and Aristotle logically for the rational character of the world.

These doctrines have influenced most Greek thinkers in one way or another. Is it possible to determine which conception is paramount in the work of Euclid the mathematician? The problem is made difficult by the absence of any direct information from Euclid himself, and also by the cosmopolitan and eclectic character of the intellectual climate of Alexandria, where Euclid lived. While scholars grant that the author of the *Elements* has widely used in his work the Aristotelian theory of demonstration, most of them would insist that his ultimate vision was Platonic in intention. For our part, the Euclidian systematization of mathematics is an application of the rational theories of both the Academy and the Lyceum, and the Aristotelian trends in Euclid are stronger than any others. This discussion must be prefaced with an account of the Alexandrian atmosphere and of the work Euclid left to posterity.

The conquest of Egypt by Alexander in 332 B.C. had important consequences for the development of learning. While Athens still remained the seat of literary interests and speculative philosophy, Alexandria became the dynamic center of scientific pursuits and the technical arts. Owing to its geographical remoteness and the political rivalry between Rome and Carthage, the Nile Delta was less open to an effective external pressure than Sicily or Greece itself. The death of Alexander in 323 B.C. and the wisdom and might of the Diadochs gradually robbed Athens of its political preponderance. Founded at a point where East meets West, Alexandria soon rose to the status of a great intellectual and commercial metropolis.

With their broad cultural horizon widened by the victorious expedition of the Macedonian conqueror, the Alexandrians came into contact with the esoteric as well as the empirical doctrines of the Persians, the Babylonians, the Assyrians, and the Phoenicians. Moreover, they had at their very door the ancient and complex knowledge of the Egyptian priests, who had been the first masters of the Greeks and who still had many things to teach in spite of their declining influence. The fusion of the Hellenic and Eastern civilizations made Alexandrian thought more cosmopolitan, but also more specialized and mystical.

On the other hand, these circumstances favored frequent exchanges between Greece and Egypt. The great philosophical schools of Athens had already given their best to the world: Platonists, Peripatetics, Stoics, Epicureans, Sophists, and Sceptics could cross over the eastern Mediterranean and widen the circle of their disciples. Yet the attraction of so many different and contradictory doctrines was tempered by the mystical interests and practical minds of the Alexandrians themselves. It is obvious that these mutual influences gave a great stimulus to intellectual pursuits which could not be ignored by the leaders of the country.

Learning was greatly encouraged by the Greek rulers of Egypt, especially by Ptolemy II Philadelphus (crowned in 285 B.C.) and his wife Arsinoe. The Ptolemics were responsible for the foundation and maintenance of the Museum and the Library, which were housed in the royal citadel. In these famous scientific institutions, eminent thinkers, scientists, engineers, alchemists, and physicians were able to carry out research and experiments, while the wise discussed philosophy and religious speculations. They imparted their knowledge to the younger men who flocked around them and then brought learning to distant cities and countries, without losing contact with their Alexandrian masters.

During that period, science learned to stand on its own merits and to develop remarkable, specialized inventions. Mathematics and astronomy were graced with the discoveries of such famous men as Euclid, Archimedes, Appolonius, Aristarchus, Erastosthenes, and Hipparchus. If the natural sciences did not produce any worthy succesors to Aristotle, the experimental genius of the Alexandrians manifested itself in the more practical sciences of engineering, alchemy, and medicine. Philosophy, however, turned its back to science and became more speculative, ethical, and religious. It lost its universal character and encouraged objective compilations of past systems, instead of constructive syntheses based on the new scientific knowledge of the time.

This situation did not seem to encourage the growth of a mathematical philosophy comparable to that of the Hellenic period. To be sure, neo-Pythagoreanism and neo-Platonism used numbers as an integral part of their structure, but the numerological aspect of these systems was less scientific than mystical in character. On the other hand, the connection of the Alexandrian mathematicians with philosophy had not a metaphysical, but a marked methodological, value. These trends are illustrated in the decisive work of Euclid the mathematician.

CHAPTER 25

Euclid and the Elements

The life and personality of Euclid have so far remained shrouded in mystery. Our scanty information about him comes from casual remarks of later commentators. Most of the mathematicians who could have taught Euclid were pupils of Plato, and it is presumed they gave him a scientific training in Athens at the Academy. It must not be forgotten, however, that the Lyceum also existed at that time, and the influence of Aristotle was felt throughout the Greek world. So if Euclid had been trained at the Academy at all, he must have been familiar with the current discussions, the textbooks used at the Lyceum, and especially the Organon, which gave to all thinkers a formal instrument of investigation and proof.

Although practically nothing is known of the early life of Euclid, there is evidence that he flourished in Alexandria during the reign of the first Ptolemy (306-283 B.C.) because he is mentioned by Archimedes, who was born just before the end of Ptolemy Soter's reign. He is even credited with the founding of a school in Alexandria where, according to Pappus, Apollonius of Perga "spent a long time with the pupils of

Euclid."[1] Such a school was unnecessary in Alexandria which possessed scientific institutions under royal patronage, and it is difficult to see, in these circumstances, how a mathematical school could survive Euclid by 2 generations. It is more reasonable to think that Euclid taught mathematics at the Museum in Alexandria, where he formed many disciples. This view justifies more readily the statement that Apollonius spent a long time in Alexandria with the pupils of Euclid, and the story of Euclid's reply to Ptolemy that there is no royal road in geometry.

An incident reported by Stobaeus shows the high conception Euclid had of mathematics. A pupil who has just learned the first propositions of geometry asked what he would get by that knowledge, whereupon Euclid bade his servant give the pupil a piece of money "since he must make gain out of what he learns." There is also the testimony of Pappus, who praised Euclid for his modesty and his fairness to other mathematicians, quoting the case of Aristaeus, to whom Euclid gave credit for his discoveries on conics without attempting to appropriate his methods.

The *Summary* of Proclus contains practically all we know about Euclid, although his remarks seem to be based upon influence rather than direct evidence. We are told that Euclid wrote several works on pure and on applied mathematics; those which can be attributed to him definitely are the *Elements,* the *Data,* the book on *Divisions,* and 2 treatises on *Phenomena* and *Optics,* dealing with applied mathematics. Many other works are unfortunately lost, among them the *Porisms,* the *Plane Loci,* the *Conics,* and the *Pseudaria* on fallacious solutions, while some others under his name are not his own compositions.

With regard to the minor works of Euclid, the *Data* developed some details of the subject matter of Books I-IV of the *Elements,* with special reference to the construction of plane figures by means of some given elements. An example of the

1 Thomas L. Heath, *A Manual of Greek Mathematics* (Oxford, 1931), p. 203.

alternative methods used here is the solution of the simultaneous equations $y \pm x = a$ and $xy = b^2$, which is another form
of the solution of the quadratic equation $ax \pm x^2 = b^2$ given
in the *Elements* (II.5,6). The initial definitions of the various
meanings of the word *given* proposed by Euclid in the *Data*
are among the interesting features of the work: straight lines,
angles, areas, and ratios are *given in magnitude* when we can
find others equal to them. Rectilineal figures are *given in
species* when their angles are severally known, and also the
ratios of the sides to one another. Points, lines, and angles are
given in position when they always occupy the same place. The
main purpose of the *Data* is obviously to help shorten the
analytical processes which are preliminary to a problem proof.
When we know that certain elements of a figure are given and
that other parts or relations are also given by implication, it
is often superfluous to determine that figure by an actual
operation. The book *On Divisions* corresponds to the description of the original work given by Proclus in his *Commentary*. The general purpose of the propositions given in strict
logical order, but often without proof, is the division of plane
figures by transversals or parallels into parts having equal or
proportional areas.[2]

Of the 2 treatises dealing with applied mathematics, the
Phenomena develops the geometry of the sphere according to
the requirements of observational geometry. It contains the
definition of the horizon, which is given for the first time as a
single technical word: "Let the name *horizon* be given to the
plane through us passing through the universe and separating
off the hemisphere visible above the earth." The *Optics* deals
with problems of perspective, explaining how figures look
from different points of view or at different distances, as compared with what they are. Heath believes that this book may
have been intended as "a corrective of heterodox ideas such

[2] This treatise was edited in 1915 by R. C. Archibald on the basis of
the original text in Arabic discovered in 1851 by Woepke, and of Fibo-
nacci's *Practica Geometriae* dealing with the division of figures, which is
supposed to have been written with the help of Euclid's work.

as those of the Epicureans who maintained that the heavenly bodies are of the size they look."[3] Like the *Elements,* the *Optics* opens with a series of definitions concerning the fundamental concepts of light and vision, and it proves a succession of propositions in strict deductive order.

Turning to the *Elements,* the presentation of its 13 books is direct and strict, as befits a school text. Without any apologetical introduction or directional principles, the first book opens bluntly with 23 definitions relating to such fundamental concepts as point, line, surface, volume, circle, angle, and figure. Without any comment, we are then given 5 postulates referring to the construction of straight lines and circles, and 5 original axioms or common notions which constitute the basis of geometrical reasoning. The difference between these types of statements is given by their content and not by any explanations. Among the postulates are the 2 famous properties of the straight line: 2 straight lines cannot enclose a space, and 2 straight lines in a plane will meet when produced, if a third line cuts them so as to form on the same side 2 interior angles together less than 2 right angles. The postulate requesting the equality of all right angles is equivalent to the principle of the invariability of figures which makes congruence possible. The axioms are statements about the equality and inequality of magnitudes.

The actual wording of these definitions, postulates, and axioms is not always necessarily that of Euclid. There have been so many transcriptions and editions of the *Elements* that scholars and copyists must have tried minor improvements in rephrasing, substitutions, and insertions. From the earliest times, however, the Euclidian straight line has been characterized by 2 postulates like those given above. Euclid's sagacity in this matter is illustrated by the failure of subsequent mathematicians to prove either of them.[4] These opening definitions

---

3 Heath, *Manual of Greek Mathematics,* p. 267.

4 The failure of all such attempts led later to the discovery of new systems of geometry and to endless logical controversies. For an attempt to solve some of these difficulties see Thomas Greenwood, *Essais sur la Pensée Géométrique* (Ottawa, 1943), for a new system of Euclidian axiomatics involving a rearrangement of the basic Euclidian intuitions.

and hypotheses are followed in the text by propositions about triangles and the mutual relations of their component parts, the first one referring to the construction of an equilateral triangle. These initial propositions prove the properties of vertically opposite angles, adjacent angles, perpendiculars, and congruent triangles. The theory of parallels requires the relevant postulate given above, and leads to the theorem that the interior angles of a triangle are together equal to 2 right angles. We come then to the areas of parallelograms, triangles, and squares, including some cases of the Pythagorean *method of applying areas.* The book ends with the famous proof (and its converse) of the relation between the square of the sides of a right-angled triangle and the square of its hypotenuse, a relation discovered, according to tradition, by Pythagoras.

The second book proceeds with the theory of the transformation of areas and proves the equality of sums of rectangles and squares to other such sums. It introduces the use of the *gnomon* for the solution of numerical problems, and the initial theorems of the geometrical *algebra* with which the Greeks solved elementary algebraic equations by means of geometrical processes and proof exclusively. Just as Book I concludes with the Pythagorean theorem of the square of the hypotenuse, so Book II leads to a generalization of the theorem for any triangle with sides a, b, c, proving the equivalent of the modern formula $a^2 = b^2 + c^2 - 2bc \cos A$ by geometrical means.

Books III and IV develop the geometry of the circle. The first begins with the definitions of equal circles, tangent, chord, segment, sector, similar segments, angle in a segment, and the archaic notion of the "angle of a segment," referring to the mixed angle made by the circle with the chord at either end of the segment. Then it proves propositions dealing with the form of a circle, intersecting circles, and tangent properties, and finishes with the beautiful demonstration of the constant value of the product of the 2 rectilinear segments $OM \cdot ON$ of a straight line, cutting a circle at any 2 points M and N and passing through any point O internal or external. Book IV

proceeds to the inscribed and circumscribed polygons con-
structible with straight line and circle, the most important
being the regular pentagon sacred to the Pythagoreans and the
regular 15-sided polygon used in astronomy.

The general theory of proportion expounded in Books V
and VI is applied to commensurable and incommensurable
magnitudes according to the Eudoxian method. A ratio is considered as a relation of size between 2 finite magnitudes of
the same kind. Book V introduces infinite magnitudes and
defines quantities in the *same ratio* or in *greater ratio,* as well
as the transformation of ratios by alternation, invèrsion, composition, separation, and conversion. It proceeds to numerical
multiples and equimultiples, and it proves the validity of the
transformation of one proportion into another. Applying in
Book VI this general theory of proportion to plane geometry,
Euclid proves the fundamental proposition that 2 sides of a
triangle cut by a third side are divided proportionally; he
shows its various consequences in the construction of proportionals and in the similarity of triangles, and finally uses the
Pythagorean theory of application of areas in its most general
form, with results equivalent to the geometrical solution of a
quadratic equation having a real and positive root. The sixth
book concludes with a remarkable generalization of the
theorem of the square of the hypotenuse, showing that proposition to be true not only of squares, but also of 3 similar plane
figures described upon the 3 sides of the right-angled triangle
and similarly situated with reference to the sides.

Books VII, VIII, and IX deal mainly with the nature and
properties of rational numbers, represented throughout by
straight lines and not by numerical signs. Following the traditional conception of the Pythagoreans, Book VII begins with
the definitions of unit, number, and the varieties of number,
including plane, solid, and perfect numbers; it then demonstrates some elementary properties and operations referring to
various kinds of numbers. Books VIII and IX relate to numbers in continued proportion (geometrical progression); the
latter proves that a number can be resolved into prime factors

in one way only, that the class of prime number is infinite, and other important propositions.

As the most finished of the whole work, Book X deals with *irrationals* understood as straight lines incommensurable with any straight line assumed as rational. It begins with this famous postulate on continuity used in the method of exhaustion, which was completed later by Archimedes and known under his name: if from any magnitude there be subtracted its half or more, from the remainder again its half or more, and so on continually, there will remain a magnitude less than any given magnitude of the same kind. The theory of irrationals was initiated and expanded by Theaetetus. According to Pappus, we owe to Euclid the precise definition, classification, and exposition of rational and irrational magnitudes. The elaborate array of definitions and proofs given in Book X must be due to the absence of a formal algebra at the time. A straight line represented all operations dealing with the solution of equations and the discussion of their roots, but, as all straight lines look alike, a detailed classification of linear definitions was necessary to cover all the operational distinctions required by the subject. The methodological contributions of Euclid to the systematic treatment of irrationals are numerous and elaborate; they are used in Book XIII for the complete determination of the regular polyhedra.

Solid geometry is treated in Books XI, XII, and XIII less systematically than plane geometry. In some proofs, Euclid allows himself more abrupt leaps, and the distinction between congruence and symmetry is not always clear; but this was the first attempt to organize solid geometry into an exact system. The required definitions are given in Book XI, where the order of propositions is very similar to that of the first 6 books. After proving a series of properties of straight lines and planes in space, it deals with parallelipipedal solids. The *method of exhaustion* is the core of Book XII, and serves to determine areas of circles and volumes of solids, as well as various proportions between their elements. This method was invented by Eudoxus (*ca.* 408-355 B.C.) in answer to Zeno's dilemma about the infinitely small. It showed that the mathematician does not require such an infinite actually, but only the possibility of arriving at a magnitude as small as he pleases by continual division. This Greek version of the modern method of limits evaluated a magnitude by calculating others close to it by defect or excess, and by using a reductio ad absurdum to eliminate the unwanted alternatives. The last Book, XIII, concerns the construction of the 5 regular solids (tetrahedron, cube, octahedron, dodecahedron, and icosahedron) and the determination of a circumscribing sphere. Some preliminary propositions have to be proved before determining the sides and angles of the polyhedra, and the relations of those sides with the radius of the circumscribed sphere.

This is the pattern and content of the *Elements* as Euclid put them together. With the exception of some original proofs and some new theorems, it adds little to previous knowledge. Whereas all pre-Euclidian mathematicians allowed their works to be weakened by deficiencies in method and content, Euclid is highly praised for his synthetic genius, logical rigor, and perfection of form, which make of the *Elements* the greatest elementary textbook in geometry of all time. Before Euclid, mathematicians had expounded many remarkable results either in special treatises covering specific fields, or in systematic collections, such as those of Hippocrates of Chios (*ca.* 470 B.C.), Leon (*ca.* 400 B.C.), and Theudius of Magnesia (*ca.* 370 B.C.), which were used as textbooks. The special treatises give an orderly exposition of investigations about definite mathematical problems. The systematic collections stress some leading propositions related to those which follow as general principles by which many properties could be proved. Such theorems were called *elements* because their function resembles that of an alphabet in relation to language. In this sense, Theudius "put together the elements admirably, making many partial propositions more general," and Hermotimus of Colophon "discovered many of the elements,"[5] as was also said later of Euclid.

The mathematical discoveries and methods of the fifth and

---

[5] Proclus *Commentary on the First Book of Euclid*, p. 67 (ed. Friedlein).

fourth centuries had outgrown the early rudimentary school texts. Further progress required a well-organized inventory of the available material, including the Eudoxian theory of proportion. This was the task of Euclid. "In putting the *elements* together, he collected many theorems of Eudoxus, improved many propositions of Theaetetus, and gave an irrefragable demonstration of statements loosely proved by his predecessors."[6] These investigations required the rearrangement of the books in the earlier texts, the redistribution of propositions, and the invention of proofs suitable to the new order of exposition. This successful effort was considered so important that Euclid is still known as the "Author of the *Elements*," as Archimedes called him.

The test of Euclid's achievement would be to compare his work with proofs given by his predecessors. In the absence of any earlier manuals, one of the best sources is Aristotle himself, for his frequent mathematical illustrations must have been taken from textbooks then in use. The comparison of corresponding statements in Aristotle and Euclid reveals the changes made by Euclid in the earlier methods. For example, as Aristotle uses Plato's definition of the straight line, this may prove that Euclid's correlative definitions of the straight line and plane are his own. With regard to Aristotle's remark about the theory of parallels involving a vicious circle,[7] Euclid seems to be the first to have solved this difficulty by formulating the famous postulate upon which he based his own system. As Aristotle gives no examples of geometrical or mechanical postulates, one may safely presume that the classical postulates relating to the straight line, the right angle, the parallels, and the construction of lines and circles have been established by Euclid himself, just as the mechanical postulates given by Archimedes at the beginning of his book *On Plane Equilibrium* should be considered as his own. These and similar examples from the works of Euclid reveal a paramount methodological concern which offers much scope to the philosophical critic of the Euclidian method and its metaphysical grounds.

6 *Ibid.*, p. 68.
7 *An. Post.* 65ᵃ 5.

CHAPTER 26

Implications of
the Euclidian Method

As a mathematician, Euclid is careful to remain within the realm of the exact sciences. Perhaps he never thought of making any philosophical statements about them. His works make no allusion to Plato or Aristotle, or even to their strictly methodological views. Yet these are enshrined in the very method of presentation of Euclid's works, especially the *Elements* to which we shall restrict our interpretative discussion.

The Euclidian method of *irrefragable demonstration* is an elaboration of the principles which both *Analytics* discuss at length. The *Prior Analytics* requires that no proposition be admitted in a system without showing its logical connection with earlier propositions already granted. Although Plato also mentioned this rule of rational necessity, he used it specifically to enable the mind to reach the ultimate elements of the Ideas through an analytical regression. For Aristotle, this rule merely served to ground the deductive process on a few initial principles stated and granted without further regression. Their types are specified in the *Posterior Analytics*[1] as definitions,

1 *An. Post.* 74b 5-77a 30.

postulates, and common notions or axioms. Euclid follows exactly this pattern in the *Elements,* which offers a systematic arrangement of geometry based on such assumed elements.

Without stating explicitly these Aristotelian rules and distinctions, Euclid abruptly begins the first book of the *Elements* with his famous definition of a point as that which has no parts. All other definitions are also given without discussion and whenever needed, usually at the beginning of a theory. This practice implies the Aristotelian view[2] that mathematical definitions are separated from existence. As such, they assert nothing about the existence or non-existence of the thing defined; they are simply answers to the question, "What is a given thing?" and do not involve existence.

Aristotle maintains further,[3] that existence is neither an essence, a genus, nor a quality. Hence the existence of a thing must be assumed or proved. It is assumed[4] when we have a clear intuition of the *what* a thing is. It is proved[5] when we show in addition the *why* it is by means of a construction. As Aristotle says, this is particularly the case in geometry, where only points and lines must be assumed to exist, while the other notions must be proved to exist through some specific additions or constructions to the mechanism of proof. This is precisely the Euclidian standpoint: the definitions given in the *Elements* are merely asserted or proved, without giving any indication as to the nature of the objects defined.

This hypothetico-deductive conception of geometry is not Platonic, for the objects expressed by the definitions are not presented in any way as reflections of ideal and eternal paradigms. Furthermore, if Euclid were a Platonist, he should have carried the process of analytic regression beyond the very notions he takes as primitive, in order to discover how the ultimate principles of the One and the Dyad required by his own system can account for points and lines and other figures. He does not go beyond points and lines at the beginning of

2 *An. Post.* 92b 12.
3 *An. Post.* 92b 14.
4 *An. Post.* 76b *sq.*
5 *An. Post.* 90b 28.

his system, although the *Elements* has much to say later about numbers. Obviously, this presentation is closer to the Aristotelian view that such notions result from abstraction applied to bodies of our ordinary experience. It is not the contemplation of the Ideas, but the usual data of the material world which gave Euclid the basic notions of geometry by a constructive abstraction, and which justify in turn their application to the physical world.

Even the biological categories of the Stagirite are involved in Euclid's definitions, where the use of the Aristotelian class concept is indeed more obvious than the use of the Platonic relation concept. Although many of Plato's geometrical definitions have an experimental origin, for him experience comes *after* the contemplation of Ideas; for Aristotle experience comes *before* the conception of abstract notions. Nothing in Euclid's *Elements* encourages the belief that the various geometrical objects assumed, constructed, or analyzed are reflections of similar substantial Ideas.

With regard to the definitions the existence of which is proved, Euclid again follows the Aristotelian directives. The assimilation of the essence of a thing with its formal cause accounts for the transition from the subjective assumption of a basic geometrical notion to its objective proof, for the constructive process involved in such a proof postulates the Aristotelian principle[6] that the knowledge of what an object or a thing is presupposes the knowledge that it is. In other words, the definition of a notion is incomplete until it is made genetic, for it is the producing cause which reveals the essence of the notion. Where existence is proved by construction, the cause and the effect appear together. In accordance with these views and earlier practices, Euclid assumes the possibility of constructing straight lines and circles in the first 3 postulates. The other notions are defined and then constructed, as for example the equilateral triangle (Bk. I, Def. 20, p. 1), the right angle (Bk. I, Def. 10, p. 11), the square (Bk. I, Def. 22, p.

6 *An. Post.* 92b 25-93a 20.

46), and the parallels (Bk. I, Def. 23, pp. 27-29). The difficulty of constructing all geometrical notions with the original Euclidian assumptions is not discussed by the author of the *Elements,* although it was probably known to earlier, and certainly to later, mathematicians.

As regards the characteristics or conditions of a correct definition, Aristotle states that: *a*) the different attributes of a definition taken together must cover exactly the notion defined; and *b*) the different attributes of a definition taken separately must refer to the thing better known or logically prior to the notion defined.[7] Thus Euclid defines a square (Bk. I, Def. 22) by means of the notions of figures, 4-sided, equilateral, and right-angled. Each of these definitions was less specific, better known, or logically preceded the term defined, and when taken together they covered exactly the notion of square. Definitions breaking either of these rules are unscientific; for example, when a notion is defined by its opposite, or a coordinate species, or a synonym, all of which are coextensive with the notion to be defined. There are several examples of such questionable definitions in Euclid: when the straight line is defined as "lying evenly with the points on itself," the expression "lying evenly" can be understood only through the very notion to be defined.

It is significant that Euclid never states a primitive notion without defining it, although such a practice is current today as a requirement of logical rigor. He does not merely assume points, lines, and surfaces; he also defines them by using intuitive notions which are not justified within the system. In doing so, Euclid improved the definitions of his predecessors only in appearance. Before him, Aristotle had criticized the definitions of a point as the extremity of a line, a line as the extremity of a surface, and a surface as the extremity of a solid, by saying they all define the prior by means of the posterior.[8] Nevertheless, Euclid must have felt that his initial definitions did not fulfill all the requirements laid down by

[7] *Topica* (vi.4) 141ᵃ 26 *sq.*
[8] *Topica* (vi.4) 141ᵇ 20.

Aristotle, for he supplemented them with the very statements Aristotle had criticized. Hence we are told (Bk. I, Def. 3) that the extremities of a line are points, that (Bk. I, Def. 6) the extremities of a surface are lines, and that (Bk. XI, Def. 20) the extremities of a solid are surfaces. Yet these supplementary statements help to understand better the Euclidian definitions, for we must consider first a solid, which is more closely related to the bodies of our experience, in order to understand correctly the definition of a solid, a surface, a line, and a point as results of successive abstractions. Similar remarks are suggested by most Euclidian definitions, including those given of geometrical notions involving a construction.

The question of geometrical constructions leads to the discussion of the hypotheses of geometry, and involves a major distinction between Plato's and Aristotle's conception of science. According to both, geometrical constructions are made logically possible and mathematically useful by the hypotheses of geometry, which are of 2 kinds: the *postulates* and the *axioms*.[9] The first are more particular to geometry, as they beg specific properties of the straight line based on some idealized intuition or generalization, and are used for subsequent constructions and logical deductions. The second assert general relations of equality and inequality between magnitudes applicable to figures, and provide an element of necessity in the process of demonstration. Euclid gives a set of propositions for each kind which he uses without discussing their logical character, but his classification of these statements reflects the Aristotelian distinction between axioms, which are self-evident, and postulates, which are not necessary but merely

---

[9] The term *axiom* used by Aristotle seems to come from the Pythagoreans, while the term *common notions* seems to be due to Democritus (cf. *Sextus,* ap. Diels, *Vors.,* A.111), who is also credited with a work on the *elements* according to titles given by Thrasyllus (cf. Diels, *Vors.,* B.11, n-p). In his *Commentary on Euclid* (p. 194), Proclus alludes to the habit of later mathematicians calling *common notions* what Aristotle defined as *axioms,* these terms being henceforth equivalent. But Aristotle also refers to the axioms as common opinions (cf. *Met.* 996b 26-30 and 997b 20), implying that such statements are required by common sense.

accidental. Furthermore, the remarks of Proclus about axioms
and postulates indicate that the Greeks were conversant with
the logical and practical technicalities involved in their
distinction.

The significance and the use of geometrical hypotheses are
heavy with philosophical implications. The argument already
mentioned concerning the Euclidian definitions could be re-
peated here: if the geometrical hypotheses reflect properties of
the Ideas, a true Platonist should have tried to justify them
by analytic regression in terms of more ultimate Platonic
principles. Furthermore, if postulates express true properties
of the relevant ideal figures, they should be stated assertorically.
Euclid proposes them as requests which are not intuitively
clear and necessary, hence their ontological weakness and
strictly hypothetical character. Finally, postulates are used
mainly to solve problems and justify constructions, but a
problem involves a request and a construction involves change,
while eternal truths are changeless and assertorical. If Euclid
were a Platonist, he should have given a different expression
to his postulates and he should have avoided the distinction
between *theorems* and *problems*, which is a fundamental feature of his method, in order to make all his statements assertorical. The weight of these difficulties induced Platonists to
explain them away with psychological arguments.[10] The fact
remains, however, that Euclid has not built the foundations
of the *Elements* according to a thorough Platonic pattern.

To be sure, the Euclidian method follows a middle course
between the Platonic conceptions expressed by Speusippus and
the pragmatic suggestions of the disciples of Menaechmus, who
invented the conics. Speusippus proposed that all mathematical
truths should be expressed as theorems, insofar as they reflect
unchangeable and uncreated relations; the practical mathematicians who followed Menaechmus maintained that all
mathematical statements should be considered as problems,
insofar as they deal with constructions and with analyses of

[10] Cf. A. Rey, *L'Apogée de la Science Technique Grècque* (Paris, 1948),
pp. 163-194.

mathematical objects. Euclid thought rightly that some mathematical propositions are straight deductions from previous ones, while others involve constructions. In choosing to distinguish between them, he follows the Aristotelian conceptions which insist on the psychological priority of experience and on the existential priority of individual objects. Indeed, the hypothetical character of the postulates and the zetetic expression of the problems entail an Aristotelian vision of the mathematical truths they assert, insofar as they point to an idealization of sense experience rather than to a repetition of preconceived realities or necessary relations.

These ontological and epistemological implications of the presentation of the *Elements* do not affect their strictly logical structure. As both Plato and Aristotle insist on the rational necessity of the deductive stages in mathematical reasoning, Euclid need not be considered as an Aristotelian simply because he uses basically the Organon in his work. It is interesting to note the structural refinements Euclid added to syllogistic practice in order to strengthen the binding character of a mathematical deduction. The elements of steps necessary to the proof of each theorem, lemma, corollary, and problem[11] are connected logically with prior statements already proved or accepted legitimately, so that one can reason backwards until one reaches the basic a priori data of the system. This analytic regression is made rigorous by the technical elimination of intuition in the detailed expression of each connecting link within and between the statements which together make up the science of geometry.

The Euclidian pattern of demonstration requires 3 fundamental steps: the enunciation, the proof, and the conclusion. These are expanded into 6 for greater clarity: (1) the *protasis* or enunciation of the proposition in general terms; (2) the *ecthesis* or specification of the particular data indicated by

11 The meaning of *theorems* and *problems* has been discussed previously. A *lemma* is an auxiliary proposition required in a demonstration without being essential in the general exposition of a theory. A *corollary* is the statement of a consequence of a particular demonstration which is not necessary for subsequent propositions. The functional distinction of these 4 types of statements scarcely favors a Platonic view of geometry.

letters with which the demonstration will be developed; (3) the *diorismos* or statement of the conditions of possibility of what is required to be proved or done in terms of the particular data, which is sometimes followed by a discussion of the limits of the proof; (4) the *kataskeve* or construction of additional elements to the original figure needed in the demonstration; (5) the *apodeixis* or proof, which draws the truth of the enunciation from the various data given or constructed with the help of previous propositions, hypotheses, and definitions; and (6) the *symperasma* or conclusion affirming that the original statement satisfies the conditions of proof.

The rational process of demonstration is *direct* by synthesis or analysis, and *indirect* by reduction or exhaustion. Synthetic reasoning explicitates the pattern of demonstration just outlined and confirms the successive logical connection of the mathematical truths. It corresponds to the objective and permanent organization of mathematics, whereas the psychological processes of invention are different. The synthetic method is the most direct in allowing the conclusion to be drawn immediately from the data and the eventual constructions, and also in exhibiting the strict rational order of truths, which is the goal of systematic knowledge. This need not mean that these truths reflect a world of substantial ideas, or that Euclid had this conception in mind in choosing a synthetic pattern of exposition, for the synthetic process is just as effective and fundamental in the hypothetico-deductive view of mathematics, which corresponds more closely to the Aristotelian tradition.

The analytic proof is a partial application of the general process of analysis, which allows one to assert the truth of a statement by a logical regression to the fundamental definitions and hypotheses. It requires 2 steps: the first is the *transformation*, which assumes the truth of the proposed theorem or problem, analyzes the particular conditions of its proof, and then shows how these conditions are provided legitimately for a direct demonstration of the original statement. The second step is the *resolution*, which discusses whether the conditions of possibility (or diorisms) of the transformed proposition are together sufficient to carry assent. In short, the analytic proof transforms a given proposition into a simpler one, shows the original data to be sufficient for making evident the simpler proposition, and explains why that proof entails of necessity the truth of the original proposition.

Indirect proof is either by *reductio ad absurdum* or by the *method of exhaustion.* The former process shows the impossibility of a proposition contradicting the original one, and concludes that the latter is true on account of the principle of contradiction. Such an indirect method is a kind of elaboration of the apagogic reasoning, which is also a process of reduction. On the other hand, the method of exhaustion reduces proofs involving infinitesimals to problems of formal logic. It proves an assumed relation of magnitude to be what it asserts by showing that both assumptions of it being greater or smaller lead to absurdity. This type of demonstration appears again as a more complex elaboration of both a reductio ad absurdum and an apagogic reasoning.

As a rule, the indirect methods, and more particularly the apagogic reasoning, followed immediately the ecthesis in the general process of proof. The disadvantage of these methods is that they assume the result to be proved, so that it must be found first by tentative methods. Such demonstrations were used when a direct proof was difficult or impossible, not because Euclid had "to convince obstinate Sophists who took pride in their refusal to accept more obvious truths."[12] The objective of Euclid was not to skirmish with schools of philosophers about the meaning and possibility of truth, but to display the strength of his deductions according to the canons of logic.

The general organization of the *Elements* and the actual order of its propositions have been influenced considerably

12 Alexis Clairaut, *Eléments de Géométrie* (Paris, 1741). Préf., pp. 10-11. In his *Essai critique sur les principes fondamentaux de la géométrie* (Paris, 1867), p. 7, J. Houel makes a similar suggestion. "Euclid's method is due to his desire to silence the Sophists; hence his habit of always proving that a thing cannot be instead of proving it to be."

by the historical evolution of geometry. Traditionally and psychologically, the easiest but not necessarily the simplest generalizations or relations were discovered first. Whenever some particular proposition was established, it was integrated into the group of known truths of the same kind. It was natural for Euclid to have this in mind in writing his work, although the geometrical truths stated in the *Elements* were not discovered in that logical order. It is logically possible to arrange the content of this work in many other ways. For example, one could begin with the arithmetical books or with more general principles, or one could group together the elementary and general propositions referring to the same theory which Euclid placed in different books, as in the case of the propositions on similarity. Thus, in combining into a single synthesis the various geometrical theories known at his time, Euclid took into account what was done previously without sacrificing the requirements of a strict deductive exposition.

The success of Euclid's effort is proved by the fact that his collection and arrangement of the *Elements* have survived centuries of controversies. Later mathematicians were able to supply only minor changes in wording or disposition. This is the case of the theory of parallels, which has caused such a storm in the history of mathematics. In this, as in any other theory, an analysis of Euclid's presentation shows that he admitted nothing that could be dispensed with, and that he left out little that matters. Of course, there are a number of imperfections in Euclid's work: many of his definitions are intuitive, as are some of his demonstrations; some capital hypotheses are omitted, as those concerning order and direction and the postulate of indeformability of figures; involved deductive proofs are often needlessly preferred to more direct arithmetical or geometrical demonstrations; finally, his systemization of geometry covers only a part of the field. Yet the brilliance of Euclid's work is enhanced by the modern conditions of methodological rigor and by the various discoveries in synthetic and metrical geometry.

CHAPTER 26

The Philosophy of Euclid

As a complete compendium of elementary Greek mathematics, the *Elements* illustrates the powerful combination of the Platonic method of analytic regression and synthesis with the Aristotelian conditions of logical necessity and demonstration. Before Euclid, philosophers had discussed and set down the characteristics of science in general and of mathematics in particular. Plato and Aristotle had pondered over the meaning of the latter, mentioned and described its features and methods, and justified it with ontological principles or epistemological considerations. In this task, they proceeded from an analysis of the rational conditions of science as well as of the results obtained by mathematicians. Neither Plato nor Aristotle would have been interested in actually improving the arrangement or the proofs of the *Elements*. The former expounded his dialectical method and used mathematics for the benefit of his Theory of Ideas and of his cosmology; the latter gave mathematical illustrations to make good his generalizations concerning the structure, principles, and method of deduction and demonstration. Both provided Euclid with the rational means of systematizing the exposition of geometry, but there is no reference to

Plato or Aristotle in the *Elements* or in the Euclidian corpus; hence the controversies about Euclid's philosophical allegiance.

A mathematician can restrict himself to the study of his field without necessarily having to choose a philosophy to account for his labors. It is possible that Euclid would be content with the title of the "Author of the *Elements*," as his works offer no direct information about his philosophy. He was acquainted with the speculations of his contemporaries because of the intellectual climate of his age and his mathematical training. Although specialization was more pronounced in Alexandria, a division of labor did not preclude exchanges between the various disciplines in the school where the influence of the masters was paramount. On the other hand, if Euclid's mathematical teachers were disciples of the Academy, it does not follow that his technical training carried with it an acceptance of the Platonic doctrines.

The suggestion that Euclid favored Platonism is made by Proclus because "he set before himself as the end of the whole *Elements* the construction of the so-called Platonic figures."[1] Proclus is careful to draw a distinction between the strictly technical aim of the *Elements* and the ultimate intentions of their author. The latter is "concerned with the cosmic figures" while the former endeavors to "make perfect for the learner the understanding of the whole geometry."[2] Heath finds fault with this distinction because the planimetrical and arithmetical portions of the *Elements* have no direct relation to the construction of the 5 regular solids.[3] Yet he admits casually that "Euclid was a Platonist"[4] when he shows that the Euclidian definition of the straight line is based on Plato's definition.

The fact remains that the *Elements* does end with the construction of the solids, a circumstance which may agree less with a rigorous exposition of geometry than with the alleged

---

[1] Proclus *Commentary on the First Book of Euclid*, p. 68 (ed. Friedlein).
[2] Proclus *Commentary*, pp. 70-71.
[3] Thomas L. Heath, *The Thirteen Books of Euclid's Elements* (Cambridge, 1908), I, p. 2 (repub. in New York, 1956).
[4] *Ibid.*, p. 168.

Platonic interests of Euclid. Consequently, the initial statement of Proclus is probably more than a mere attempt to connect the Alexandrian with Platonic philosophy. This idealistic interpretation of Euclid is also shared by some historians[5] who try to show that the whole structure of the *Elements* is a practical illustration of the Platonic conception of science in general and of mathematics in particular.

On the other hand, it cannot be said that Euclid's systematization of geometry is merely an elaboration of the Aristotelian syllogistic and theory of proof. It does entail a number of considerations closer to the Aristotelian than to the Platonic world view, and it does present itself as an application of Aristotle's logic to the exposition (but not to the invention) of geometry. Euclid seems to have organized the geometrical elements in such a way as to encase them neatly in Aristotle's *Analytics,* where the logic of classes predominates. There is a taste of the biological conceptions of the Stagirite in Euclid's definitions involving physical intuitions or experiments, when the distinction between genus and species is used to avoid a confusion of the levels of abstraction. The primacy of the class concept asserts itself more formally when one remarks that the *Elements* neglect relational arguments, spatial postulates, and constructibility conditions required by modern axiomatics.

Although Euclid in fact uses a relational logic in his constructions and proofs, such reasoning is a natural condition of the activity of the mind and the development of mathematics proper. The logic of relations was not formalized before the nineteenth century, although Aristotle speaks of conditional arguments and the Stoics had established a practical theory of the hypothetical syllogism. Hence, Euclid does not share Plato's concern for the status and use of relations as such. He is quite satisfied with the more positive organization of the geometrical elements on the broad basis supplied by intuitive

[5] Cf. A. Rey, *L'Apogée de la Science Technique Grècque* (Paris, 1948), and L. Brunschvigg, *Les Etapes de la Philosophie Mathématique* (Paris, 1947), pp. 93-98.

concepts copied from idealized experiments or constructed logically with these as material. This Aristotelian outlook prevailed in the systematization of the higher geometrical theories developed by Euclid's successors. Instead of stressing the relational structure of the new fields, they described and organized them with the help of categories or classes more pliable to an analytical and syllogistic treatment.

The actual disposition of the mathematical theories making up the body of the *Elements* provides a further argument against the alleged Platonic vision of Euclid. His work begins neither with number, the most immediate reflection of the number-forms, nor with the elementary triangles with which Plato constructs the material world. For this purpose, Euclid used concepts which Plato would consider as intermediate between number and the elementary triangles, but which Aristotle would obtain more directly from the external world by abstraction and construction. Expanding this realistic approach, Euclid devotes the first 4 books of his work to a simplified systematization of what may be called a natural geometry. He introduces much later. the theory of irrationals, with which a Platonist would have started his exposition. What is most significant, he bases the theory of irrationals on geometric considerations, which reverses Plato's wish to justify geometry by means of numbers. In other words, Euclid used the only existing methods of geometrizing the continuum instead of attempting to fulfill the Platonic dream of its arithmetization.

This factual priority of geometry might be explained on strictly methodological grounds, yet it involves an attitude of mind which does not fit with the over-all Platonic outlook. Moreover, the loose connection between planimetry and stereometry suggests that Euclid incorporated in the *Elements* the Pythagorean theory of the regular solids for the sake of mathematical completeness, rather than for the satisfaction of his alleged Platonic faith. Hence, the construction of the regular solids does not appear as the crowning of a strict Platonic endeavor, but rather as the result of an Aristotelian effort to rationalize the very concepts obtained by abstractions from the solids or bodies presented to us by the external world. The intimate connection between this effort and the use of classes in the structural development of the *Elements* is a further indication of a prevailing Aristotelian intention or influence.

In conclusion, it can be truly said that Euclid is situated in the Aristotelian rather than the Platonic perspective, although he combines the methodological results of both. The rule of logic strengthened by the Platonic dialectic of numbers became supreme with Euclid, who submitted geometry to its canons. As a consequence, the place given by Aristotle to geometry in the classification of the sciences remained unchallenged until the birth of modern analysis. Indeed, the intimate combination of logic and geometry made the latter almost a real science. By showing or constructing its objects, Euclidian geometry was considered for centuries as the pattern of all motion in the universe, although Euclid himself does not present his mathematical system as a constituent of reality.

Selected Bibliography

In addition to standard works on Greek philosophy or mathematics, the following books can be consulted for a more detailed presentation of the material in this book.

Apostle, H. G., *Aristotle's Philosophy of Mathematics.* Chicago: Chicago University Press, 1962.

Boyer, Carl B., *The Concepts of the Calculus: A Critical and Historical Discussion of the Derivative and the Integral.* New York: Columbia University Press, 1949. (Also in paperback as *The History of the Calculus,* New York: Dover Publications, Inc., 1959.)

Brumbaugh, Robert S., *Plato's Mathematical Imagination: The Mathematical Passages in the Dialogues and Their Interpretation.* Bloomington, Ind.: Indiana University Press, 1954.

Farrington, Benjamin, *Greek Science: Its Meaning for Us.* New York: Penguin Books, 1953.

Heath, Thomas L., *A History of Greek Mathematics,* 2 vols. London: Oxford University Press, 1921.

————, *A Manual of Greek Mathematics.* London: Oxford University Press, 1931.

————, *Mathematics in Aristotle*. Oxford: Clarendon Press, 1949.

————, *The Thirteen Books of Euclid's Elements* (2nd ed.), 3 vols. New York: Dover Publications, Inc., 1956.

Neugebauer, O., *The Exact Sciences in Antiquity* (2nd ed.). Providence, R. I.: Brown University Press, 1952. (New York: Harper Torchbook, 1962.)

Sarton, George, *A History of Science: Ancient Science Through the Golden Age of Greece*. Cambridge, Mass.: Harvard University Press, 1952.

————, *A History of Science: Hellenistic Science and Culture in the Last Three Centuries, B.C.* Cambridge, Mass.: Harvard University Press, 1959.

Van der Waerden, B. L., *Science Awakening*. Groningen, Netherlands: P. Noordhoff, 1954.

Wedberg, Anders, *Plato's Philosophy of Mathematics*. Stockholm: Almquist and Wiksell, 1953.

Index